Personnel Practices for the '90s

A Local Government Guide

Edited by
John Matzer, Jr.

PRACTICAL MANAGEMENT SERIES
Barbara H. Moore, Editor

Personnel Practices for the '90s
Capital Financing Strategies for Local Governments
Creative Personnel Practices
Current Issues in Leisure Services
The Entrepreneur in Local Government
Ethical Insight, Ethical Action
Hazardous Materials, Hazardous Waste
Human Services on a Limited Budget
Long-Term Financial Planning
Managing New Technologies
Pay and Benefits
Performance Evaluation
Police Management Today
Practical Financial Management
Productivity Improvement Techniques
Risk Management Today
Shaping the Local Economy
Successful Negotiating in Local Government
Telecommunications for Local Government

The Practical Management Series is devoted to the
presentation of information and ideas from diverse
sources. The views expressed in this book are those of
the contributors and are not necessarily those of the
International City Management Association.

Library of Congress Cataloging-in-Publication Data

Personnel practices for the '90s: a local government
    guide/edited by John Matzer, Jr.
        p.   cm.—(Practical management series)
    Bibliography: p.
    ISBN 0-87326-055-4
    1. Local government—United States—Personnel
management. 2. Local officials and employees—United
States. I. Matzer, John. II. Series.
    JS358.P47   1988   88-7648
    353.9'31—dc19   CIP

Printed in the United States of America.
939291908988
54321

Foreword

Local government managers, human resources directors, and professors of public personnel administration have consistently turned to ICMA for state-of-the-art material on personnel management issues and practices. Among our most popular publications has been the book *Creative Personnel Practices*, edited by John Matzer, Jr.

Last year, recognizing that the field is constantly changing, Jack undertook what he intended as a revision of that book. What ultimately took form, however, was an entirely new volume reflecting the personnel issues that will affect local governments in the 1990s. Furthermore, he found such a wealth of material on compensation practices that he created a companion volume, *Pay and Benefits: New Ideas for Local Government*, dealing entirely with that subject.

Personnel Practices for the '90s: A Local Government Guide looks at the changes that are affecting the workplace—demographic shifts, downsizing requirements, legal imperatives—and describes personnel practices that have been successful in organizations of various kinds. It provides up-to-date information and ideas on such questions as drug abuse and drug testing, AIDS in the workplace, privacy rights, smoking, and immigration legislation. And it looks at the influence of changes on basic personnel management responsibilities—training, performance appraisal, and incentive programs, for example.

This book is part of ICMA's Practical Management Series, which is devoted to serving local officials' needs for timely information on current issues and problems.

We are grateful to Jack Matzer for his work in compiling the volume, to Sandy Chizinsky Leas for her editorial guidance, and to the individuals and organizations who granted ICMA permission to reprint their material.

William H. Hansell, Jr.
Executive Director
International City
   Management Association

Personnel Practices for the '90s: A Local Government Guide

The International City Management Association is the professional and educational organization for chief appointed management executives in local government. The purposes of ICMA are to enhance the quality of local government and to nurture and assist professional local government administrators in the United States and other countries. In furtherance of its mission, ICMA develops and disseminates new approaches to management through training programs, information services, and publications.

Managers, carrying a wide range of titles, serve cities, towns, counties, councils of governments, and state/provincial associations of local governments in all parts of the United States and Canada. These managers serve at the direction of elected councils and governing boards. ICMA serves these managers and local governments through many programs that aim at improving the manager's professional competence and strengthening the quality of all local governments.

The International City Management Association was founded in 1914; adopted its City Management Code of Ethics in 1924; and established its Institute for Training in Municipal Administration in 1934. The Institute, in turn, provided the basis for the Municipal Management Series, generally termed the "ICMA Green Books."

ICMA's interests and activities include public management education; standards of ethics for members; the *Municipal Year Book* and other data services; urban research; and newsletters, a monthly magazine, *Public Management,* and other publications. ICMA's efforts for the improvement of local government management—as represented by this book—are offered for all local governments and educational institutions.

About the Editor and Authors

John Matzer, Jr., is a consultant to local government. Previously he was City Administrator, San Bernardino, California; Distinguished Visiting Professor, California State University—Long Beach; Deputy Assistant Director, U.S. Office of Personnel Management; City Manager, Beverly Hills, California; Village Manager, Skokie, Illinois; and City Administrator, Trenton, New Jersey. He received B.A. and M.A. degrees from Rutgers University, New Brunswick, New Jersey, and he has taught graduate courses in public administration at a number of universities.

Following are the affiliations of the contributors at the time of writing:

David E. Bowen, assistant professor of management and organization, School of Business Administration, University of Southern California.

George E. L. Barbee, The Consumer Financial Institute, a division of Price Waterhouse.

Larry Besnoff, law firm of Pechner, Dorfman, Wolffe, Rounick, and Cabot, Philadelphia.

Paul L. Cary, Toxicology and Drug Monitoring Laboratory, University of Missouri Hospital and Clinics, Columbia, Missouri.

Ruth Colvin Clark, manager of training in information services, Southern California Edison Co., Rosemead, California.

Suzanne H. Cook, associate professor of management, Arizona State University, Tempe.

Lennie Copeland, Copeland Griggs Productions, San Francisco, California.

Richard H. Deane, associate professor of management, Georgia State University, Atlanta.

Robert H. Elliott, professor, Department of Government, Auburn University, Montgomery, Alabama.

Robert W. Goddard, director of publications, personnel development departmemt, Liberty Mutual Insurance Companies, Boston.

Larry E. Greiner, professor of management and organization, member of the board of directors of the Management Analysis Center, a division of the Academy of Management.

Ellen K. Harvey, counseling psychologist, Office of Organization and Human Development, General Accounting Office.

Eric L. Harvey, executive director, Performance Systems Corporation, Dallas.

Robert P. Hey, staff writer, *The Christian Science Monitor.*

Alicia Johnson, editorial staff, *Management Review.*

Rosabeth Moss Kanter, Class of 1960 Professor of Business Administration, Harvard Business School.

Delaney J. Kirk, professor, North Texas State University, Denton.

Patricia McLagan, principal, McLagan & Associates, Inc., St. Paul, Minnesota.

J. B. Miles, Washington editor, *Computer Decisions.*

James D. Powell, professor, North Texas State University, Denton.

Robert K. Robinson, lecturer, North Texas State University, Denton.

Ned Rosen, president, Teamworkers, Inc., Lighthouse Point, Florida, and Washington, D.C.

John R. Schultz, deputy associate director, General Government Division, General Accounting Office.

Maxine M. Wade, accountant, Drive Train Division, John Deere Waterloo Works, Waterloo, Iowa.

Thomas M. Wilson, assistant professor of government, Auburn University, Montgomery, Alabama.

Ron Zemke, senior editor, *Training,* The Magazine of Human Resources Development.

Contents

Introduction

John Matzer, Jr.

Personnel management in local government is continuously evolving in anticipation of and in response to changes in the nature and composition of the workforce, external social and economic pressures, organizational structures, and technology. At the same time, human resources managers must respond quickly to such new personnel issues as AIDS, employee drug abuse and drug testing, smoking in the workplace, privacy rights, and the Immigration Reform Act. All of these changes, of course, have an impact on employee training and development, performance appraisal systems, and employee motivation and incentives.

Personnel Practices for the '90s: A Local Government Guide is designed to give today's managers the information and ideas they need to ensure that the human resources programs in their organizations are capable of accommodating these changes. It explains the implications of new legislation affecting human resources policies, describes programs that have worked for governmental and corporate organizations, and provides suggestions for implementing new practices at the local level.

Although this book was originally intended as a revision of ICMA's popular book *Creative Personnel Practices*, the coverage here is entirely new. Furthermore, the topic of pay and benefits emerged as such an important topic that a companion book, *Pay and Benefits: New Ideas for Local Government*, is devoted solely to compensation issues. Together with a third volume, *Performance Evaluation: An Essential Management Tool*, edited by Christine S. Becker, these books provide comprehensive treatment of new developments in human resources management.

The articles that follow review the state of the art in nontechnical terms to provide local officials, human resources practitioners, and students with information on new personnel developments and contemporary practice.

Changes in the workforce and workplace

Personnel management has evolved from a basic clerical function concerned with routine employment and record-keeping tasks to a human resources function that emphasizes managerial, humanistic, and behavioral needs. Human resources management encompasses management and career development, forecasting personnel needs, strategic planning, job design, and the use of data-based computer systems. Greater attention is being given to the decentralization of personnel activities. At the same time, human resources professionals are an integral part of top management and are expected to play an active role in making organizations more effective. The opening section of this book looks at the context of human resources management today—the transition to a service orientation, organizational downsizing, workforce changes, age bias, women in the workplace, and career plateauing.

A common complaint of line managers is that the personnel department does not meet their needs, which include assistance in developing new systems and technical skills that fit their particular departments. In the opening selection, David E. Bowen and Larry E. Greiner argue that the perceived ineffectiveness of the human resources function stems from an orientation toward *production* rather than *service*, and they recommend action steps for fostering a service orientation. Only with this outlook can human resources professionals help the organization prepare for future challenges.

Among these challenges has been the need for public organizations to reduce costs through downsizing, or systematically reducing the workforce. Reducing the size of an organization is difficult and can result in low morale and employee stress, accompanied by performance problems. Downsizing challenges managers and human resources professionals to find ways to accomplish this goal with minimum disruption to the employees and the organization. A sound downsizing approach provides a unique opportunity to change the direction of the organization.

In "Downsizing with Dignity," George E. L. Barbee discusses why and how organizations are reducing their workforces. Alternative downsizing strategies include layoffs, downgrades, lateral assignments, early retirement programs, hiring freezes, pay and benefits freezes, furloughs, attrition, outplacement, reductions in hours or pay and benefits, and job sharing. Downsizing and the movement toward leaner organizations mandate modifications to personnel systems. Performance appraisals must improve. Career paths must change. Pay systems must eliminate their management bias. Employees must be more responsible for their own work. Staying streamlined requires a strengthened human resources function.

Another challenge to human resources management has been the pressure of social, demographic, economic, and other changes. Employee litigation, shifts in employee attitudes and lifestyles, and the changing nature of work are just a few manifestations of those changes. The workforce is aging, growing more diverse, becoming more educated, and expressing new values and expectations. Corresponding changes in the workplace include employee involvement programs, organizational restructuring, job sharing, alternative work schedules, and "intrapreneurship." At the same time, upward mobility is no longer guaranteed; bloated managerial structures are being trimmed back; and a new management philosophy is emerging. Ron Zemke examines four factors that affect human resources development—external social forces, the nature and composition of the labor force, organizational structure, and technology. Rosabeth Moss Kanter's article, "The New Workforce Meets the Changing Workplace," discusses the strains and dilemmas stemming from new workplace practices—participation and pay, innovation versus management control, and the tension between equal opportunity for women and the increasing absorptiveness of work.

The new workforce contains an increasing percentage of women, minorities, and immigrants. It has been estimated that these groups will make up more than 80 percent of the net additions to the workforce between 1986 and the year 2000. According to the most recent projections by the U.S. Bureau of Labor Statistics, blacks, hispanics, and other nonwhite groups will account for about 57 percent of the growth in the labor force during that same period. While education levels in the workplace are on the rise, the pool of functionally illiterate adults grows at about 2.5 million people a year. The Hudson Institute's Workforce 2000 report predicts that in 1990 more than 50 percent of the jobs being created will demand post-secondary training. Very few jobs will be created for those who cannot read and use mathematics. The diversity of the workforce and the growing mismatch between employers' needs and the skills available in the labor pool present further challenges to human resources professionals. Conflicting needs of women who work and have families need to be reconciled. The problem of extensive illiteracy must be addressed. Blacks, hispanics, and other minority workers need to be integrated into the workforce. The minority rights movement of the 1960s and 1970s and the rise of career-oriented women in the 1970s and 1980s will continue to have an effect on human resources management. Lennie Copeland describes common errors in managing a multicultural workforce and outlines what every manager needs to know to be effective in this setting.

Although the 1964 Civil Rights Act, the Equal Employment Opportunity Commission guidelines on sexual harassment, the Equal Pay Act of 1963, and the Pregnancy Discrimination Act of 1978 give women employees protections against discrimination, women continue to face both overt and subtle forms of discrimination. Comparable worth and sexual harassment remain major personnel issues, and upward mobility for women is still restricted. Alicia Johnson discusses the barriers faced by female managers and presents suggestions for eliminating discrimination against women in hiring and career advancement.

The Bureau of Labor Statistics reports that the United States will soon have the oldest workforce in recorded history. One problem associated with the aging workforce is an increase in age discrimination. Older employees are filing age discrimination complaints with the Equal Employment Opportunity Commission and suing in state and federal courts. Robert P. Hey highlights the importance and extent of age discrimination on the job, particularly as they relate to early retirement plans. Employers need to be sure they do not have personnel policies and procedures that discriminate against older workers.

A problem associated with the older workforce is that the baby boom generation is meeting a career-ladder obstruction, which is further aggravated by a decline in middle management positions. Downsizing and the movement toward flatter and leaner organizations have reduced the availability of middle management jobs. Furthermore, job-skill obsolescence has become particularly prevalent for those over the age of thirty-five. The Hudson Institute's Workforce 2000 report estimated that everyone entering the workforce by 1990 will have to be retrained two or three times in the course of his or her career. Ellen K. Harvey and John R. Schultz discuss career plateauing, which occurs as the opportunity for promotion declines and employees neglect to develop and expand their technical, managerial, or career skills. Harvey and Schultz discuss the nature and causes of career plateauing and comment on several forms of intervention.

Employee performance, motivation, and training

Receding revenues and spiraling costs have stimulated a search for ways to increase employee productivity. Managers need to understand how to motivate employees and improve their performance, yet changing employee attitudes and needs have complicated performance evaluation and the design of motivation programs. Researchers and courts have found serious flaws in many appraisal systems, leading to efforts to develop accurate performance measures on which to base personnel decisions. In addition to improving performance appraisal systems, managers are continually challenged to develop effective motivational techniques. Part 2 explores performance appraisal practices, incentive and reward programs, employee attitude surveys, ways to help troubled workers, and employee training and development.

Performance appraisals continue to serve as the basis for selection, promotion, transfer, training, retention, and pay decisions. In addition, appraisals are used to influence reward systems, measure an employee's productivity, develop an employee's career path, and determine the need for counseling. Developing employee potential demands a systematic connection between behavior and rewards. Feedback from appraisals provides motivation and permits employees to improve performance.

On the other hand, the appraisal process is subject to subjectivity and discrimination, and employees are challenging their ratings in court when they are used as the basis for denial of promotions or pay increases or for termination. The courts are scrutinizing and penalizing discriminatory aspects of performance appraisals, because the law requires that all procedures used to measure performance must be valid and job related. Human resources professionals are confronted with the need to develop appraisal systems based on measurable performance standards. Experience has also demonstrated the need for frequent coaching, separate appraisals for different purposes, and the use of goal setting for improving performance. Robert W. Goddard identifies flaws in performance appraisal systems and suggests ways to make them as objective and productive as possible. A checklist then walks the reader through some factors to consider in developing performance appraisal systems that will be effective in improving individual and organizational effectiveness.

Studies generally agree that most workers are satisfied with their jobs. But this does not mean that the workers are motivated to be productive. Increased productivity depends on motivational systems that are tailored to meet individual needs, encourage desired behavior, and build satisfaction as a result of high performance. Improved productivity is related to management's understanding of what motivates employees within the context of the roles they perform. Three strategies that have proven successful are maintaining positive expectations, providing feedback, and matching consequences with behavior. Maxine M. Wade explains how to motivate and retain employees through a combination of flexible benefits, job enrichment, and mentor/management development. Robert W. Goddard describes how financial and psychological reward systems are being restructured. Motivation and reward practices should be designed to fit the needs of particular persons working under particular conditions, and managers may need to experiment with a range of individual, group, and organizational techniques.

Attitude surveys are one means used by many organizations to help meet employee needs, increase productivity, and motivate and communicate more effectively. These surveys have proven to be effective in identifying changing employee needs, values, perceptions, and expectations. They can identify probable causes of employee dissatisfaction, turnover, absenteeism, and other problems, and they are one way of encouraging more objectivity in designing reward systems. Typical survey questions deal with the effectiveness of management, communications, pay, benefits, and supervisory practices. Effective attitude surveys are designed with involvement by employees and are conducted frequently. Frequent surveys can tell employees that management cares, but they also can identify problems that cannot be solved immediately and aggravate already disgruntled employees. Management should decide what they want from a survey and carefully communicate survey results, including an explanation of what they can and cannot do. Ned Rosen presents a useful primer on what managers should know about employee attitude surveys.

Employee performance problems are often due to psychological, medical, family, legal, financial, drug, or alcohol problems. Most unresolved personal problems eventually manifest themselves in poor job performance and employee attitude problems. They can show up in accidents, absenteeism, tardiness, increased disciplinary actions, poor work quality, and increased workers compensation, disability, and health insurance claims. It has been estimated that one out of every six employees, at some time, has a personal problem that affects performance. In order to minimize the impact of such problems, supervisors need to be trained to identify declining performance and help employees obtain assistance. J. B. Miles describes types of personal problems and offers suggestions on how to help troubled workers.

Closely related to performance problems is the question of discipline. Some organizations have discovered that traditional approaches to discipline fail to generate commitment to the organization and its goals. They recognize that little of value comes out of the belief that discipline and punishment go hand in hand. In some organizations the traditional punitive approach has been replaced by systems that require acceptance of personal responsibility, individual decision-making, and self-discipline. Eric L. Harvey discusses the deficiencies of the traditional punishment approach to discipline and describes the basics of a "commitment approach." Such systems make supervisors responsible for reinforcing good performance and informing problem performers about the consequences of their decision not to meet the organization's goals.

Workforce and workplace changes also have had a significant impact on training and career development. A trend has been toward training that is focused, specific, and closely integrated with emerging personnel issues such as AIDS, substance abuse, employee privacy, and sexual harassment. Organizational downsizing and delayering and the decline in middle management jobs have placed renewed emphasis on training and career development. The movement toward a comprehensive approach to human resources management, along with innovative training technologies, has provided many new opportunities for management development and training.

Career development has assumed new importance for mid-level managers whose organizations are downsizing or restructuring and who need to explore new career options or develop new skills. Few frameworks are available for conceptualizing, designing, and implementing career development activities. Organizational design, job design, reward systems, performance appraisal systems, and employee control systems all affect the type of career development system an organization needs. A primary objective is to recognize the impact of organizational and career instability while preserving an employee's commitment to the organization. Career development involves looking beyond the work at hand toward a set of long-term employer-employee interactions that will improve mutual performance and satisfaction. Human resources professionals must design career development programs that prepare employees for change and help them identify new career paths and skills for future jobs. Patricia McLagan contributes some thoughts on what professional development means today and why it is beneficial for the organization as well as for the individual.

Other employee development programs encompass employee training, education, and development and offer the potential for improving performance, morale, and job satisfaction. Critical factors in the success of an employee development effort are the proper identification of training needs and the ability to create and deliver training that will achieve its defined objectives and be applied in practice. Managers and human resources staff need to establish effective methods of defining needs and evaluating methods and results. They must also analyze where the training dollars go and ways to make training pay off on the job. Human resources professionals are being challenged to determine the effective use of new training technologies and to determine the true cost of training programs. Ruth Colvin Clark describes nine situations in which training failed to transfer to the job and offers tips on how the problems could have been avoided.

Employee issues

Both public and private employers are struggling with an increasing number of complex employee issues. Legal issues include drug and AIDS testing, employee privacy, immigration legislation, and sexual harassment. Other issues are smoking in the workplace, substance abuse, stress disabilities, ethics, workplace hazards, and interactions between men and women at work. All of these issues require innovative personnel policies and practices. The accompanying table shows, by industry, the percentage that have specific policies and practices relative to some of these issues. Organizations are recognizing the importance of communicating to employees what

Table 1. Workplace issues by industry.

	All organizations	Manufacturing	Transportation/communications/utilities	Wholesale/retail trade	Finance/insurance/banking	Business services	Health services	Educational services	Public administration
Do drug testing of employees (with probable cause)	24.8%	30.8%	11.9%	38.0%	11.3%	15.8%	48.3%	27.2%	35.7%
Do drug testing of employees (without probable cause)	8.5	1.9	25.1	11.1	0.9	1.9	0.0	17.4	20.6
Do drug testing of job applicants	14.2	30.4	34.3	21.9	1.9	1.0	1.4	1.5	24.7
Have a formal policy on substance abuse	67.1	68.9	78.9	70.8	55.2	63.1	87.6	59.1	78.0
Conduct or sponsor training for substance abusers	25.4	29.5	34.4	17.0	4.4	9.4	51.5	34.6	46.5
Have an EAP that handles substance abuse problems	37.9	31.7	47.5	19.5	23.9	21.2	69.4	43.3	72.5
Do AIDS antibody testing of employees	2.5	0.0	0.0	0.3	0.0	0.3	0.1	0.1	19.1
Do AIDS antibody testing of job applicants	1.5	1.1	12.3	0.0	0.0	0.3	0.3	0.0	2.8

Have a formal AIDS policy	7.4	2.1	0.6	3.6	6.5	2.4	20.6	11.4	16.2
Have an AIDS education program	18.4	1.8	6.9	1.8	9.0	20.6	59.4	23.6	37.5
Have a policy that limits smoking at work	68.8	65.8	55.2	80.5	66.6	59.9	89.0	72.6	72.3
Have a policy that bans smoking at work	11.0	17.7	5.0	4.4	13.9	12.6	13.7	9.7	5.6
Do not hire smokers	3.7	6.9	0.1	0.0	0.2	17.8	0.0	0.0	3.8
Have a formal policy on sexual harassment	69.4	73.9	52.7	56.4	56.1	65.5	81.8	84.5	85.2
Have a formal affirmative action plan	71.8	76.9	96.1	45.8	72.3	53.0	78.9	73.7	78.2
Have a formal code of ethics	56.0	38.2	39.8	51.1	65.1	64.5	52.6	62.2	69.1

Source: "Workplace Issues: Testing, Training, and Policy," by Dale Feuer, *Training*, October 1987.

constitutes acceptable and unacceptable behavior, either by modifying existing personnel policies or by creating new ones. Other responses to new employee issues include employee assistance programs, employee education and communication, and wellness programs. Part 3 examines a wide range of issues and responses.

Privacy in the workplace is a major personnel issue, and workers are asserting their right to be let alone by their employers. The practices in question are medical screening, surveillance, employment references, disclosure of personal information to other employees, and confidentiality of records. Lawsuits, huge jury awards, and demands for privacy legislation indicate the scope of the privacy issue. Governments and the courts are defining the right of organizations to collect, use, and release personal information on employees, and employers are adopting guidelines for handling information. Personnel professionals need to understand the legal issues involved in employee privacy and institute strict controls over the gathering and use of personal data. Suzanne H. Cook discusses the personal dimensions of privacy, information gathering, legal issues, and recommendations to help safeguard privacy.

With an expected increase in the incidence of AIDS cases nationwide, AIDS in the workplace and AIDS discrimination rank at the top of today's personnel concerns. Federal, state, and local laws mandate that employers provide reasonable accommodation for employees suffering from AIDS. The U.S. Supreme Court has ruled that employees with infectious diseases are handicapped within the meaning of the Federal Rehabilitation Act. Confidentiality and mandatory AIDS testing are among the new legal battlegrounds. Few organizations have personnel policies and practices covering employees with AIDS, although many organizations sponsor AIDS education programs. Approximately thirty of the nation's largest employers have endorsed a ten-point bill of rights on AIDS issues calling for education to dispel fears, urging that medical records be kept confidential, and pledging not to test for the AIDS virus in hiring. Recommendations for coping with the AIDS crisis in the workplace are offered by Robert H. Elliott and Thomas M. Wilson. Employee health benefits, co-workers' concerns, pre-employment inquiries, and termination decisions are concerns of personnel management in dealing with AIDS.

Substance abuse by employees results in poor performance, reduction in service quality, and increased employer costs. Employees with drug and alcohol problems have higher absentee and accident rates, use health benefits at a higher rate, and file more workers' compensation claims. It has been estimated that one in every ten employees suffers from alcohol or drug problems. Employers are subject to expensive liability claims when people are injured by employees under the influence of alcohol or drugs. Many organizations have adopted formal policies on substance abuse and require employees to take drug tests under certain circumstances. Employers also sponsor training programs to help supervisors identify and deal with substance abusers. Employee assistance programs, which provide professional treatment for substance abusers, are on the increase. Drug testing of employees has come under attack. Seven states have laws limiting drug tests, and the Supreme Court has agreed to decide whether testing government employees violates the Fourth Amendment's guarantee against illegal searches and seizures. The absence of standards and high error rates for drug testing have further complicated the problem of substance abuse in the workplace. Paul L. Cary outlines the elements of a comprehensive, occupationally based substance abuse program. He also discusses the elements of a complete substance abuse policy and legal issues in drug detection programs.

Increasing recognition has been given to the right of employees to work in a reasonably smoke-free environment. Most organizations now limit smoking to some degree. Many employers believe that smoking increases health insurance costs, absenteeism, maintenance costs, and accidents. In some states nonsmoking employees are eligible for workers' compensation or disability benefits, and unemployment benefits have been awarded to employees who felt that smoke injured their health. The courts have held that employers have an obligation to provide employees with a healthful work environment. Richard H. Deane addresses the health, productivity, and legal issues associated with smoking and outlines a plan of action for employers, including a smoking policy.

Sexual harassment continues to be a major issue in the workplace. *Redbook* magazine reported that 92 percent of 9,000 women polled believed sexual harassment to be a problem. More than one-third of the women who replied to a City of Los Angeles confidential questionnaire cited instances of sexual harassment in the workplace. Seventy percent said filing complaints would be fruitless, and 61 percent feared retaliation if they reported it. Sexual harassment includes unwelcome sexual advances, requests for sexual favors, and other verbal or physical conduct of a sexual nature under several conditions: (1) when submission to such conduct is made a condition of employment, (2) when submission to or rejection of sexual advances is used as a basis for employment decisions, or (3) when such conduct creates an intimidating, hostile, or offensive work environment. The courts are widening the definition of sexual harassment, and employers who know or should have known about such conduct are responsible for the actions of supervisors and other employees. Employers need to develop strong policies on sexual harassment and institutionalize a complaint mechanism. Supervisors and employees need to be educated about sexual harassment. Robert K. Robinson and two colleagues define sexual harassment, discuss the scope of the problem, and recommend what employers should do.

Still another concern for employers, especially since the passage of the Immigration Reform and Control Act of 1986, is identifying unauthorized aliens. The law makes it a federal crime to hire illegal aliens, creates an amnesty program to grant legal status to aliens in the country since January 1, 1982, and imposes new penalties on employers who discriminate against workers on the basis of national origin or citizenship. Employers have to document the identity and authorization to work of all new hires, with stiff penalties for hiring unauthorized foreigners, failing to keep proper records, and discriminating against minorities. Larry Besnoff presents highlights of the act, discusses the antidiscrimination provisions, and recommends actions for employers.

Conclusion

Changes in the workforce and workplace present many challenges to human resources professionals and local government managers. To meet current and future needs, human resources managers must:

1. Analyze the implications of workforce and workplace changes
2. Become more service-oriented and decentralize HR functions
3. Engage in human resources planning
4. Develop comprehensive HR information systems
5. Monitor organizational behavior and attitudes
6. Assume responsibility for the evaluation and maintenance of the organization's culture
7. Provide advice on ethical issues
8. Apply advanced techniques in the humanistic and behavioral science areas to work design, reward system design, career management, and other personnel activities
9. Establish a pluralistic organizational culture
10. Foster a climate of equal employment opportunity
11. Develop performance appraisal systems that use objective performance standards and encourage coaching/counseling
12. Design reward programs based on objective interpretations of employee motivations
13. Adopt personnel policies and practices that address such issues as AIDS, drug testing, smoking in the workplace, employee privacy, and sexual harassment
14. Strengthen employee development programs to address problems caused by downsizing, career plateauing, and the need for new job skills.

Human resources management will continue to evolve as we enter the 1990s. Local governments that are innovative and creative in the development and implementation of human resources policies and practices will be able to maximize the potential of their most valuable asset—the people who make up the organization.

PART 1

Changes in the Workforce and Workplace

Moving from Production to Service in Human Resources Management

David E. Bowen and Larry E. Greiner

The human resources (HR) function is frequently the recipient of both good news and bad news these days. The good news is that in an era of Japanese management, search for excellence, and strong corporate cultures, the importance of human resources to organizational effectiveness is increasingly recognized. Indeed, an effective human resources function is viewed by executives and business critics alike as the key to successful management in our emergent high-tech, services-based, global economy. The bad news is that although the HR function is now receiving attention equal to its production and marketing counterparts, it continues to attract severe criticism from line managers. They frequently complain that HR does not provide the help they need, that HR uses esoteric techniques, that HR is "out of touch" and "paper-ridden," and that HR is an unnecessary source of "costly overhead."

In this article we argue that the perceived ineffectiveness of HR in many organizations stems from the performance of the HR role with a "production" rather than a "service" orientation. In other words, the HR function is carried out as if it were a manufacturing operation turning out uniform products for a homogeneous market rather than a service organization providing unique offerings matched to diverse client needs. HR is seen as producing rather than serving, while clients (inside and outside the organization) are viewed as demanding, but not receiving.

Assertions about HR effectiveness

We will make three assertions about the limited effectiveness of HR and the reorientation required if HR is to move closer to its clientele. These assertions come from our interviews with top corporate managers and HR executives, from our consulting experience, and from feedback from executives in seminars in which we have discussed the role of HR in their organizations.

Assertion I: Corporate management and line managers often view their HR groups as performing ineffectively   We recently asked a CEO of a medium-size company if we could talk to him about HR in his company. His reply was "Sure. I'd love to talk to you about our 'Horrendous Results' guys." He believed that HR was similarly labelled by many CEOs in other companies. Furthermore, he told us that two months after asking his VP of HR to look into perks for his top team, he received a costly proposal of perks for the entire company.

Assertion II: Ineffective HR groups display more of a "production" than a "service" orientation in performing their work   Both line managers and top corporate officers report that HR responds more to the demands of their own technologies than they do to the needs of their clients. Examples include HR's production of the same trait-based appraisal rating forms for all departments and the same MBO programs for all manufacturing plants, regardless of differences in task activities and skill requirements across departments and plants. HR is described as caught up in turning out an endless stream of uniform personnel manuals and regimented training materials.

Assertion III: If HR groups act with a "service" orientation, they will perform their role more effectively   We believe that if HR groups were managed like businesses that provide a high-quality service— e.g., research hospitals, gourmet restaurants, and "blue chip" consulting firms, they would less often be criticized as narrow and out of touch with their customers. Recent descriptions of how service businesses provide quality service to *external* customers can guide the way HR provides a service to *internal* customers—namely, line managers and workers on the firing line. These emerging service models can be used to reorient HR from production to its original and intended mission: functioning as a staff activity that *serves* the line organization.

In support of these assertions, we will first explain why a production orientation to HR currently exists in many organizations. We will then present four key features of a service orientation in today's service businesses. Next we will apply these same features to

HR in order to highlight the radically different mission and structure that a service orientation implies. In closing, we will propose a change strategy that begins with an audit of HR's effectiveness and orientation toward its clients. We encourage the reader to compare his or her own experiences with what we report here.

Why a production orientation?

A production orientation in HR has been shaped by a number of historical, legal, and educational forces.

Industrial era management models   Management principles developed in the 1930s for the manufacturing sector still guide many of today's executives. These classic principles of scientific management include protecting the core technology from outside disturbance, standardizing of the product line, measuring quantity of output, staffing with specialized labor, and targeting short-term return on investment. Top management has been conditioned to view these principles as desirable in the operation of all functions. In other words, the purpose of HR is the same as the purpose of manufacturing: to produce a product. If an HR group lacks these production characteristics, the head of HR might easily be replaced by someone from Manufacturing or Sales who "knows how to get things done."

The training of HR specialists in graduate schools   The last decade has seen a proliferation of Ph.D.s in industrial-organizational psychology who have entered the HR function with "production expertise" in psychological tests, behaviorally anchored rating scales, cafeteria pay plans, quality circles, and so on. These educated scientists resemble automobile-assembly workers who specialize in brake linings, steering assemblies, and drive trains. In both cases, the well-trained expert knows a lot about tools, parts, and procedures, but fails to see the overall perspective for the product and its intended use by a demanding customer.

Legal requirements   A changing legal environment in the 1970s has required standard personnel practices. The need for corporate compliance with EEO, OSHA, and ERISA has reinforced HR's role as a centralized monitoring activity where top management, the legal department, and government regulatory agencies have replaced line operating managers as HR's most important clients. Moreover, line managers have reluctantly deferred to HR as the group that will keep them out of trouble with the law.

Economic competition and productivity pressures   Everyone agrees that corporate management should assess HR's effectiveness, just as it does that of other business functions. However, heightened economic competition in the 1980s has prompted the growing use of a "bottom-line mentality" to measure HR's ability to achieve tangible short-term outcomes. HR's effectiveness is frequently assessed by the number of people trained for dollars expended, the number of people hired per offers extended, the amount of reduction in turnover, this year's absenteeism compared with last year's, and the settlement rate for EEO complaints.

All these forces have, over time, shaped a production orientation for HR. Employees within HR have even come to accept it as a way of life. But is there another alternative? We propose that HR be shaped by a new force in our society: a services-based economy that is replacing the industrial one. We will describe the basic ingredients of a service business and then discuss its implications for the human resources function.

What does "service" look like in service firms?

Management researchers in marketing and organizational behavior have recently detailed how the dynamics of the service sector differ from those of the manufacturing sector. Senior executives, such as Lynn Shostack at Bankers Trust Company and G. M. Hostage at Marriott, have also described their experiences in managing service businesses. These accounts point to four basic differences between products and services, which can be summarized as follows:

Services are intangible A service is an act performed by one party for another. A service provides the customer with an experience, while a product offers the customer physical ownership. For example, the student receiving a college education can neither touch nor measure it directly. Customers of a service rely heavily upon cues surrounding its *delivery* (physical setting, the rapport between employee and customer, and so forth) in forming an assessment of its value. These cues can be referred to as the "climate for service"; research has demonstrated how crucial the climate for service is in shaping customers' views of service quality. (See Benjamin Schneider and David Bowen's study of bank branches appearing in *Journal of Applied Psychology*, August 1985.)

Management's task is to manage the delivery of and climate for service so that customers feel they have acquired something of value. It is important when providing intangible services, such as teaching, that the service provider be interpersonally competent and an effective communicator. The effective teacher is able to make abstract intangible concepts appear desirable and understandable; the quality of "being educated" is not measured by a grade received or the number of papers written.

Services are produced and consumed simultaneously In the manufacturing sector, there is a delay between production of a product and its consumption in the market, given the lengthy distribution chain between manufacturer and customer. Services, however, are typically consumed at the moment of production; examples of such services include health care, education, banking, entertainment events, hair salons, and restaurants. In these settings, services are exchanged face to face between employee and customer. Unlike manufacturing, service operations are not created in an impersonal environment where the customer is not aware of how the "product" is produced.

Simultaneous production and consumption also makes it impossible to "stock" services as inventory—a situation that, in turn, makes it difficult for management to coordinate supply with demand. When a sporting event is held in a half-empty stadium, no mechanism is available for storing vacant seats for a future event. Simultaneous production and consumption also require service management to respond to *individual* customer preferences at the point of sale. The teacher can tailor his or her remarks to the class, given their personal needs and moods of the moment, while the consultant must adjust to the frowns of a disgruntled client. The manufacturer produces a predesigned, fixed product that cannot be tailored to the personalities of individual users.

Customers participate in producing services   In many service organizations, customers help to create the service they receive. For example, the reliability of a doctor's diagnosis often depends on how well the patient describes his or her illness; supermarket shoppers fill up their own carts before store employees cash them out; and restaurant goers act as their own waiters and waitresses at a Sunday brunch. In these examples, service customers act not only as consumers, but also as co-producers. They may even act as sole producers of the service, as when bank customers use automated teller machines.

Managing service businesses requires adroit management of customer behavior as well as employee behavior. Because the customer does the work without being paid, effective customer participation in a service clearly provides a means for increasing productivity not available to manufacturing operations. However, customer participation may also pose challenges for management. Customers often need to be "socialized" into the roles that management expects them to play, such as when a flight attendant demonstrates safety procedures on an airplane.

Services are nonstandardized   The labor intensity of service operations leads to more variability in output than occurs when machines dominate the production process. The consumer of mass-produced Sony video products can rely on their uniform quality, but the patron of a beauty shop will always insist upon "one last look in the mirror" before leaving. Service managers find it more difficult to maintain quality control than do managers in manufacturing organizations because customers perceive more risk with intangible services than they do with physical products.

The above four characteristics (intangibility, simultaneity, customer participation, and nonstandardization) set services apart from manufacturing. They describe fundamental differences in both *what* is exchanged between the firm and customer and *how* the exchange takes place. We can now examine what the HR function would look like if it were based on these characteristics.

A service orientation in HR

The ideal HR group with a service orientation would respond to the dynamics of organizing very differently from an HR group with a production orientation. The two groups would differ in their descriptions of their missions, their planning, their staffing, and their structure.

Mission   Here's how each group would view its mission:

Production. We are turning out tangible, uniform products for consumption by an undifferentiated market that we assume needs our products.

Service. We are creating a service for the client that will meet changing needs over time and is unique to each client's situation.

The mission of a service-oriented HR group is to provide line managers with a service, rarely with a specific, tangible product. If line managers report "difficulties in the performance appraisal process," a production-oriented response might be to begin production of "behaviorally anchored rating scales" and to start the planned obsolescence of trait-based forms. On the other hand, a service-oriented response might begin with a view that functions like performance appraisal are primarily intangible concepts and only secondarily products. Performance appraisal should be viewed as a complex process of evaluating and coaching that must be tailored to the task requirements and people skills in a particular work setting.

Another way of expressing these mission differences is to say that a service orientation focuses on the *goals* of HR management (e.g., effective reward systems and EEO compliance), whereas a production orientation focuses on *means* (e.g., cafeteria pay plans and quotas). Focusing on goals is consistent with a mission of serving intangible needs; focusing on means will result in a short-sighted generation of formal programs.

Planning   Now let's look at the way each group would describe planning.

Production. We are best equipped by training and experience to determine the human resources needs of the corporation and then to produce formal systems, programs, and policies to meet these needs.

Service. We work with the line manager to develop tailored services to fit the evolving needs of each client's situation.

A production-oriented HR group follows an "inside-outside" strategy in designing programs for line managers. Program design is driven by the interests and competencies of HR, not by the needs of line managers. There is a clean division of labor in production-oriented HR: The staff produces and line managers consume. Conversely, service-oriented HR staff views line managers as "co-producers" and "partial employees" of the HR function.

HR's training performance evolves quite differently under these two orientations. In a production approach, the HR staff builds a limited inventory of "canned" programs that it provides in standardized format to all customers. In a service approach, line managers participate in a needs analysis and in the design of customized training. Moreover, during training, participation and feedback from trainees are used to modify the training design. "Outsider" participation may make HR's task more difficult, but it offers the advantage of enhancing managerial and employee commitment to HR's efforts. For example, if engineers in R&D complain about how their performance is appraised, HR should not immediately assume that a new appraisal form is the answer. Instead, the real solution may lie in training R&D supervisors in more effective ways of setting goals and giving feedback to highly educated employees.

Staffing   In the area of staffing, too, the two groups differ from each other.

Production. We employ a large number of specialists who will design and package the most up-to-date products in their areas of expertise.

Service. We employ a few generalists who act as client-executives serving a variety of client needs over a lengthy period of time.

Employing generalists is a move away from having an HR staff composed of "product champions." It is a shift toward a lean staff that retains only a few key specialists while contracting with outside specialists for extraordinary HR needs. A staff of generalists is better equipped to deal with varying demands that arise. In contrast, a production-oriented staff of specialists—with their dependence on a limited inventory of prepackaged programs—cannot respond effectively to unanticipated demands.

The client-executive stands out in comparison with the HR specialist acting as an expert in compensation or training. Instead of possessing a narrow range of technical skills, the generalist is a diagnostician who addresses a broad range of problems. While the HR generalist spends most of his or her time in the field, the client-executive gives exclusive attention to the full range of HR needs expressed by line managers in a few organizational units. Knowing that local ownership will lead to further projects from the same client, he or she seeks to involve these managers in determining a plan of action.

Structure   In their viewpoints on staffing, production and service directly oppose each other:

Production. We remain centralized and specialized to produce a coherent and uniform approach throughout the organization.

Service. We are decentralized in order to get close to the customer so we can sense and respond to his/her needs.

Who *is* the customer? In a production orientation, corporate management and the EEOC often receive attention before the line manager does. In a service orientation, line managers require equal billing to or top billing over the HR customer. The critical functions of R&D, manufacturing, and sales take place in the field, not in corporate headquarters. Decentralization of HR decision making is therefore a prerequisite for serving the line manager well. Unless the HR generalist is close to a line executive, it is difficult to build an ongoing relationship.

Another benefit of decentralization is that the line executive feels more accountable for human resources decisions affecting his or her unit. No longer can the line executive's sole concern be to produce widgets while unloading human resources practices on a central staff. Similarly, the HR executive cannot walk away from the consequences of his or her actions.

Implementing a service orientation

Up to this point, we have described an ideal state for the HR function to aim for if it is to achieve a service orientation. But what are

---

Action steps for implementing a service orientation to HR

Audit the effectiveness of HR and its orientation
Sell top management on a service orientation
Educate HR staff in service delivery
Educate line managers on their role in a service orientation
Implement two-way design of HR menu
Develop service-oriented effectiveness criteria
Be aware of service-product balance issues
Know the business

the practical steps required to shift an HR group from a production to a service orientation?

Conduct an orientation audit   The first step is a diagnosis of the "state of HR" within the organization. How good a job is HR viewed as doing? How do people feel about how HR goes about its business? This step is a test of two of our opening assertions: that HR is frequently judged as ineffective and that it has a production orientation.

The "auditors" should include not just top corporate managers but line managers and outside consultants as well. The orientation audit assesses the degree to which HR has a production orientation relative to a service approach. This audit can be conducted in survey and interview format with questions drawn from our preceding descriptions of production versus service orientations. Here are some sample questions: To what extent do line managers participate in the design of HR offerings? To what extent is the HR staff decentralized? Is the HR staff composed more of generalists than of specialists?

Sell top management   Reorientation of HR from production to service will require a top-down change effort. The starting point is to sell top management on implementing a service orientation. This sales effort will be easier if the audit clearly depicts HR as ineffective and operating in a production mode. If this is not the case, the following two sales tactics may prove useful. First, top management can be reminded that HR was originally created as a staff activity to *serve* line managers, not to direct and control them. Second, if a topflight, service-oriented HR group can be created, it can provide a "role model" for other staff functions to emulate. Many of the same production-oriented problems occur in accounting, MIS, and strategic planning groups at the corporate level.

Educate the HR staff   The HR staff needs to be reeducated if it is to know what a service orientation looks like in practice. They need to understand why HR's output is more intangible than a performance appraisal form or a psychological test. They also need to know how to explain and sell services, not just packaged products, and how to involve line managers in the design and delivery of services.

If the HR staff is to enact these service principles, they must reorient themselves by adopting new "core values" that support a service orientation. We think it would be constructive for HR management and staff to identify their present core values and contrast them with the values necessary for a service orientation. One such value is to "let the client take credit" instead of saying, "Look at all

---

Core values of HR service

Remember that the client is king or queen
Work hard for the client
Go to the client
Trust the client
Provide total service
Involve the client
Retain integrity
Stay with the client
Let the client take credit
Remember that a satisfied client is the best referral

---

the good things I did for you." A sample group's listing of service core values appears in the accompanying sidebar.

Educate line managers regarding their role   Quality service is provided collaboratively by service provider and customers who act as co-producers and partial employees in service creation. However, this raises two troubling questions: Are line managers *competent* to act as co-producers with the HR staff? Are line managers *willing* to act as co-producers? On the competency question, HR and line managers must first inform each other of the roles they expect each other to fill. Line managers may require special training in how to perform a "needs analysis," or they may need to know more about alternative goal-setting techniques. This is similar to a doctor-patient service relationship in which the doctor serves the patient, but the patient co-produces by describing symptoms to the doctor, working through a plan of treatment, and self-administering medication as prescribed.

Although line managers who are currently dissatisfied with HR may gladly join in the design and implementation of HR services, others may require additional motivation. One reason HR has become so centralized and out of touch may be that many line managers chose long ago to hand over their human resources management responsibilities to the HR staff. To provide any service involving customer participation, those providing the service must convince the customers that they are better off doing some of the work themselves rather than having the service provider do it all. One source of reinforcement is to have top management send clear signals that it holds line managers accountable for effective HR management. Another means for motivating line managers is to point out that the time and costs of participation are usually outweighed by benefits of greater commitment and control over events.

Two-way design of HR menu   This action step stems from the notion that quality services are "customized" rather than standardized. Tailored HR services require the line manager's active participation in the design of HR's *menu* of offerings. We emphasize the importance of HR's providing clients a menu as opposed to force-feeding them HR's "soup du jour" or "daily special." Just as quality menus offer different choices to adults, children, and the diet-conscious, a quality HR menu is varied and flexible in its application. For example, the line manager may prefer team building over a confrontation meeting, or cross-training over job rotation, or recruiting a new manager over training an existing one. The exact form of any of these choices is determined through intensive dialogue between line manager and HR executive.

Develop service-oriented effectiveness criteria   New criteria must be developed to assess the effectiveness of HR if it is to behave in a service-oriented manner. Traditional effectiveness indicators, such as number of employees trained per budgeted dollar or number of minorities advanced this year over last, reflect the use of short-term, countable criteria common to a production orientation. Overreliance on quantity as a measure of effectiveness fails to assess whether services were provided in a quality manner. Periodic sampling of client perceptions through questionnaires is one important way to measure HR success. Other success indicators include the frequency with which clients refer HR to new clients in the organization and the number of new projects requested by existing clients.

Finally, it might also be interesting to see how HR would fare if its clients were asked the following hypothetical question: How would you feel if your firm's HR function were deregulated; would you continue using it, or would you turn to outside sources? This question would obviously be tested if HR charged for its services instead of being assessed through fixed overhead. However, we should mention that HR's clients might be equally unsuccessful in finding an outside consultant with a service orientation. Consultants in the HR area are often caught up in manufacturing a "product" line—e.g., workbooks, slides, and videotapes—that can be sold in bulk to organizations, thus avoiding the income limits of labor-intensive consulting. HR as a product rather than a service seems to be the all-too-common orientation among HR practitioners, both internal staff groups and external consultants.

Be aware of service-product balance issues   Our call for a service orientation should not be heard as a total condemnation of product characteristics. Two important issues should be raised regarding an appropriate balance between service and product:

1. *Service drives production.* Personnel policy manuals, performance appraisal forms, and the like do not disappear with a service orientation. But whatever HR produces should be driven by the client's needs rather than by HR's attempt to keep up with the latest developments in HR programming. Production is concept- and customer-driven, not technology- and fad-driven.
2. *Service is not servility.* Serving a client's needs is far different from being a servant to the client's needs. A competent HR staff should not "give in" or "sell out" to the client in a misplaced effort to serve with a collaborative spirit. The effective HR practitioner contributes a valuable expertise that line managers lack. He or she must guard against becoming the manipulative arm of the client.

Know the business   This action step should appear on anyone's list of ways to improve HR. Line managers often lack respect for HR because HR managers appear unknowledgeable about marketing, finance, and technology. The effective HR executive must know his client's products, people, systems, and business terminology. The jargon of an HR specialist will have to be replaced by a language the client uses and understands. In sum, HR will have to demonstrate a "nuts and bolts" awareness of the line managers' jobs if it is to remain credible.

Accepting the challenge
We are challenging HR groups to move both backward and forward in rethinking their future direction. In a "backward" sense, we are calling upon HR to return to what it was initially intended to do: Act in a staff capacity providing a needed *service* to line management. In a "forward" sense, we are urging HR to draw on what has been learned about how quality service is provided in a services-based economy. This transition will not be easy, but if HR does not take the initiative to influence its own destiny, line management may take a less constructive path toward solving its growing frustration.

Selected bibliography
Other sources that discuss the shortcomings of corporate HR include Harish Jain and Victor Murray, "Why the Human Resources Management Function Fails" (*California Management Review*, Summer 1984) and Kenneth F. Misa and Timothy Stein, "Strategic HRM and the Bottom Line" (*Personnel Administrator*, October 1983).

Two sources that comprehensively describe organizational dynamics in the service sector are Christopher H. Lovelock, *Services Marketing* (Prentice-Hall, 1984) and John A. Czepiel, Michael R. Solomon, and Carol F. Suprenant (eds.), *The Service Encounter: Managing Employee/Customer Interaction in Service Businesses* (Lexington Books, 1985).

Downsizing with Dignity

George E. L. Barbee

At a party recently I ran into a Fortune 500 company CEO whom I had not seen in a while. Noticing that he seemed uncharacteristically withdrawn, I asked him what was bothering him. He confided that within the next year or two he would have to release several thousand employees. Among them would be long-time friends and colleagues, fellow members of business and social organizations, and, especially troubling, a mentor who had supported him on his rise to success.

During many sleepless nights, he thought about the tough questions he'd have to answer as he "downsized"—reduced the workforce of—his company. How to downsize quickly so his company could be more profitable? How to downsize with minimal disruption to those leaving and those remaining? How to ease the trauma facing valued employees and their families? How to downsize with dignity?

The plight of this CEO is an increasingly common one and will become more so in the years ahead. Although the reasons vary, many companies are developing downsizing programs to contain costs.

The downsizing trend began in the '70s as corporate America tightened its belt to cope with the recession. Although it was predicted that as the economy recovered employees would regain their jobs, this did not turn out to be true. In fact, many companies dis-

"Downsizing with Dignity: Trends in Employee Reduction Programs," reprinted with permission from *Price Waterhouse Review*, vol. 30, no. 3, 1986. The author of the article notes that Price Waterhouse's Consumer Financial Institute division is the largest independent provider of financial planning programs in the United States and a leader in innovative personalized employee communication services.

covered that staff reductions had not significantly hurt productivity but had significantly improved profits.

Why are companies downsizing?

Today corporations are downsizing for many reasons, the predominant one being cost containment. Large numbers of companies are experiencing rising compensation, benefits, and pension costs with no corresponding increase in revenues. To reduce expenses, organizations are being restructured, corporate pyramids are being flattened, and jobs—particularly middle-management positions—are being combined or eliminated.

Rising competition has contributed to the downsizing trend. With inexpensive goods from abroad flooding the marketplace and domestic competitive pressures increasing, corporations in all industries are striving to maintain competitive prices through leaner operations. This is especially true for companies in recently deregulated industries that were suddenly subjected to intense price competition and were forced to cut costs to survive.

Mergers, acquisitions, and divestitures are another important catalyst for downsizing. Combining entities typically have layers of duplication in management functions and need to eliminate redundant positions, and companies divesting themselves of units must usually let staff go.

The threat of takeovers is also a major motivation for downsizing: As corporate raiders search for targets, corporations must often put their houses in order to protect their independence. And companies that have successfully defended themselves from takeover attempts frequently incur large debts in the process—debts that are often paid off in part by reducing the workforce.

Another contributing factor to the downsizing revolution is technology. As factories, administrative functions, and executive offices become automated, many employees are being phased out. This trend is likely to continue as advanced computer and artificial intelligence systems are developed.

Also likely to perpetuate downsizing is the coming of age of the baby-boom generation. Baby-boomers climbing the corporate ladder often find their progress blocked because of older employees on the payroll. And the number of senior workers may multiply as people live longer, healthier lives and the mandatory retirement age rises. A major challenge for corporate management now and in the next several decades, therefore, will be to make room for those rising through the increasingly crowded ranks.

How are companies downsizing?

Just as doctors must choose among various treatments for seriously ill patients, so too must CEOs, CFOs, and human resource executives determine the most appropriate treatment for curing ailing companies. The courses of therapy being prescribed by cost-cutting U.S. companies include radical surgery, elective surgery, and preventive medicine.

Radical surgery: Terminations and plant closings "Radical surgery"—terminations and plant closings—may be needed to cope with unanticipated events requiring immediate staff reductions. Examples include sudden price drops, product obsolescence, takeovers and divestitures, and economic circumstances such as unfavorable foreign exchange developments. Radical surgery may also be necessary for companies experiencing financial or sales losses as a result of litigation or catastrophic events.

Under these circumstances, companies target groups of employees who will be released. These groups might include employees in specific divisions, plants, or geographic areas or employees who have not been performing well.

To avoid adverse employee and community reactions, companies must move quickly to adopt programs that make the best of a bad situation. Timely communications packages, career or outplacement counseling, and financial planning programs, for example, demonstrate that despite troubled times, the company is concerned about employees' welfare. This is important for the morale of both departing and remaining employees.

Companies releasing large numbers of workers often distribute to employees information kits communicating the reasons for termination programs and expressing sympathy for the personal effects of such programs. Follow-up communications may provide information about severance payments, retirement benefits, Social Security, state unemployment programs, and any other financial resources that terminated employees need to know about.

Some companies also provide targeted financial planning analyses to employees. These reports are customized for each departing employee and include specific details regarding company-provided sources of income that will be received at termination and during the months that follow. To help employees supplement this information, companies often provide worksheets regarding noncompany sources of income. Employees can then integrate and organize all their personal financial information to better develop post-termination financial strategies.

Candid communications about company crises and assistance in adopting financial plans for altered circumstances can ease the pain of termination and help employees through the transition.

Elective surgery: Early retirement programs Less drastic measures may be adopted by companies not involved in crisis conditions but aware that staff cutbacks will be necessary in time. Industries that foresee trends indicating probable loss of business are implementing "elective surgery" programs, or procedures to encourage early retirements in a less threatening, more gracious manner than terminations or layoffs.

Under such programs, targeted groups of employees are presented with the option of remaining with the company or taking advantage of early retirement inducements. By offering employees financial incentives to voluntarily move on to something new, these companies achieve their overall cost containment objectives while avoiding negative perceptions by their workers and the general public.

A popular method of encouraging early retirements is a "window," or limited-period, incentive program. Under this type of program, groups of employees meeting company-specified age and service requirements are offered early retirement "sweeteners," which may include a combination of lump-sum severance payments, pension bonuses, and extended medical and insurance coverage. Selected employees are generally 55 years old or more and eligible for pensions; however, some companies present incentives to younger employees who might be inclined to try something different, such as changing jobs or careers or starting their own businesses.

Typically, employees selected for the program have only 30 to 90 days to decide whether to stay put or take advantage of the incentives offered. To help employees make this decision, many companies provide a variety of counseling services. For example, some offer outplacement counseling and assistance in finding new jobs or adjusting to not working.

Other companies provide financial planning services that help employees answer the question "Can I afford to retire?" and assist them in making decisions about their pension, benefits, and tax options. Such financial counseling can be an important factor in the success of an early retirement incentive program for a number of reasons.

Reluctance to elect early retirement frequently stems from financial uncertainty. Many individuals would be hard pressed to assess their current financial condition, much less project their income for the years ahead. Personal financial planning and professional counseling enable individuals to organize their finances and evaluate their economic position.

Often, employees considering early retirement are surprised to discover how financially secure they really are. When analyzing all their sources of income—working spouse income and benefits, company profit-sharing and savings plans, investment income, Social Security—they find that they are much better off than they thought. Once relieved of their financial uncertainty, they feel more economically self-reliant and comfortable about moving on to something new.

Financial counseling helps an employee decide whether to accept the employer's offer by addressing questions crucial to early retirement elections, such as: How will my retirement and pension plans help me? How heavily can I depend on my savings and investments? What Social Security benefits can I expect? How will inflation affect me in the years ahead? What are the income tax effects of my retirement benefit options?

In addition to providing employees with peace of mind regarding their long-term financial status, financial counseling also helps workers analyze the effects of various critical—and often irrevocable—decisions that must usually be made very quickly. These decisions include: What pension plan payment option is best for me? Should I roll over distributions from company plans into an IRA? Should I take a lump-sum retirement distribution? When should I begin collecting Social Security? Should I sell my home?

Beyond relieving employees of some of the anxiety associated with downsizing, financial planning programs provide peace of mind to employers. The executive who can't sleep at night because of concern over departing employees' welfare gains comfort knowing that the company has made an effort to ease employees' transitions and alleviate financial doubts.

Financial planning provided in connection with downsizing programs is cost-effective, helping companies achieve their cost containment goal. As one executive offering early retirement incentives to several hundred employees told me, "If only two of the 300 employees selected for the program accept our offer, the cost of providing financial planning services will be repaid." In fact, companies in which hundreds of employees elect early retirement can save millions of dollars in salary, pension, and other benefits costs.

Many companies choose in-depth personalized reports, group seminars, or a combination of the two as the most economical methods of providing financial planning. These methods are less time-consuming and less costly than one-on-one counseling for large numbers of geographically dispersed employees during a period when time and cost savings are of the essence.

Company human resources departments are sometimes called upon to provide financial advisory services to employees. However, external advisers are frequently engaged for a number of reasons. First, employees are less likely to feel pressured or resentful when dealing with an objective third party. Second, they are often more comfortable providing confidential financial information to people outside the organization. In addition, external advisers may be better able to communicate information about company developments and programs on an unemotional level during what may be a traumatic period for all concerned.

Preventive medicine: Financial planning   Longer-term—or "preventive-medicine"—activities that help companies contain costs include financial planning programs for employees in their 30s, 40s, and 50s. While early retirement windows are intended to encourage immediate staff reductions, often in response to specific events, early financial planning programs are a proactive method to promote ongoing timely or early retirements.

When employees begin financial planning earlier in life, they are better able to accumulate wealth. By taking advantage of compound interest and well-reasoned investment strategies throughout their working lives, they become less dependent on their employer for financial security. In addition to helping employees achieve economic well-being—and fostering good employee relations in the process—financial planning also offers the company several cost containment advantages.

In the short term, by enhancing communication about and appreciation of employee benefits, financial planning programs reduce the pressure on companies to provide additional benefits. Promoting informed decisions about existing employee benefits also helps employers reduce corporate spending on redundant or unnecessary benefits. Moreover, financial planning programs themselves serve as a low-cost, highly valued benefit at a time when more costly benefits, such as health care, are being cut back. Financial planning programs also benefit the company in the long term: Employees who feel financially self-reliant are more likely to retire on time or earlier than those who don't.

Productivity may also be enhanced by financial planning programs. Lack of financial planning leads to economic uncertainty that may divert employees' attention, and employees attempting their own planning often find the process stressful and time-consuming. When freed of some of their financial planning responsibilities, employees can devote more energy and attention to company matters.

Executives who have gone through the agony of downsizing programs are taking steps to ensure that the experience will not have to be repeated; by helping employees plan for their financial well-being, they may be able to avoid downsizing programs through the voluntary attrition of financially secure individuals. And if downsizing programs prove to be necessary, the goodwill that has been generated over the years by employer-sponsored financial planning assistance can minimize employee morale problems.

Downsizing with dignity

Downsizing is never a pleasant process, but there are ways to minimize negative effects. Developing programs that offer support to employees—and help relieve both employers and employees of the anxiety they often feel during the downsizing period—is the key to downsizing with dignity.

Training
in the '90s

Ron Zemke

"Seers and prophets come out of the woodwork in times of uncertainty," begins a *Fortune* magazine article on the business of trend spotting and future forecasting. True to our turbulent times, as Peter Drucker has dubbed this decade, there is no shortage of specialists ready and willing to tell corporate America, or anyone else who will listen, what tomorrow will bring....

More than 150 private research institutes and think tanks in the United States claim to be involved in some aspect of future research. A few corporations even employ staff futurists. There are so many futurists in this country that they have their own professional association: the Washington, DC-based World Future Society, which claims some 20,000 dues-paying members.

There is nothing new about crystal-ball gazing, of course. But sheep entrails, star configurations, tossed coins, dealt cards, creased palms and refuse in the bottom of teacups are yesterday's news. Today's seers eschew the arcane in favor of computer extrapolations and trend-analysis technology. The result, however, is the same: prognostication. And the more startling, the better. Who, after all, is interested in hearing that tomorrow's prospects look just like today's?

The future and HRD

Literally thousands of published reports and predictions on the future are available. Government agencies, associations, private re-

Adapted with permission from the January 1987 issue of TRAINING, The Magazine of Human Resources Development. Copyright 1987, Lakewood Publications, Inc., Minneapolis, MN (612) 333-0471. All rights reserved. This article is based, in part, on research on future trends conducted by the author and Dana Gaines Robinson, president of Partners in Change, Pittsburgh.

search organizations, foundations, corporations, universities and individual, wandering seers all contribute their dime's worth to the pile. The task of sorting out the predictions for a specific field, like human resources development, is a matter of looking at the reams of compiled and projected information others have assembled, and putting it into a context.

One reasonable anchor for looking at the future is the past. Someone, probably a history professor with an enrollment problem, observed correctly that unless we understand our past we are doomed to repeat it. In the short history of HRD, at least four factors have shaped everyday practice. From broadest to most narrow, they are (1) external social forces, (2) the nature and composition of the labor force, (3) organizational structure and (4) technology. Changes in these same arenas will continue to shape the field.

External social forces

It is an understatement to assert that organizations do not exist in a vacuum. What transpires in the courts, legislative bodies and government agencies of this country can have a dramatic impact on management practices. And that is as true in the training room as it is on the factory floor or in the executive suite. Minority rights and feminist issues, for instance, have required employers to address training to legal pitfalls in performance appraisal and hiring practices, as well as formerly unheard-of concepts such as fair employment practices and sexual harassment.

Unionization   Unions are not popular with young people today. The decline of factory jobs in general has led to the lowest union membership in decades. But it is important to remember that an avowed goal of the AFL-CIO is to organize the "pink ghettos," as large offices full of data-entry workers, telephone salespeople and so on are called in the '80s.

The growing legion of low-paid, low-skill service workers is seen as another opportunity area for the unions, though the generally transient nature of many service workers is a considerable barrier.

White-collar workers, especially technical professionals and first-line supervisors, are considered vulnerable to union organization as well. If schoolteachers, university professors and nurses can be organized, why not computer programmers, chemists or quality-control inspectors? One school of thought suggests that such organizations might take the form of the old guild structure, with closed professions, apprenticeships and contract labor as opposed to "owned" employment.

Many organizations are finding that they can contain and minimize the threat by "taking a page from the union book"—that is, by having formal grievance procedures, published pay scales, established career ladders, acceptable working conditions and competitive pay.

Regulation   For most of the past decade, the federal government has been reluctant to impose new regulation on American business. Instead, the *deregulation* of industries—transportation, banking and telecommunications—has been grabbing most of the attention.

But at the same time, some current regulations are being enforced with more precision. The U.S. Department of Transportation, for example, took the Kentucky State Highway Department to task for denying female employees access to road-crew jobs. Such pinpoint enforcement is likely to continue.

Despite a more sympathetic federal administration, few organizations seem anxious to dismantle compliance apparatus already in place. And state and local bodies have become other additives in our food.

Two-thirds to three-fourths of the work force of 1990 will be made up of working parents, and as many as 25% will be responsible for the care of an aging parent. These "dependent-heavy" householders will be willing to trade off salary for a broad range of benefits and protections, from day care to extended family health coverage. Flexible work arrangements and assurance against transfers will also hold appeal.

Consumerism   By 1990, says the Department of Commerce, the 35-to-54 age group will be the principal retail consumer group in the United States. These consumers spend freely now. Chances are they will continue to spend, not save, and to demand "fun," excitement and high quality in their purchases. They are a vocal and fickle group, showing little brand loyalty and exhibiting severe fad-following behavior. This is the group responsible for the second-mortgage explosion in the United States today.

The texture of the economy   We live in a service economy. Seventy-three percent of all jobs and 65% of the GNP come from organizations that perform rather than produce. And according to the U.S. Department of Commerce, the trend away from manufacturing and toward a service-based economy shows no sign of abating.

As the economy becomes more service centered, consumers are becoming more service sensitive. The quality of service that accompanies a product is a key to customer satisfaction. Manufacturers that see service as a competitive advantage are "wiring" the factory into the service loop. Some put customer service units in the factory. Others routinely circulate service complaints to line personnel. Some even send supervisors to the field to meet wholesale and retail customers. The result: less distance between factory and consumer, which leads, presumably, to responsiveness to customer needs and innovation at the factory level.

Some traditional manufacturing organizations are diversifying into services. General Motors Acceptance Corp., according to some criteria, is the largest lending institution in the country. Ford Motor Co. has been in the savings and loan business for some time. Many manufacturers are going out of the fixed-assets business (building and running factories) and segueing into the business of marketing the technologies they already have developed.

Global economy   You don't need a futurist to tell you that U.S. companies are moving their manufacturing functions overseas. Foreign joint ventures, with U.S. companies supplying capital and technological know-how, should increase.

Changes in the work force*

Average age of the work force
In 1975	28 years
In 1990	40 years

The work force by 1990
Women	45%
Minorities	15
Foreign "guest" laborers	20
Children of single-parent households	25
White collar	55

Education levels in the 1990s workplace
High-school graduates	75%
College graduates	33
Advanced degrees	9
Functionally illiterate	18

Today's work force is
Less...	*More...*
Mobile	Health-conscious
Loyal	Self-centered
Thrifty	Experience-seeking
Obedient	Challenging

Tailoring employment in 1990
Permanent part-time	50%
Flextime	25
Home workers	10

*Figures are the author's extrapolations from various data sources.

The work force

Changes in the nature and composition of the labor force have had a significant impact on HRD. During World War II, the severe shortage of adult males in the labor force brought women out of the homes and into the factories—and created a need for the corporate training department. In the late 1950s and early 1960s, the need for more managers than colleges and universities could produce led to the first concerted efforts in management training and development. The minority rights movements of the 1960s and 1970s led to changes in the training of supervisors and managers, as did the ascent of career-oriented women in the 1970s and '80s. It's a safe bet that these types of changes—and the need to react to them—will continue to affect HRD.

In January of 1975, Leonard Silk, economics analyst for *The New York Times*, wrote that "The closing decades of the 20th century will be characterized by a conflict between economic efficiency and social equity, the demands of productivity and the needs of people." The truth of this prediction is borne out in the changing nature of workplace demographics and in the wants, needs and values of the people who work for a living. There are seven aspects of the work force of tomorrow that we need to think about: the aging of the work force, increased workplace diversity, changing educational levels, changing values, employee expectations, supervisors' views and a new sense of loyalties.

The aging work force   According to the U.S. Bureau of Labor Statistics, we are about to experience the oldest work force in recorded history. By 1990, 70% of the work force will be in the 25- to 54-year-old bracket. At the same time, there will be a smaller proportion of workers 55 and older.

The "pig in the python" is becoming a serious career-ladder obstruction for the "baby boom" generation. The universal corporate carrot—the promotion—is growing ever more elusive. More and more people are chasing fewer and fewer management jobs. As today's 30-year-olds discover that the next chair is occupied, and the next and the next—with none of the occupants due to retire soon—retaining good employees will become a bigger problem.

There is also pretty good evidence that job-skill obsolescence becomes more severe after age 35. Researchers Gene Dalton and Paul Thompson have found that professionals who reach age 35 without regular promotions—i.e., plateaued professionals—receive steadily worsening performance reviews as time passes.

Valuable technical professionals once moved into management and supervisory positions rapidly enough that their technical obsolescence was a moot point. But the oversupply of people seeking management jobs and the decreasing need for managers now make upward mobility an iffy aspiration. The problem becomes how to keep these professionals up-to-date.

An aging work force also means that the supply of cheap, entry-level labor is drying up. Fewer and fewer young people will be available to bus dishes, flip burgers, carry luggage, and sell records and clothing to their peers for minimum wages.

In some regions of the country, fast-food chains are advertising in hopes of enticing the few remaining full-time homemakers off the bench and into the game—at least part-time. A McDonald's franchise in Darien, CT, buses teens in from the Bronx, 28 miles away, to keep its restaurants running. Zayre's, a discount department store chain in the Northeast, runs direct-mail recruiting campaigns aimed at attracting high school students to part-time jobs. But these are temporary measures, not long-term solutions.

Just how *do* we keep the burgers frying, the platters flying and the candy wrappers off the floor of the neighborhood Cinema 6, without this traditional labor supply?

Growing work-force diversity   The work force of tomorrow will be even more diverse than the work force of today. By the year 1990, most forecasters agree, there will be more women, more minorities and more handicapped individuals in the mainstream of the work force. The growth of the country's Hispanic and Asian populations, coupled with a projected increase in dependence on "guest" workers (foreign nationals with green cards), could lead to serious communication problems.

How do we make skillful employees of guest workers? Are we willing to concede a permanent employee underclass? Are we ready to pour money into the reading, writing and arithmetic training that could be required to bring permanent foreign workers into the personnel mainstream?

The "Ozzie and Harriet" nuclear family, already confirmed by the last U.S. Census as a minority life-style, will account for only 15% of U.S. households in 1990. At the same time, one in four working people will have been raised in a one-parent household. Some sociologists are suggesting that supervisors and managers from "traditional" family backgrounds will have trouble relating to those from a different background.

Another pertinent figure comes from the FBI's crime statistics. Forty-two percent of the crimes committed in this country today are committed by people under 21 years of age. One estimate suggests that, given the number of young people who have been involved with some form of crime over the last 15 years, 20% of the labor pool of tomorrow could have a felony history. "We won't hire any of *those*," you say? Then just who will you hire and train?

If you don't see a big connection between the new diversity of the American work force and your HRD efforts, ask yourself this question: How dependent is your management and supervisory and customer service training on the empathy derived from shared values, culture and heritage between supervisor and employee?

Changing education levels   In some ways we are becoming over-educated for the work to be done. In the mid-1970s, we were producing twice as many teachers as there were teaching jobs. Today we are overproducing lawyers, MBAs, dentists and doctors.

In 1990 there will be about 15 million college graduates and 12 to 13 million jobs available that require a college education. Forty-five percent of these graduates will be from technical or occupation-specific fields. In 1975 there were 10 qualified candidates for every middle-management job available, according to Anthony Carnevale, economist for the American Society for Training and Development. By 1990 the ratio is expected to reach 30:1.

At the same time, we are facing the results of several years of deterioration in the public school system. A recent study by the University of Texas concluded that 26 million adult Americans are "functionally illiterate"—they can't read or write well enough to fill out a job application or do enough arithmetic to count change. Jonathan Kozol, author of *Illiterate America,* estimates that another 46 million adults are "marginally" literate—they function at about the fifth-grade level in basic skills. A U.S. military report estimated that 27% of Army enlistees can't read training manuals written at a seventh-grade level.

According to Kozol, the pool of functionally illiterate adults grows at about 2.5 million people a year. Included in that number are one million high school dropouts, 700,000 high school graduates and 800,000 illegal immigrants. That means by 1990, at the current rates, two million functional illiterates will have graduated from high school and joined the ranks of job seekers.

Stop for a moment and calculate the print dependency of the last training program you put on the boards. Worse yet, how much did it depend upon the ability of the trainees not only to read and write, but also to add and subtract?

Changing values   It's no longer surprising to hear that the values of people in the work force are changing. Some attribute it to the social upheavals of the '60s and '70s, others to changes in parenting and schooling. Whatever the cause, the common assumption is that we face a workplace populated by people whose values are somewhat different from those of previous generations of workers.

Where we once were loyal, credulous, thrifty and essentially obedient, we have become self-centered, distrustful, more prone to spend than save and more challenging of authority.

A University of Michigan study found that 77% of people polled believe that "people get ahead on personality today" as opposed to getting ahead by hard work or any associated work-ethic values (e.g., track record, contributions to the company, etc.)

The same study found that a "happy home life" outweighed "job satisfaction" 2:1, and that "living in a nice place" outweighed a job promotion by the same ratio. Recruiters have noted a growing tendency for professionals and managers to reject job offers that require relocation to a less desirable locale despite significant increases in responsibility and pay.

A 25-year longitudinal study of young managers' values and attitudes by Douglas Bray, former director of basic human resources research at AT&T, found:

1. A continuously decreasing desire to "climb the corporate ladder" (54% of the young AT&T managers Bray studied in 1950 scored high on measurements of this desire vs. 34% in 1975).
2. A decrease in desire to "lead others" (49% vs. 22%).
3. A decreasing "need for approval from others" (68% vs. 37%).

These findings and others like them have led some to speculate that there is a new generation of managers who don't particularly want to be leaders *or* followers, and who aren't especially interested in "getting ahead" in the strict traditional sense (see "Brave New Managers," TRAINING, June 1986).

Employment expectations   While employees expect work to be tailored to their wants, needs and lifestyles, organizations are increasingly using people on an "as needed" basis to control costs. The result is a trend toward part-time employment, desirable from both the employees' and employers' perspectives, which is predicted to escalate until as much as half of the work force is permanent part-time. The trend soon will include a sizable percentage of professionals, administrators and supervisors, as well as clerical and blue-collar employees.

Several experts, including John Naisbitt, expect job sharing, variable and frequent leaves of absence, long-term temporary contracts and multiple job holding to be common, if not the norm, by 1990. "Home workers," so-called telecommuters working from their "electronic cottages," as well as people doing various kinds of factory-type piecework at home, may account for one in 10 employed people.

According to a study by a data processing association, about 12% of all systems analysts and computer programmers working in the United States today are contract professionals; that is, they actually work for a company that leases them out to other organizations. Demand for analysts is expected to grow 120% by 1990. Demand for computer operators is supposed to grow by 90% and for programmers by 87%. The study suggested that 71% of corporate DP managers already have trouble finding people to fill openings.

It is difficult enough for the supervisor of a group of "captive" technical employees to manage and motivate the troops. How will they deal with the performance problems of leased employees? By the same token, how does a manager in the leasing firm monitor and appraise the performance of leased employees when the latter spend most of their time on the client's premises, working on projects the manager may be prohibited by contract from knowing about in any detail?

Supervisors' views   If the first-line supervisor will continue to be a key player in tomorrow's successful organization, it is important to know how supervisors are faring today. It is not news that first-line supervision is one of the toughest jobs an individual can have. The supervisor is at the bottom of the authority structure and at the top of the complaint chain.

Several research efforts suggest that life for the incumbent first-line supervisor is no bed of roses. A study by Opinion Research Corp. of Princeton, NJ, reported that first-line supervisors see themselves as "on-the-spot" between labor and management, lacking control over their work, low on organizational "input" and poorly equipped to manage.

To be specific, ORC reports that more than 60% of supervisors say their bosses do a poor job of telling them how they are doing. Only 40% think their company does an adequate job of telling them what and how the organization is doing. Less than 50% feel they were adequately prepared to supervise.

Loyalty   It's become a cliché that loyalty to one's employer, in the traditional sense, is becoming a thing of the past. Some pundits attribute the loss to a different set of values among baby boomers and younger employees. Others point out that the long-term security companies once offered in *exchange* for loyalty is also becoming a thing of the past.

A study of graduating college seniors with business and professional degrees concluded that they wanted "stimulation, advancement and a voice in what they do and how things are done." Asked what they would do if they took a job and found those wants unmet, 60% said they would "look for another company to work for."

Organizational structure

The way organizations are structured has an impact on both the content and delivery of training. When decentralized approaches are fashionable, training at a distance becomes the act to be mastered. Content changes as well: Participation, self-direction and leadership become curriculum items. When centralization is the password of the week, supervision, team building and communication are content concerns. Centralization also frequently produces the need for the corporate college and a strong, centralized training department.

Downsizing/de-layering   Today, for reasons both economic and social, the traditional pyramidal organization is quickly losing layers and luster. The result is "downsized" and "reconfigured" organizations.

Automation, decentralization, "demassing" and the changing nature of the work force are conspiring to create the need for new and different work structures. Between 1981 and 1983, half of the nation's 1,000 largest companies eliminated at least one layer of management, according to *Fortune* magazine. General Motors and Chrysler reported eliminating three, and Ford five layers.

In a 1986 survey of TRAINING readers, 26% of respondents reported that managers in their organizations tend to have more direct reports than they did five years ago; 52% said today's managers are more accountable for results; 54% said their organizations' managers appear more stressed; and 48% reported that managers are working more hours. Sixty-three percent said managers are expected to increase output with no increase in staff; 25% said managers regularly work weekends to keep up. One in three respondents reported that some managers in their organizations are working at or near burnout level. It is tempting to conclude that all the delayering and downsizing is beginning to take a toll on the surviving managers.

Companies such as Ralston Purina, Eaton and Cummins Engine have had experimental "leaderless" production teams in place since the early '70s. It appears that more participative working relations through innovations like leaderless, temporary and participative group structures is an idea whose time may have arrived.

The Japanese scare of the late '70s and early '80s, and the accompanying accounts of how Japanese workers take responsibility for productivity and quality, led to experimentation with participative approaches such as quality circles. One of the offshoots, courtesy of Swedish manufacturers including Volvo and Saab, has been a movement away from the traditional assembly line toward a team-assembly process.

As the downsizing movement continues and alternatives to assembly operations increase, employees will need to be more able to self-manage. Some theorists suggest that in order to avoid obsolescence and to be most productive in the new work structures, employees will have to develop "clustered" skills—skills beyond the narrowly focused ones provided by today's version of technical training.

Technology

Changes in technology, both hard and soft technologies, have always had a significant impact on HRD—and not just in terms of the content of training programs but in the way programs are built and delivered. Programmed instruction was a soft technology that affected the training field in the 1960s; the cheap and easy-to-use microcomputer was a hard technology that produced a major impact in the 1980s. In the '70s, the marriage of the videocassette and the concept of behavior modeling changed the way we designed, developed and packaged interpersonal and other behaviorally specific skills training.

Hard technologies for the 1990s   Computers, robotics and other forms of advanced technology will continue to have a significant impact on the manufacturing workplace. According to various estimates, between $300 and $500 billion will be spent on office automation and advanced manufacturing automation over the next decade. One estimate by the Department of Commerce puts fixed capital plant and equipment investment for the next 10 years at 10% to 15% of the GNP. The common analogy: The robotics industry today is where the auto industry was in 1910. Some experts suggest this period of rapid innovation will last from 30 to 50 years.

Future Shock author Alvin Toffler and others have used the term "demassing" to characterize the flexibility of scheduling and production that advanced automation is expected to bring to manufacturing. Some predict that advanced automation also will result in smaller, more decentralized manufacturing facilities.

Automation is decreasing the number of people it takes to manufacture hard goods, and changing the kinds of skills needed in the manufacturing environment. Production workers increasingly will become "automation technicians" who will need a broad range of troubleshooting abilities and complex cross-training. Today's robotics technicians need knowledge of hydraulics, mechanics, electronics and programming. They must be able to troubleshoot across *all* of these disciplines.

The role of supervisors will change as well. They will have to be comfortable supervising work they don't necessarily understand or help perform.

Soft technologies for the 1990s   In addition to the obvious soft technologies—like computer and robotics programming—that are needed to make the automated workplace go, supervisors must learn to access data bases and handle complex scheduling and operations management problems that will require the use of a computer to solve. Manufacturing managers and supervisors will need much larger tool kits of management skills. The soft technologies usually mentioned in connection with the "factory of the future" are dynamic programming, short-interval scheduling (SIS), local-area networks (LAN), just-in-time scheduling (JIT) and manufacturing automation protocol (MAP).

One of the less frequently addressed new soft technologies is the development of "smart" tools. The U.S. Air Force already uses smart tools to assist human technicians in the diagnosis and repair of sophisticated equipment. Who will build smart tools and expert systems (computer programs that function like human experts, providing advice and instruction) in organizations, and how will employees be trained to use them? And what are the pros and cons of teaching technicians to be dependent on smart tools instead of carrying expertise around in their heads?

Several instructional technology journals are already predicting that the advent of practical expert systems development tools will have a significant impact on both public education and industrial training.

Which future? Your future

How do we know which pieces of this whole puzzle we should take to heart? Rule of thumb: the ones that make the most sense in your experience, for your industry and your organization.

There is, it sometimes seems, a fatalistic, *fait accompli* assumption behind any prediction of what might be. And therein lies the enigma: The future is what we make out of the complexity of the here and now, as well as the thousand and one surprises that invariably lie beyond the next hill. In the words of novelist Joseph Conrad, "The mind of man is capable of anything—because everything is in it, all the past as well as the future."

Further reading

Albrecht, Karl, and Ron Zemke. *Service America! Doing Business in the New Economy.* Homewood, IL: Dow Jones-Irwin, 1985.

Bell, Chip. "Training and Development in the 1980s," *Personnel Administrator*, August 1980.

Dalton, Gene W., and Paul H. Thompson. *Novations: Strategies for Career Management*, Glenview, IL: Scott, Foresman and Co., 1986.

Drucker, Peter. *Managing in Turbulent Times*, New York: Harper and Row, 1980.

Hatakeyama, Yoshio. *Manager Revolution: A Guide to Survival in Today's Changing Workplace.* Cambridge, MA: Productivity Press, 1985.

Houze, William C. *Career Veer*, New York: McGraw-Hill Book Co., 1985.

Howard, Ann, and Douglas Bray. "AT&T: The Hopes of Middle Managers," *The New York Times*, 21 March, 1982.

Morgan, Brian S., and William A. Schiemann. *Supervision in the '80s: Trends in Corporate America*, Princeton, NJ: Opinion Research Corp., 1984.

Naisbitt, John. *The Year Ahead: These Ten Trends Will Shape the Way You Live, Work & Make Money in 1985*, Washington, DC: The Naisbitt Group, 1985.

Piercy, Nigel (Ed.). *The Management Implications of the New Information Technology*, Beckenham Kent, GB: Croom Helm Ltd., 1984.

Rukeyser, Louis. *What's Ahead for the Economy*, New York: Simon and Schuster, 1983.

Toffler, Alvin. *The Adaptive Corporation*, New York: McGraw-Hill Book Co., 1985.

Weiss, Alan Jay. "HRD in the Information Age," *Training*, October 1981.

Zemke, Ron. "Delayed Effects of Corporate Downsizing," *Training*, November 1986.

The New Workforce Meets the Changing Workplace

Rosabeth Moss Kanter

A popular cliché about the design of American work systems holds that the problems of work can be solved by a shift to a more participative, entrepreneurial workplace. This shift, the argument runs, would solve two problems. It would create more opportunity for the ambitious "new workforce," and it would restore international competitiveness by tapping new sources of creativity and enterprise.

Limited workplace reform, in that view, is all that is needed to respond to the growing expectations of the changing workforce. The desires of the labor force for meaningful work and the desires of employers for greater innovation and productivity could be satisfied simultaneously—a happy situation, indeed.

This essay views the situation more pessimistically—or, at least, sees it as more complex and difficult. It is in the nature of social systems that "solutions," particularly limited ones, beget new "problems," as the impact of a limited change begins to be felt in other parts of the system. And chipping away at one part of a structure may cause cracks in other parts.

Just as Daniel Bell identified the "cultural contradictions" of capitalism,[1] I attempt here to identify three "organizational contradictions" engendered by attempts to implement participative-entrepreneurial management principles. I argue that efforts to give employees more opportunity to contribute new ideas raise questions

Revision of a paper presented at the 1985 meeting of the American Sociological Association, Washington, D.C. Special thanks to Cynthia Ingols for excellent assistance. "The New Workforce Meets the Changing Workplace: Strains, Dilemmas, and Contradictions in Attempts to Implement Participative and Entrepreneurial Management," reprinted by permission of John Wiley & Sons, Inc., from *Human Resources Management*, Winter 1986, Vol. 25, Number 4, pp. 515–537. ©1986 by John Wiley & Sons, Inc.

about how pay is determined and how the payroll should be divided. Second, I question whether or not the new entrepreneurial management modes are compatible with the command orientation and bureaucratic-hierarchical trappings of today's organizations. And third, I suggest that the very spread of the new forms of work threatens equal opportunity goals. If the new workplace emphasis on greater involvement makes earnings dependent on initiative, then the time demands of work could increase. If this occurs, then those who shoulder the burden of out-of-work responsibilities (primarily women) could be excluded from "equal opportunities."

In short, while workplace reform has the potential to fulfill many of the expectations of the new workforce, it also points to more fundamental problems in the design of organizations. The ideal-typical twentieth century bureaucracy could be showing cracks and strains, tensions and contradictions which point to the need for a new concept of the corporation.

This article is by necessity speculative. Although I have summoned evidence to support my analysis, the issues dealt with in this article hover under the surface of observable phenomena. By definition, these issues cannot be visible to the actors who experience only parts of them. It is the task of sociologists to find the wider patterns, the larger implications, contained in the fragments of new experience that begin to present themselves in times of rapid change.

I will first provide some background on the new workforce and the changing workplace. Then I will explore the three principal tensions arising out of the confluence of workforce and workplace, concluding with some reflections on the dilemma that change poses to both the new workforce and new workplace alike.

Background: Workplace reform

In the 1970s, the corporation was under attack for being unresponsive to the needs, values, and abilities of a changing workforce. The profile of the American workforce had changed in important ways since the mid-1960s, in both demographic characteristics (female and minority participation, age, and educational attainment) and in expectations (more career-minded, more rights conscious, and more concerned with "meaningful" work.[2]

Beginning in the early 1970s, many analysts pointed to a growing mismatch between the characteristics of the workforce and the ability of the workplace, as then typically constituted, to satisfy the new expectations. One labor economist argued, in a book appropriately subtitled *The Great Training Robbery*, that the payoff from education was declining because of a growing scarcity of "desirable" jobs;[3] too many jobs were too narrow to use the skills and capacity of the workforce.

Furthermore, promotion opportunities (one of the major sources of increase in pay, challenge, and influence in a large corporation) were thought to be declining. Increased competition from a larger number of aspirants, an aging workforce postponing retirement, and a slower-growth economy prevented the organizational pyramid from expanding to accommodate all those seeking the "better" jobs.

Even recently, popular management publications have made dire predictions about the problems about to occur as the baby boom generation reaches middle management, only to find their route upward blocked by bosses who would not step aside. Commentators wondered how these newcomers would assassinate their bosses.

The old workplace, then, was seen as inhospitable to the new workforce.

At the same time, there were also signs that the corporate workplace was beginning to change in ways that would better suit the new workforce.

The impetus for these changes was only partially a response to the existence of new employee characteristics and attitudes, except where these were made the subject of government decrees, as in the case of equal employment opportunity. Even among the most progressive companies, for whom workplace reform was a longstanding interest predating popular concerns, change was a response to business concerns and competitive pressures as much as or more than to a recognition of employee needs, though these companies had in place more mechanisms than their counterparts for collecting data on workforce changes.

For example, General Motors was influenced to begin a Quality of Work Life program with the United Auto Workers in 1972 because of experience with much higher productivity and quality in plants that had experimented with degrees of worker involvement in the 1960s; the bottom-line benefits to the company were clear. The program was helped along by adverse publicity from the wildcat strikes at the Lordstown Vega plant, and then given a real boost by the success of Japanese cars in the U.S. market after the second energy crisis.[4] Indeed, the speed of workplace reform in the U.S. was significantly increased after the "discovery" of the importance of certain human resource management practices in Japanese firms.

While it is very difficult to document the real extent of use of new forms of workplace organization across American corporations, there are indications from company surveys that new workplace practices such as these have been spreading in use since the 1970s and even beginning to be seen as normative:[5]

1.   Employee involvement programs, including, but not confined to, quality circles and problem-solving teams in which employees are vested with more responsibility for and authority

over changes that will improve performance. In some cases, they participate in organizational governance or sit on task forces making recommendations or decisions in areas well beyond the employees' usual jobs.

2. "Matrix" organization structures and project-team-based organizations;
3. Organizational restructuring to reduce layers of the hierarchy, often layers in the middle, which significantly enlarges job scope, creates closer communication with the top, and gives greater responsibility without waiting for promotion;
4. Programs to stimulate innovation and entrepreneurship, such as internal venture funds which allow people to start businesses within the umbrella of the large corporation; and
5 Flextime, part-time work, and job sharing, to allow people to exercise more choice over hours worked in order to accommodate non-work interests or responsibilities.

As practices like these spread, they do indeed better match the needs and expectations of the new workforce, enabling them to use skills, find meaningful work, and balance work and family responsibilities. *But each problem solved also creates new strains.* As the new forms spread, they begin to conflict with other, often unexamined premises about corporate organization. As new forms take hold, they can pose challenges to the legitimacy of still other corporate practices, reaching further into fundamentals and becoming more threatening to those who benefit disproportionately from the status quo.

Because the pace of social change is uneven, some organizations are much further along in facing these problems than others. The most reform-minded, or "progressive," are much likelier to experience these contradictions and dilemmas because of their longer experience with workplace changes. Other corporations are only at the beginning stages of implementing new workplace practices.

As stated earlier, I identify here three principal dilemmas stemming from new workplace practices:

1. *The impact of greater employee participation on the legitimacy of pay systems*—raising questions about how pay is determined and how the payroll is divided;
2. *The impact of the desire for innovation and entrepreneurship on the legitimacy of management controls;* and
3. *The tension between equal opportunity for women and the increasing absorptiveness of work.*

My observations are drawn from several sources: ongoing field work on the change problems in major corporations, including detailed documentation of over thirty "change episodes"; a survey of 1,618 member organizations of all sizes, of the American Management Association;[6] a comparison of 45 companies nominated by experts as innovative in human resource areas with a matched control group of 40 similar companies, including a survey on implementation of new work practices;[7] access to in-company surveys and expert commentary; and the literature.

Strain #1: Participation and pay

The new workforce has more education, at all levels; expects a greater voice in decisions at work; and wants opportunities beyond the job to use skills. At the same time, the new workplace is characterized by a requirement of higher levels of employee effort and mechanisms to stimulate this effort. For example, in the American Management Association company survey, it was discovered that almost half used cross-training and about one-third had quality circles, project teams, or the heavy use of task forces—all mechanisms for giving employees opportunities to participate beyond the job and to get involved in innovative activities. As employees contribute beyond the job, then rank and job definitions should become less important as determinants of how much employees contribute. At this point, the legitimacy of traditional distribution of pay is called into question—and with this, the legitimacy of the traditional hierarchy.

This is a major change. Employees have always expressed great concerns about pay, but the basic premises of the system appear to have been accepted. Employees wonder about the fairness of the distribution of rewards, but not the basis for determining how much each job is paid in the first place. For example, in one in-house survey of 12,000 employees of a large manufacturing company, there was a prevalent feeling that poor performance was tolerated, especially in the upper ranks, and high agreement that "who you know" counts for more than "what you know." But there was little indication that anyone challenged the setting of pay levels.

Traditional pay systems are based largely on the cost of hiring (market forces), later rationalized into grading systems based on levels of responsibility (internal equity). While there was generally a small merit component in the traditional system, increases in pay largely came with promotion, thereby contributing to the dramatic emphasis on upward mobility in American corporations.

But the legitimacy of traditional systems is beginning to erode. The introduction of new work systems responding to the new labor force and the pressures on U.S. industry to become more competitive in an international marketplace both drive forward, giving people enlarged opportunities to contribute and then rewarding them for that contribution. Intensely competitive situations require organizations to engage more of the effort of their workforce and, along with this, to find new ways to create incentives for increased performance.

Six new pay issues are emerging to rattle the iron cage of bureaucracy. *These challenges all move pay away from a status basis toward a contribution basis*, wreaking havoc with hierarchy in the process.

The important issue is not how many organizations actually use each alternative, but the fact that so many alternatives and experiments co-exist.[8] Each begins from a different premise, but in total they underline dilemmas for established notions of organization.

Pay-for-performance   Merit pay, or pay-for-performance, is by far the most common "new" pay principle in American organization, generally the first one adopted when compensation systems are "modernized" to reward contribution.

Merit pay is an essentially conservative approach to the allocation problem. It accepts—indeed, builds on and thus preserves—the status and category distinctions already defined by the organization. In its most common form, it retains—even enhances—the power of superiors over subordinates, as they dole out raises based on their judgments of contribution. In its individualistic bias, merit pay is also consistent with traditional corporate ideology, which holds the individual responsible for his or her fate.

But when the merit component of pay moves beyond a very small increment, there can be radical implications. When a merit pay system creates wide enough ranges, it is entirely possible that paychecks can reverse hierarchical statuses, with "subordinates" paid more than their bosses. And if it builds on real contributions to enhancing organizational achievements, rather than on supervisors' subjective assessments of whether a person does an established job well, then it can be one step more toward loosening the shackles of bureaucracy and challenging the hierarchy.

For example, one public sector pay-for-performance system established remarkably broad pay ranges for jobs with bases of $40,000 to $100,000 (field interviews). The total range is now 40 percent away from a midpoint established in comparison with "normal" pay identified by an external salary survey. People can dip 20 percent below or rise 20 percent above, depending on performance against specific, quantifiable objectives. One result is that job category and official hierarchy have much weaker meaning as determinants of earnings. The top of the range is more than the chief executive is making, and at least two people are paid more than he is.

The impact of a system like this on productivity and entrepreneurship can be considerable. The impact on work relationships is more subtle. After all, people don't wear their paychecks over their name badges; authority relationships cannot have the same meaning when people know that they out-earn their boss.

The boss is thus forced to move from a relationship of authority to one that is more collegial. But there are positive implications for the boss as well. If the subordinate can earn more than the boss while staying in place, then one of the incentives to compete with the boss for his or her job is removed. Gone is the tension that can be created when an ambitious subordinate covets the boss's job and will do anything to kill off the boss. In short, if some of the *authority* of hierarchy is eliminated, so is some of the *hostility* of hierarchy.

There are some organizational precedents for situations in which people in "lower" ranked jobs are paid more than those above, but it is not a comfortable situation for most traditional corporations. There is evidence from surveys that traditional corporations consider these situations a source of problems.[9] They do not want the gaps between hierarchical statuses to be closed. If merit pay is meaningfully implemented in organizations, then it can meet resistance from those who wish to maintain traditional practices.

Performance bonuses   The performance bonus approach creates a variety of income-earning opportunities for the enterprising by adding special incentives for specific contributions. And these bonuses further loosen the relationship between pay and job status.

High technology firms are particularly dependent on the contributions of individual innovators who could sometimes just as easily leave to start their own firm. So entrepreneurial incentives are a particular necessity in these organizations.

For example, a 1983 random sample of the 105 Boston-area firms employing scientists and engineers compared the "high tech" ones dependent on R&D for new product development with their more traditional, established counterparts. The high tech firms tended, on average, to pay a lower base salary but offer more financial incentives of other kinds, such as cash bonuses, stock options, and spot awards—independent of job levels. Furthermore, the most successful firms did more of this.[10]

Entrepreneurial pay   The third challenge revolves around entrepreneurial pay—how to share the returns with people who provide added value to the organization by creating something new.

The attempt to provide the new workforce with entrepreneurial opportunities within an established corporation, including the higher income-earning opportunities that entrepreneurs have when they start their own businesses, has led to a very different kind of compensation system operating within some traditional corporations. In a style that is pay-for-performance to its fullest extent, special venture participants can earn a return, just like founder-owners do, on the marketplace performance of their product or service. While this alternative is still relatively rare (only 6.9 percent of the 1,618 AMA member organizations surveyed had special venture funds or entrepreneurial opportunities), interest is growing.[11]

Typically, such schemes allow people to start a business with the support of the parent company. They are paid a base salary, generally equivalent to their former job level, and they are asked to put part of their compensation "at risk"; their percent "ownership" is determined by the part they put at risk. Sometimes the return is based solely on a percentage of the profit from their venture; sometimes it comes in the form of internal "phantom stock" pegged to the parent company's public stock price.

Pay-out may occur at several intervals in the development of the venture, and not simply after the seven to twelve years it can take to earn a profit in the new venture. "Milestones bonuses" for meeting established targets may be used, with further incentives added for timeliness—if you're late, the payoff goes down.

Entrepreneurial pay, like other new forms, threatens hierarchy. It is "embarrassing," in the words of a senior bank officer, when people can earn more than their boss. But it is equally tense in the other direction, when lower-level employees get a 6.8 percent increase while their manager gets a 30 percent bonus for results that lower-level employees know they helped create. People are getting angry and are beginning to push hard for a more equitable arrangement.

Gainsharing   The fourth response to the new workforce and the new workplace gives workers at the lowest levels a direct return on their contributions, as a group rather than on an individual basis.

In theory, gainsharing is a simple idea. Employees should share in the gains from contributions they make to improving the company's performance.[12]

In practice, the term gainsharing refers to a cluster of programs with some features in common: sharing with groups (as against individuals), based on explicit formulas with objective measures (as against subjective judgments or flexible criteria), and always involving at least the hourly workforce (as against only salaried managers and professionals). The unit whose performance is measured may be the whole organization, subdivisions of it, or single facilities. What's important is that the whole group benefits from overall performance.

Gainsharing programs come in three major variants—Scanlon, Rucker, and Improshare—though many companies develop versions of their own. All of the plans are compatible with the presence of unions, and all are found in both union and non-union environments.

Data on how many organizations use gainsharing and how many employees participate in programs are difficult to come by. Eleven percent of the 1,618 organizations in the AMA membership survey had some sort of gainsharing in operation.[13] A survey of high tech firms showed that over half had cash or stock awards for individuals, but only six percent had gainsharing or group profit-sharing.[14] Bullock and Lawler estimate that the total number of implemented plans ranges from 500 to 1,000 but they found only 33 cases described in enough detail to study.[15] On the other hand, interest seems to be going up. Timothy Ross, head of an institute devoted to studying gainsharing, estimates that several thousand companies have some sort of gainsharing, involving probably millions of employees, but says that he cannot be more specific about the numbers, because "Gainsharing is being used now as an umbrella concept to also mean profit-sharing and pay-for-performance, and people will have to define their terms before we can even begin to make an accurate count. But in just the private companies the institute alone is working with now, we're probably talking about 40-50,000 people right there."[16]

Unfortunately there is little hard evidence to explain why gainsharing plans work. Bullock and Lawler speculate that plans "change the culture of the organization . . . transform(ing) individuals, working on their own tasks and largely unaware of how their jobs interface with the whole of the organization, into groups of employees which suddenly have a much broader understanding of and commitment to the total enterprise."[17] Although there is some disagreement in the literature with scholars such as Geare arguing money is the primary motivator,[18] most gainsharing experts believe that employee participation is the key for effective change.[19] I will go one step further. For gainsharing plans to work, a particular organizational structure and corporate culture is required, including open discussion of the plan to gain employee acceptance; establishment of cross-unit teams or task forces to develop the plan; and adoption of suggestion systems. Gainsharing programs also require open communication about company goals and performance. If employees' pay is based in part on profits, they need to know where the company stands and how their percentage is calculated.

Pay for skill   A fifth wrinkle on traditional pay practices was designed specifically with the new workforce in mind, and it also challenges conventional hierarchical assumptions: pay for jobs mastered.[20] Pay for skill provides individual incentives for employees to rapidly upgrade their performance—while creating strong teams that are virtually "self-managed."

The system used by one manufacturing company is heavily team-based (field interviews). Teams have responsibility for all aspects of production: operating the machinery, working with suppliers, inspecting the product for conformance to quality standards, and keeping records. With this kind of responsibility, it clearly helps every member of the team to have highly-skilled colleagues capable of fully sharing the load.

All in all, pay-for-skill is a clever approach. It stresses individual responsibility but does not have the drawbacks of other pay-for-performance systems that pit team member against team member in contention for the highest ratings. Because there is no limit to the number of people who can reach the highest pay levels, there is little formal inducement to maintain a monopoly of skills or withhold training from newcomers in order to preserve a superior position. It creates a community of nominal peers with a broad range of skills who decide among themselves how best to deploy those skills.

A system like this also runs counter to the goal many neo-Marxist critics attribute to modern corporations: to "de-skill' jobs so as to keep some people confined to lower pay levels and to make it easier to accommodate turnover, ensuring that a reasonable proportion of the workforce is always new and thus always paid at lowest rates.[21] Both of these efforts of "de-skilling" keep the total wage bill low. How does an organization economically "justify" doing the opposite? Because of a work environment that better utilizes human skills, productivity improves and more than saves the additional costs of higher average wages on the shop floor. To do this, a new organization structure is required, one that challenges conventional notions of hierarchy.

Comparable worth   As more and more women have entered the workforce without closing the pay gap between women and men, activists have picked up the comparable worth banner.[22] Comparable worth as an employee rights' issue is compatible with the other "new pay" issues that arise from workforce and workplace changes. But its threat to the legitimacy of hierarchy is even greater.

Most of the ferment in pay reflects attempts by employers to improve organizational performance while controlling fixed payroll costs. And that's all. Organizational change is often not a goal, even if it is an unintended side effect, and it is often resisted by managers. The fact is that various forms of contribution-based pay also tend to shake up the hierarchy, challenge traditional authority relations, and weaken the meaning of organizational status—that's a source of trouble to most corporations. The threat of comparable worth, in the eyes of many executives, is the massive organizational readjustments it may entail, even more than the cost of equalizing pay across certain jobs.

Performance or contribution-based pay would seem to be highly compatible with the principle behind comparable worth: to ensure equivalent pay for jobs that create equivalent value for the organization. Measures of status—the "market" price to hire for certain positions, the "standing" of the job in an organizational hierarchy, the "social status" of typical job incumbents—should be less important, if we adopt a comparable worth principle, than the contributions made to carrying out organizational purposes.

Organizations are gradually coming to accept the necessity of gearing pay to performance and giving employees a "cut" of the extra value they produce. But they are also trying to confine this to rather minor changes, so that jobs do not have to be repositioned in a status structure.

Recall that merit pay comes as a percent increase above a predetermined salary level defined by job status. Incentive pay for special contributions is offered as a bonus above base salary. The return to internal entrepreneurs who build new ventures may be calculated with the pre-venture salary in the equation. Even gainsharing may be distributed as a function of wage level.

Clearly, for some organizations, the development of a new pay policy is also an occasion for organizational changes. Jobs may be reevaluated to adjust the level of base pay; the supervisory ranks may be trimmed as employee teams take on more responsibility; a new venture structure goes along with opportunities to earn entrepreneurial returns. But—and this is an important point—organizations do not necessarily have to reconsider the relative positioning of jobs in the hierarchy in order to have contribution-based pay. They can preserve some of the old status order while overlaying the new contribution principle.

The old status order is at the heart of the comparable worth issue. And that's why comparable worth—a principle that should be swimming in the mainstream of the movement to reward contribution—is instead felt to be one of the ultimate challenges to the calculation of pay. If pay-for-performance systems rattle the hierarchy, comparable worth threatens to shake it to the core.

Overall, the new pay issues make clear the difficulty of maintaining a traditional command-and-control hierarchy once actual contribution becomes the basis for the distribution of pay. The emerging participative-entrepreneurial incentives for increased performance satisfy a number of the expectations of the new workforce, but their existence also makes it harder to sustain the authority or the privilege of position.

Strain #2: Innovation versus management controls

The second strain involves a more basic incompatibility between the management systems required for innovation and entrepreneurship and those associated with continuation of already-established organizational operations.

The new workforce expects greater meaning, a feeling of making a difference. This feeling comes from the desire to innovate. For example, one highly placed executive in a well-regarded company, who was successfully climbing the management ladder, commented in an interview that the only thing he felt he would really be remembered for in the corporation and that he would remember about his work was a special assignment in which he had an opportunity to propose a major reorganization of a function.

The new workplace is also designed around the theoretical value of entrepreneurship and innovation—the theme of well over half of 400 major corporate meetings included in a 1983–1985 data base that is still being developed. Economic pressures have caused organizations to be more interested in new products, new services, and new systems. And this interest is compatible with the desires of the workforce for creative contributions.

But it is very difficult to accommodate this goal within the large corporation geared to stability, control, and maintenance of ongoing operations.[23] In those organizations that have deliberately established workplaces along entrepreneurial principles, there is a growing tension between the existence of such pockets of change and the traditional hierarchy.

The creation and exploitation of new products, new processes, or new systems has four special requirements and unique situations to manage because of characteristics of the innovation process itself.[24] Understanding the requirements of innovation makes clear why entrepreneurship challenges the legitimacy of the classic command-and-control hierarchy.[25]

Uncertainty   The innovation process involves little or no precedent or experience base to use to make forecasts about results. Hoped-for timetables may prove unrealistic. Anticipated costs may be overrun. Results are highly uncertain.[26] This situation thus requires:

1. Committed visionary leadership willing to initiate and sustain effort on the basis of faith in the idea.
2. The existence of "patient money," or capital that does not have to show a short-term return.
3. A great deal of planning flexibility, to adjust the original concept to the emerging realities.

Knowledge intensivity   The innovating process is knowledge intensive; it relies on individual human intelligence and creativity. New experiences are accumulated at a fast pace; the learning curve is steep. The knowledge that resides in the participants in the innovation effort is not yet codified or codifiable for transfer to others. Efforts are very vulnerable to turnover, because of the loss of this knowledge and experience. This situation thus requires:

1. Stability among the participants involved in an innovation effort, especially the venture manager or visionary leader.

2. A high degree of commitment among all participants as well as close, team-oriented working relationships with high mutual respect, to encourage rapid and effective exchange of knowledge among participants.
3. Intense and concentrated effort focused inward on the project.

The need for different types of structures may depend on whether the innovation is primarily concerned with the generation of new knowledge or the reformulation of existing information. For example, Kazanjian and Drazin argue that the implementation of a manufacturing innovation required both the creation of knowledge and the integration of current knowledge from the manufacturing organization.[27] In this case study, the company established a separate unit, staffed with a team of people from inside and outside the organization, to generate new knowledge. At the same time, the organizer of the innovative process built multiple bridges to the manufacturing division, assuring access to existing manufacturing knowledge. The degree of separation of an innovative unit and the need for linkages from it to the larger organization may depend on the balance between new knowledge and the integration of existing knowledge.

Competition with alternatives   In the innovation process, there is always competition with alternative courses of action. (The pursuit of the air-cooled engine at Honda Motor, for example, drew time and resources away from improving the water-cooled engine.) Furthermore, sometimes the very existence of a potential innovation poses a threat to vested interests—whether the interest is that of a salesperson receiving high commissions on current products, or of the advocates of a competing direction. Indeed, observers point to "political" problems as one of the major causes for the failure of corporate entrepreneurship.[28] This situation thus requires:

1. Champions or sponsors who will argue for the course of action, who will sustain the vision.[29]
2. Coalitions of backers or supporters from a number of areas willing to lend credence (and resources) to the project.
3. Sufficient job security throughout the organization that innovations are not seen as position-threatening.

These roles and the need for job security act as a constellation of roles and conditions rather than as singular conditions.[30]

"Boundary" crossing   The innovation process is rarely if ever contained solely within one unit. First, there is evidence that many of the best ideas are interdisciplinary or interfunctional in origin—as

connoted by the root meaning of entrepreneurship as the development of "new combinations"—or they benefit from broader perspectives and information from outside of the area primarily responsible for the innovation. Second, regardless of the origin of innovation, they inevitably send out ripples and reverberations to other organizational units, whose behavior may be required to change in light of the needs of innovations, or whose cooperation is necessary if an innovation is to be fully developed or exploited. Or there may be the need to generate unexpected innovations in another domain in order to support the primary product, like the need to design a new motor to make the first Apple computer viable. This situation thus requires:

1. Enlarging the focus of participants in the innovation process to take account of the perspectives of other units or disciplines. (What I call "kaleidoscope" thinking is at the heart of the creative process in innovation—the use of new angles or perspectives to reshuffle the parts to make a new pattern, thus challenging conventional assumptions.)
2. Early involvement of functions or units that may play a role at some later stage of the venture or innovation effort.
3. A high degree of commitment by functions or players outside of the innovation-producing unit to the innovation.
4. A high degree of interaction across functions or units—and thus more interunit teamwork.
5. Reciprocal influence among functions.

Overall, then, it is not surprising that research on the problems of new corporate ventures tends to attribute failures to such common factors as the requirements for inappropriate planning/analysis and pressure for faster results; turnover on the venture team and lack of committed leadership; the politics of gaining sponsorship within the corporation (or the perils of getting the "wrong" sponsorship); and interfunctioning conflicts that either slow the process down, or steer the project in an inappropriate direction.[31]

The tension between command and mutual adjustment systems   Traditional corporate management works to hold things in place, preventing deviation from established practice, once rules are made. It is compatible with a "command" system in which every person and every function knows its place. When this type of management results in high degrees of compartmentalization of responsibilities and limited contact between a large number of differentiated statuses (distinctions of level, of function, of unit), I have referred to it as *"segmentalism"*—an approach to organizing and managing that discourages change, even in the face of obvious problems.[32]

But the entrepreneurial process requires instead more reliance on the particular persons involved, closer working relationships, the ability to depart from tradition, and a governance system that is one of continual negotiation and mutual adjustment among all participants with something to contribute to the effort. This approach to organizing can be called *"integrative"*—an emphasis on bringing people together rather than separating activities or people—and the governance system called a partnership or *mutual adjustment* model.

A single proposition in organizational theory holds that under conditions of low uncertainty and high predictability about both inputs and outcomes, it is effective to manage by rules, paperwork, and other impersonal means administered through clearly established centers of command. But under conditions of high uncertainty and low predictability, it is more effective to manage by personal communication and negotiation—in part because of the sheer inability to issue enough commands to cover every contingency.

Thus entrepreneurship requires a system of management by mutual adjustment instead of a system of management by command. Management by mutual adjustment, in turn, relies on integrative organizational conditions: a close working relationship among all participants, mutual respect fostered by the absence of status differences, overlapping responsibilities, and concern for joint goals. It is partnership-oriented and allows for temporary alliances among equals instead of submersion of parties in a hierarchy—e.g., joint ventures vs. acquisitions, borrowing or renting assets rather than owning them.

All established organizations clearly need both systems. They need a *command* system for those areas where repeating the past is necessary, where predictable products or services are to be turned out reliably and uniformly according to an established blueprint, and where efficiencies are to be gained through a learning curve derived from numerous repetitions. And they need a *mutual adjustment* system wherever innovation is desired, problems need to be solved, and new techniques or methods are sought.

Maximizing *both* efficiency and innovation is required for an organization to be adaptive.[33] Even in a fairly new company developing new products in a growing market, both systems play a role. Mitchell Kapor, the young founder and first CEO of Lotus Development Corporation, a highly successful software firm, acknowledged this need for two simultaneous management systems:

To be a successful enterprise, we have to do two apparently contradictory things quite well: We have to stay innovative and creative, but at the same time we have to be tightly controlled about certain aspects of our corporate behavior. But I think that what you have to do about paradox is embrace it. So we have the kind of company where certain things are very loose and other things are very tight. The whole art of management is sorting things into the loose pile or the tight pile and then watching them carefully (*Boston Globe*, 1/27/85).

Organizations where administrative command systems dominate sometimes establish a separate system for entrepreneurship and innovation and run, in effect, two organizations side by side. One example is the "parallel organization" concept in use in the employee involvement or quality-of-work-life programs in many companies—a second, participative organization of temporary task forces added to the operating organization with its clear specification of roles and responsibilities and its numerous distinctions between functions and levels.[34] While full-blown parallel organizations were used by only 8.5 percent of the 1,618 organizations in the AMA survey, well over a third had a more limited variant in the form of quality circles.[35] Another example is the establishment of new venture units in large corporations that operate by different principles than the organization running established businesses, like GM's Saturn subsidiary or the separate organization that developed the IBM PC.

If the innovating unit is kept separate—to preserve its autonomy, acknowledge its special management requirements, and keep it from "contaminating" the parts of the organization devoted to routine operations—then it can soon draw fire as a privileged elite, threatening to the maintainers of the routinized organization and a target of resentment for other participants. Pressure mounts to dissolve it, to absorb it back into the established hierarchy and subject it to the established rules. This drama has been played out in the entrepreneurial divisions of two computer companies and a pharmaceutical firm, among the cases I examined, and it has been a common fate of new venture units.[36] Perhaps this is why under seven percent of the organizations in the AMA survey had internal venture funds for entrepreneurial opportunities.[37] On the other hand, if the entrepreneurial process is carried out alongside the command-and-control process for ongoing operations, then there is the likelihood of behavioral spillover from the mutual adjustment mode, which undermines traditional authority relations in the hierarchy. Once having tasted the freedom to participate in decisions, work across organizational boundaries, and envision alternatives, it is difficult to accept management by command.

But as tasty as participative-entrepreneurial management may be to some segments of the new workforce, it is less palatable to others because of the connections between the workplace and other societal institutions.

Strain #3: Equal opportunity for women vs. time demands in desirable positions

As organizations move to more participative and entrepreneurial modes, creating a new workplace of high involvement and rewards for special contributions, another tension is introduced. This one does not so much involve a challenge to the legitimacy of established hierarchies as it does a challenge to the ability of organizations, as presently constituted, to fulfill another goal of the new workforce: career success for women.

Ironically, the new workplace may itself be a detriment to meeting equal opportunity goals—unless organizations, along with the wider institutions of society, change in more profound and fundamental ways.

The new workforce contains an ever greater proportion of women with ever greater education and ever greater aspirations. But the very people who are pressing for higher level positions also carry with them heavier out-of-work demands, particularly centering around family responsibilities. Accumulated evidence indicates that women still do the bulk of the family work, even if men bear an increasing share.

At the same time, relatively few of the new workplace systems involve flexibility and time off or direct support for family responsibilities. If anything, the major thrust is in the opposite direction. Most of the new workplace systems *increase* the absorptiveness of work. The chances to earn performance bonuses, or share in productivity gains, or get funding for special entrepreneurial ventures or participate in innovations—all of these increase, rather than decrease, the time demands. The most desirable jobs all seem to take the most time, as Jencks found when he related hours of work to job satisfaction.[38]

The modern corporation is what Coser called a "greedy organization."[39] As new work alternatives take hold, they make it *more* so, at the same time that a large group in the workforce wants it *less* so. Despite the career consciousness of the younger generation of women, there still exists a conflict between demands of work and demands of family, and there is evidence that career ambitions begin to taper off in the 30's as women express a desire for children. The careers they have been educated to want, however, do not accommodate less than fully committed—and to a certain extent, even overburdened—people.

There is also evidence that the amount of leisure is dropping *faster* than the increase in hours worked, indicating, in part, that out-of-work responsibilities have not declined as work hours go up. A 1985 Harris survey identified a steady and inexorable decline in leisure. Since 1973, the median number of hours worked by Americans (in paid work) increased by 20 percent while the amount of leisure time available to the average person dropped by 32 percent.[40] Among the groups with the longest hours of work are those in the most "desirable" occupations: entrepreneurs in smaller businesses, especially retailing, at 57.3 hours per week; professionals, at 52.2 hours per week; and those with incomes over $50,000, at 52.4 hours per week. Clearly, the "best" jobs are the most time-demanding.

This is not only because of what the corporation imposes on employees, but also what employees themselves seek under options to get access to more challenging and interesting work or to participate in organizational problem-solving.

When work is more interesting, people take it home. In one organization, secretaries on a task force found themselves carrying piles of paper home for the first time in their careers (field interviews). The task force was exciting, its mission interesting, and suddenly they had a project with goals that required reflection beyond the time permitted in the office. It is also common to see members of quality circles using their lunch hour to hold meetings because they are committed to the goals of the group.

In addition, more challenging, more entrepreneurial, more participative positions carry with them the requirement for more communication and interaction.

I have already pointed to the intensivity of innovation—the requirement of a cohesive team that exchanges new knowledge frequently, as it is developed. In addition, groups take longer to do certain kinds of work than do individuals, even if the quality of the solution is higher. One needs more time for meetings in a participative-entrepreneurial workplace; where job territories overlap, people might report to more than one manager, and projects require the coordination of a number of people, each with specialized responsibility. Furthermore, management tasks are different under a more participative system. People need to spend more time selling ideas rather than commanding. They need to spend more time with subordinates explaining the goals, keeping them up-to-date with timely information, and making sure they understand where their pieces fit into the whole task.

Especially in the higher ranks of management—the levels to which women aspire but where equal opportunity goals are least likely to have been met—evidence suggests that the highest proportion of an executive's time is spent communicating, often in short fragments on a large variety of topics.[41]

In the emerging corporation, sheer communication, and therefore time demands, are up. One electronics firm, in a fast-paced business with a great deal of need for communication across diverse entities, established its own in-house helicopter service to link 17 New England facilities. Concerned about travel time and costs, the company established an elaborate teleconferencing system to allow people to communicate without travelling (field interviews). But instead of reducing travel costs, the teleconferencing capacity actually *increased* them, because more people, who could communicate more easily, found even more reasons to get together.

Finally, when I asked successful innovators in my studies for *The Change Masters* what their accomplishment *cost*, their answers were revealing: gaining weight, getting a divorce, getting in trouble with the family.[42] The bestselling account of the development of a new computer at Data General, *The Soul of a New Machine*,[43] widely used as an example of effective innovation in a high participation organization, documents the extraordinary lengths to which people with highly absorbing work over which they have control will go to do that work: 60-, 90-, 100-hour work weeks, with people occasionally going into the laboratory in the middle of the night when they had an idea. Of course, these employees were young males without families. But the fact that this work style is engendered by providing great opportunity for challenge and excitement may also eliminate the possibility that women can achieve in such jobs.

Therefore, we see a conflict between two kinds of change. Equal opportunity opens up hopes of higher positions for women, but new work systems (designed with many of the same liberal goals in mind) may increase the barriers to getting them. There was for a time some evidence that organizations characterized by high-participation, high-involvement work systems also created more opportunities for women, because of the values of the organization and the ways in which bureaucratic structures inhibited women concentrated in "stuck" (low mobility) positions from ever getting access to opportunity. But recent data from Silicon Valley show the paucity of women in significant positions in some of the most entrepreneurial companies in the country.[44] It becomes clear that women do not automatically do better in high participation environments unless there is also significant support for the additional responsibilities they bring with them.

There is a clear strain in the system here. As organizations loosen up and begin to operate on less hierarchical premises, giving more people an opportunity to participate in decisions, tackle challenging projects, and take on exciting tasks, they also absorb more of people's time and energy. If organizations are allowed to absorb more of the person without providing support for other responsibilities, then they will either become more antagonistic to the family than they have been in the past, or they will eliminate the prospect of ever reaching equal opportunity goals in the more challenging, higher level, and better paying positions.

Conclusion

Social and organizational change is fraught with dilemmas, tensions, and contradictions because of the impossibility of decoupling pieces of a system. A minor change over there sends ripples to the activities over here. A problem solved here creates new, unanticipated problems over there. Gradually, the structures that have supported one form begin to crumble and crack, even when only minor renovations are desired.

I have rejected the premise that the "new workforce" itself presents the problem. Instead, I have argued that the new workforce finds itself involved in a "new workplace"—created in response to forces such as global competition. This new workplace involves opportunities for greater employee initiative, for entrepreneurial effort, and for greater participation in problem solving. However, this new workplace cannot exist easily in the conventional command-and-control hierarchy of status and authority relations that has been the dominant organizational form in the twentieth century.

I have identified three principal strains. First is the shift from status to contribution as a basis for pay, as the new workplace attempts to improve performance and allow initiative to be expressed. Second, entrepreneurial management modes that take advantage of employee initiatives are incompatible with the command orientation and bureaucratic-hierarchical trappings of organizations. Third, the thrust of the new workplace is on greater employee participation, making earnings dependent on initiative. Greater participation could so increase the time demands of work that those shouldering the burden of out-of-work responsibilities (primarily women) could be excluded at the time that the rhetoric offers them "equal opportunity."

All three strains represent the major tensions that organizations, particularly large corporations, need to manage as we enter the last decade of the century.

The cracks in the old system are showing. What will happen is still to be determined. Conservative keepers of the old way could attempt to patch the cracks and fortify the walls against the new challenges, thereby shoring up an obsolete system. Or we could witness the gradual crumbling of the traditional hierarchy and the reshaping of the work-family nexus.

Notes

1. D. Bell, *The Cultural Contradictions of Capitalism* (New York: Basic, 1976).

2. R. M. Kanter, "Work in a New America," *Daedalus* 107 (1978): 47–78.

3. I. Berg, *Education and Jobs: The Great Training Robbery* (New York: Praeger, 1970).

4. R. M. Kanter, *The Change Masters* (New York: Simon & Schuster, 1983).

5. Goodmeasure, Inc., *The Changing American Workplace: Work Alternatives in the 1980s* (New York: AMA Membership Publishing Division, 1985); R. Levering, M. Moskowitz, and M. Katz, *The 100 Best Companies to Work for in America* (Reading, MA: Addison-Wesley, 1984).

6. Goodmeasure, *Changing American Workplace*.

7. R. M. Kanter and D. V. Summers, *The Roots of Corporate Progressivism*, report to the Russell Sage Foundation, 1984.

8. See E. E. Lawler, *Pay and Organization Development* (Reading, MA: Addison-Wesley, 1981).

9. J. W. Steele, *Paying for Performance and Position: Dilemmas in Salary Compression and Merit Pay* (New York: AMA Membership Publishing Division, 1982).

10. J. R. Schuster, *Management Competition in High-Technology Companies* (Lexington, MA: Lexington Books, 1984); and "Compensation Plan Design: The Power Behind the Best High-Tech Companies," *Management Review* (May 1985): 21–25.

11. Goodmeasure, *Changing American Workplace*.

12. B. E. Graham-Moore and T. L. Ross, *Productivity Gainsharing* (Englewood Cliffs, NJ: Prentice-Hall, 1983); R. J. Bullock and E. Lawler, "Gainsharing: A Few Questions, and Fewer Answers," *Human Resources Management* 23 (1984): 123–40.

13. Goodmeasure, *Changing American Workplace*.

14. M. F. Spratt and B. Steele, "Rewarding Key Contributors," *Compensation and Benefits Review* 17 (1985): 24–37.

15. Bullock and Lawler, "Gainsharing: A Few Questions."

16. Personal interview, 1986.

17. Bullock and Lawler, "Gainsharing: A Few Questions."

18. A. J. Geare, "Productivity from Scanlon-Type Plans," *Academy of Management Review* 1 (1976): 99–108.

19. M. Schuster, "The Scanlon Plan: A Longitudinal Analysis," *Journal of Applied Behavioral Science* 20 (1984): 23–28; Bullock and Lawler, "Gainsharing: A Few Questions."

20. E. E. Lawler, "Reward Systems," in J. R. Hackman and J. L. Suttle, eds., *Improving Life at Work* (Santa Monica, CA: Goodyear, 1977); H. Tosi and L. Tosi, "What Managers Need to Know about Knowledge-Based Pay," *Organizational Dynamics* 14 (1986): 52–64.

21. H. Braverman, *Labor and Monopoly Capitalism* (New York: Monthly Review Press, 1974).

22. E. R. Livernash, ed., *Comparable Worth: Issues and Alternatives* (Washington, D.C.: Equal Employment Advisory Council, 1980).

23. H. Stevenson and D. Gumpert, "The Heart of Entrepreneurship," *Harvard Business Review* 63 (1985): 85–94.

24. Kanter, *Change Masters*; J. B. Quinn, "Managing Innovation: Controlled Chaos," *Harvard Business Review* 63 (1985): 73–84; A. H. Van de Ven, "Central Problems in the Management of Innovation," *Management Science* 32 (1986): 590–607; Kanter, "What Makes the Thousand Flowers Bloom: Social, Structural, and Collective Determinants of Innovation in Organizations," *Research in Organizational Behavior* 9 (1987).

25. R. M. Kanter, "Supporting Innovation and Venture Development in Established Companies," *Journal of Business Venturing* 1 (1985): 47–60.

26. Quinn, "Managing Innovation."

27. R. K. Kazanjian and R. Drazin, "Implementing Manufacturing Innovations: Critical Choices of Structure and Staffing Roles," *Human Resource Management* 25 (1986): 385–404.

28. N. D. Fast, "The Future of Industrial New Venture Departments," *Industrial Marketing Management* 8 (1976): 264–273.

29. J. Galbraith, "Designing the Innovating Organization," *Organizational Dynamics* 10 (1982): 5–25.

30. Kazanjian and Drazin, "Implementing Manufacturing Innovations."

31. E. Von Hippel, "Successful and Failing Internal Corporate Ventures: An Empirical Analysis," *Industrial Marketing Management* 6 (1977): 163–174; Z. Block, "Can Corporate Venturing Succeed?" *The Journal of Business Strategy* 3 (1982): 21–33 and "Some Major Issues in Internal Corporate Venturing," in J. A. Hor-

naday, J. A. Timmons, and K. H. Vesper, eds., *Frontiers of Entrepreneurship Research* (Wellesley, MA: Babson College, 1983); E. L. Hobson and R. Morrison, "How Do Corporate Start-up Ventures Fare?" in *Frontiers of Entrepreneurship Research*; Fast, "Future of Industrial New Venture Departments"; I. C. MacMillan, Z. Block, and P. N. Subba Narasimha, "Obstacles and Experience in Corporate Ventures," Working Paper, New York University, 1984; Quinn, "Managing Innovation."

32. Kanter, *Change Masters.*
33. P. R. Lawrence and D. Dyer, *Renewing American Industry* (New York: Free Press, 1983).
34. B. A. Stein and R. M. Kanter, "Building the Parallel Organization: Toward Permanent Structures for the Quality of Work Life," *Journal of Applied Behavioral Science* 16 (1980): 371–388.
35. Goodmeasure, *Changing American Workplace.*

36. Fast, "Future of Industrial New Venture Departments."
37. Goodmeasure, *Changing American Workplace.*
38. C. Jencks, "What Is a Good Job? A New Measure of Labor Market Success," paper delivered at the Annual Meeting of the American Sociological Association, Washington, D.C., 1985.
39. L. Coser, *Greedy Institutions* (New York: Free Press, 1974).
40. L. Harris and Associates, "Americans and the Arts," report to Phillip Morris, Inc., 1985.
41. H. Mintzberg, *The Nature of Managerial Work* (New York: Harper and Row, 1973).
42. Kanter, *Change Masters.*
43. T. Kidder, *The Soul of a New Machine* (Boston: Atlantic-Little, Brown, 1981).
44. E. Rogers and J. K. Larsen, *Silicon Valley Fever* (New York: Basic, 1984).

Learning to Manage a Multicultural Work Force

Lennie Copeland

Trend-watcher John Naisbitt says, "The big challenge of the 1980s is not the retraining of workers but the retraining of managers." The rapidly changing demographic makeup of the American work force is one reason why this is true. Now, for the first time in history, white males are the minority—only 46 percent. The U.S. Department of Labor projects that within just a few years, 75 percent of those entering the work force will be minorities and women.

The labor pool is not only changing, it is shrinking. In the 1990s, there will be four to five million fewer entry-level workers each year than in 1980. The consequences are clear. Organizations that want the most productive employees will have to put aside old definitions of "corporate fit" and employ people of different colors and cultures. They will have to compete for women, minorities and others who are different from the norm in age, appearance, physical ability and lifestyle. But that's not all. They also will have to develop and retain them.

Erroneous assumptions

Diversity is emerging as one of the most serious issues in the workplace today, yet most employers are not prepared to deal with it. Nor are their managers. Many managers grew up having little contact with other cultures. They are actually "culturally deprived," and their graduate-school texts did not cover the kinds of situations that arise in today's multicultural settings.

Most traditional models of human behavior and management

methods—as well as many of the recommendations in best-sellers such as *The One-Minute Manager* and *In Search of Excellence*—are based on implicit assumptions of a homogeneous white male work force. The most widely taught theories of motivation mirror the white male's own experience and attitudes. Some of those methods can be startlingly counterproductive when applied to women or to blacks, Asians, Hispanics or American Indians. For example:

A manager, thrilled with a new technique developed by one of his American Indian employees, rewarded her with great fanfare and congratulations in front of her peers—just as the management books suggest. Humiliated, she didn't return to work for three weeks.

After learning that a friendly pat on the arm or back would make workers feel good and motivated, a manager took every chance to pat his subordinates. His Asian employees, who hated being touched, avoided him like the plague. Several asked for transfers. (If he had treated female employees this way, he could have had other problems on his hands.)

Fresh from a course on delegation, a production supervisor asked his primarily Filipino staff to alert him to any problems with some new equipment. Instead, they used masking tape and other makeshift remedies to get the machines working.

Concerned about ethics, a manager declined a gift offered him by a new employee, an immigrant who wanted to show gratitude for her job. He explained the company's policy about gifts. She was so insulted she quit.

In a similar situation, a new employee's wife (an Eastern European) stopped by the office with a bottle of champagne, fully expecting everyone present to stop and celebrate the new job. When people said "hello" and returned to work, she was mortified. Her husband quit within a few days.

Trying to implement his company's policy of participatory management, a manager asked his Hispanic employees to work together to come up with solutions to some problems. Bitter ego battles ensued, as well as incidents of insubordination. Work came to a stop. This manager found he had undermined his own authority. In an ingenious "save," he appointed Hispanic women to facilitate the teams. The women were able to get input from the men by asking their "advice" and funneling their ideas to management.

Managing diversity

Some organizations are taking aggressive steps to meet the demographic challenge of the 1990s. Digital Equipment Corp. has a "director of valuing differences." Honeywell has a "director of workforce diversity." Avon has a "director of multicultural planning and design."

Many companies, such as Bank of Boston and GTE, offer management courses dealing with race and gender. Mobil set up a special committee of executives to select high-potential women and minorities for critical line positions, moving them from staff functions to the mainstream of the oil business. Security Pacific Bank has established minority networks and support groups to encourage personal and professional growth of minority managers. The Equitable has business resource groups that meet with CEO John B. Carver to discuss issues pertaining to women, blacks and Hispanics. Carver signs off on the groups' suggestions and directs a senior manager to execute them. At the end of each quarter, he reviews progress.

"It is absolutely clear that we have to manage diversity right now and much more so in the future," says David Kearns, president and CEO of Xerox Corp. "American business will not be able to survive if we do not have a large diverse work force, because those are the demographics—no choice! The company that gets out in front of managing diversity, in my opinion, will have a competitive edge."

The current interest in multicultural diversity is embraced by equal employment opportunity specialists, who view it as the chance the EEO never had. It puts their issues in the mainstream. In a company that values diversity, says Daisy Chin-Lor, director of multicultural planning and design at Avon, "EEO goes beyond numbers. It takes on real meaning. Valuing diversity is more than EEO-driven, it's part of the management process."

But simply throwing different people together does not create a productive work environment—or even a genuinely diverse one. People tend to cluster with people like themselves, those with whom they feel comfortable and who confirm old stereotypes. It is harder to manage a group of people who have different wants and ideas about how work is to be done. Prejudice and cultural misunderstandings cause conflict, bad decisions and poor results. Productivity may decline unless diversity is deliberately managed and managed well.

The reality today is that most organizations must deal with diversity at entry levels simply because of the demographics of the labor pool. At the same time, organizations need diversity at the top, where more complex tasks need different perspectives. The upshot is that effective managing of diversity is a requirement at all levels.

Beyond equality

Managing diversity is conceptually different from equal employment opportunity, which was primarily a battle against racism and prejudice. To *value* work-force diversity is to manage in a way designed to seize the benefits that differences bring.

In the past, experts say, we actually conspired to ignore differences. Advocates of civil rights downplayed cultural heritage because differences were regularly used as evidence of minority group inferiority. Well-meaning whites went along with the conspiracy because they were embarrassed by differences that they indeed did see as marks of inferiority. Consequently, "we are all equal" came to mean "we are all the same." Even now, many of those who say they value diversity take umbrage when actual differences are discussed. There's a fine line between recognizing cultural norms and promulgating stereotypes.

The consequence of viewing all people as the same is that the majority culture is seen as the standard. Those who don't conform are regarded as not measuring up to that standard. For example, equality for women at work came to mean that women had to become like men: aggressive, competitive, wearing dark suits, talking about sports. "The problem with measuring everyone against that white male standard," says Gerald Adolph, a management consultant and principal at Booz Allen & Hamilton, "is that you set up a sizable portion of your work force for failure."

Being blind to differences is not the aim. As Price Cobbs, a management consultant and coauthor of *Black Rage* puts it, "When people say, 'I don't even notice you are black,' what they are really saying is 'You have overcome that handicap,' or 'I don't value the difference—I see you as just like me.' It is just as bad to ignore differences as it is to emphasize them, or to treat them as deficits, or to treat everyone in a group as the same."

Santiago Roderiguez, head of affirmative action at Stanford University, says that fair treatment is more important than equal treatment. "Part of being a professional is being analytical, making choices, discerning between options and acknowledging that people are stimulated by different needs, operating with different styles. A good manager knows that individuals react differently for a variety of reasons, one of which is culture."

Still, some consider it demeaning to say that different people in the workplace have different needs. Avon's Chin-Lor counters with a wonderful analogy: "If I were planting a garden and I wanted to have a number of flowers, I would never think of giving every flower the same amount of sun, the same amount of water and the same soil. I'd be sure to cultivate each individual type of flower differently. Does that mean that the rose or the orchid is less because I have to do more with them? Certainly not!"

What every manager needs to know

If managers are to be trained to value diversity, what do they actually need to learn? What barriers must they overcome to work effectively with people who are different from themselves or different from the mainstream?

Many EEO and human resources development professionals seem to agree that four major problem areas need attention: (1) stereotypes and their associated assumptions, (2) actual cultural differences, (3) the exclusivity of the "white male club" and its associated access to important information and relationships, and (4) unwritten rules and double standards for success, which are often unknown to women and minorities.

Stereotypes and assumptions   Some experts say stereotypes are not necessarily bad—it's what we do with them. I disagree. Stereotypes are bad because they are so powerfully effective in preventing differentiated thinking about people who belong to the stereotyped group. As defined by Gordon Allport in his classic book, *The Nature of Prejudice,* "A stereotype is an exaggerated belief associated with a category. Its function is to justify (rationalize) our conduct in relation to that category."

Stereotypes hurt individuals when invalid conclusions are reached about them and when those conclusions remain untested and unchanged. Take this scenario: A white male manager walks through the office, passing two black men talking at the watercooler. He is slightly irritated. Why are they standing there wasting time? A moment later he passes two women coming out of the ladies room talking. He wonders what they are gossiping about and hopes they get back to work quickly. He comes upon two white men leaning on the walls of a cubicle, also talking. He thinks nothing of it.

What are his assumptions? The women and minorities are "goofing off," but the white men are talking business. Since he hasn't really listened to the conversations, he doesn't realize that the women and the black men were talking business while the white men happened to be talking about their children. Instead, his misinterpretation of what he saw will only strengthen his bias that women and minorities don't work hard enough.

Many stereotypes have some basis in truth, but there are so many exceptions that it is a mistake to apply notions about a group to any one individual. Even when an individual seems to fit a stereotype, it's important to analyze all the assumptions that are being made. For example, take an Asian engineer who is quiet, modest and hard-working. He avoids eye contact and doesn't speak out in brainstorming sessions. When he applies for a promotion, he doesn't really sell himself. His boss's conclusion: "He is a good technician, but he lacks management skills."

It's entirely possible that the white manager fails to realize that the Asian has successfully (if indirectly) led many of his team's projects for some time. He could be coached in areas where he is lacking, as a white candidate would be. And what about the criteria the boss is using to define "management skills"? Is aggression really needed, or might intelligence, persistence and the ability to foster group collaboration be equally or more effective in getting to the same goal? Managing a diverse work force requires managers to learn new ways to recognize talent. This means laying aside some assumptions and looking beyond style at results.

Unwritten rules Each organization has its own culture, and that culture reflects attitudes about what is important, how the organization does its work, how employees are to behave and how they are to be rewarded. In most companies, the values are male, white and based in European traditions, not because these ways are better than others but because the organization reflects the values of the people who control it. It is important for all employees to know what those values are because they define the ground rules for success.

In some organizations many of the rules are explicit, even written. In most, however, the rules are ambiguous, unwritten and may be completely inconsistent with written policy. A problem for women and minorities is that they aren't aware of many of the rules that are obvious to people in the mainstream. White men may not share the rules because it never occurs to them that everyone is not aware of them or because they don't want to seem patronizing.

Even when coaching women and minorities, managers sometimes inadvertently contribute to failure. In one company, men would train other men by putting them on the equipment and then coaching them. But they trained women by showing them how the equipment worked without giving them "hands-on" practice. In another company, men training men used correct technical terminology for the equipment, but when they trained women they referred to the "gizmo" or the "thingamajig with the little curlicue on top." They assumed that the women could not handle technical terminology and thus hindered their training.

A team is a winning team only when all the players know the rules. Because so many white male managers are only subconsciously aware of the rules and double standards, they need to learn to identify their organizations' culture and rules and learn how to pass on that information to women and minorities. This means providing all employees with what they need to know about career advancement, communication, leadership, management, organizational culture, power, networking, interpersonal skills and all the other unwritten rules, norms and cues for success.

But this does not mean that women and minorities should do all the changing. An employer who recognizes the value added by diversity will strive to nurture differences, not reduce everyone to white male clones. Valuing diversity may mean changing the rules to accommodate differences in style and perspective. The aim of sharing the rules is to give everyone choices, recognizing that no organization is going to change completely overnight. Employees who know the rules can proceed to take care of their careers while they (and management) work to change the system.

Membership   Relationships are central to achievement, and being a member of the "club" is as important as hard work and competence. When a white man and a woman (or minority employee) are competing for a promotion, the decision maker may be heard to say, "I just don't know Mary as well as Bob." Most of us prefer to have lunch and socialize after work with people most like ourselves. As a result, people in the mainstream fail to include those who are different and thus exclude them from important information and relationships.

Women and minorities complain that they must prove themselves while white men automatically assume membership in the club. They are kept in training too long, given just one more assignment, one more test. White men are given promotional opportunities sooner under the assumption that they will rise to the occasion. The catch-22 is that when people are not given challenging assignments, they never have the chance to learn by experience or to develop the track record that will reduce others' feelings of risk about them.

Managers impede their own people this way. They need to learn to make deliberate efforts to include people in work-related and social events. Managing the diverse work force requires conscious team building, networking and mentoring to bring others into the mainstream.

Cultural differences   It's obvious that cultures are different. No one disputes that some people prefer sushi to tacos or wiener-schnitzel. Why then do so many managers (and management gurus) assume that what works with one employee will work with others? Cultural differences affect the values people bring to the workplace. Different people feel differently about their roles in an organization, how they can make a contribution and how they want to be recognized for their efforts.

What motivates one worker might completely inhibit another—for example, rewarding people who don't like to be touched with pats on the back, or publicly recognizing people who don't like to be isolated from the group. Workers unintentionally humiliated in this manner may become less productive. Then, typically, the manager who made the mistake will fall back on stereotypes to explain an employee's disappointing behavior: "Well, what can you expect, Hispanics are like that."

In some multicultural workplaces, many diverse people work side by side: Laotians, Cambodians, Vietnamese, Chinese, Korean, Salvadorean, Guatemalan, Mexican, Peruvian and so on. Managers in these mixed settings may ask, with some panic, "How can I possibly learn about all these cultures?" Experts answer, "Of course you can't learn everything there is to know about all cultures, but the more you know, the better able you will be to do your job. If you don't understand and value your employees, how can you hope to motivate and supervise them?"

It's also important to understand your own culture, whether you are Indian, Asian, Hispanic, black or white. Many whites, particularly those of European heritage, don't think of themselves as having a culture. They think "culture" is something quaint that minorities have.

Promoting differences

Says Xerox's Kearns, "There's a lot of discussion about compromise in promoting women and minorities, and I would like to get it out of our vocabulary because it's not necessary. If you give people the right experiences, then the normal measurement system of competence and results will prove itself."

Many people expect women, minorities and others outside the mainstream to do all the adapting. But it has to be a two-way street. While women and minorities must perform, build relationships, learn the rules and work to become members of the club, managers must share the rules, invite people into the club, accommodate cultural differences, create climates that support diversity and establish systems that enable different types of employees to succeed.

Valuing diversity is an established mode of operation in some companies and unheard of in others. But even the most progressive organizations have some offices, divisions or regions of the country where more work needs to be done. Plenty of companies have given lip service to the idea of managing a diverse work force, but end up with few changes because they have failed to establish accountability.

Kearns insists that making sure you have the right balance in your work force at all levels "is something you have to measure and you have to target just like you do profits or market share." At Xerox, he went about this by identifying successful white males and studying where they had been and what they had done to get ahead. Then Kearns set targets and put in place a process to ensure that women and minorities got the same types of experiences.

Four essentials in managing a diverse work force are really a matter of changing old habits:

1. Periodically stop and ask, "What's going on here? What assumptions am I making?"
2. Make sure all your employees are invited into the club.
3. Share the unwritten rules and change them to nurture diversity.
4. Be sensitive to individual differences: appreciate diversity.

Women Managers: Old Stereotypes Die Hard

Alicia Johnson

When Jane Evans was named president of Butterick/Vogue Patterns in 1974, there were several male vice-presidents. They hadn't met her, but after her name was announced for the job they went to a men-only club, got roaring drunk, and decided to quit *en masse*. Evans called them together, told them she'd heard about this, and asked them to give her a chance. "'As far as I'm concerned,' I told them, 'you have more to prove to me than I have to prove to you.'" The confident president bet them that in a year they would say she was the best boss they had ever had, that they had achieved more in that year than ever before, and that they had had more fun in that year than ever before. A year later, she got a check for $50 and a bouquet of roses for winning the bet.

Although Evans' experience at Butterick happened [in 1974], today's female managers still face obstacles. Now a general partner with San Francisco's Montgomery Securities Fund specializing in leveraged buyouts, Evans says female-dominated positions are becoming "ghetto jobs." These include the service-related fields with little or no line management opportunity or profit/loss responsibility. She explains, "If women continue to enter only these jobs, such as human resources and public relations, they will continue to have difficulties reaching top management positions."

Moving out of "ghetto jobs" into high-profit areas such as financial management and marketing is only one solution to the problems facing women at work. To make progress in corporate America, many successful women have had to give up on the idea of marriage and family. And even those who did not give up the idea soon realized that maternity usually carries a greater burden than paternity.

Do women stand as good a chance as men to reach the top levels of management? For this issue, *Management Review* talked to a number of impressive women who have broken through barriers, managers such as Susan Boren, vice-president of human resources for Dayton Hudson, and Virginia Littlejohn, president of Littlejohn Johnson.

Beginning in the 1960s, the women's movement pressed for legislation forcing employers to open their doors wider to women. This movement produced such measures as parental leave mandates and protection against sexual harassment and unfair pay, promotion, and hiring practices.

Felice Schwartz, founder and president of Catalyst, a New York-based research and advisory organization that helps corporations further the career and leadership development of women, comments, "A number of companies are making backup lists to ensure they are including women [in the pool of management candidates], because we are moving out of a period of abundant supply of talent from the baby-boom generation." Progressive employers are helping both men and women by offering childcare assistance, flexible work schedules, and nonsexist performance appraisal systems.

While great strides have been made, it's evident that woman managers are, for the most part, stuck. Corporate managements now must analyze women managers' current situation, respond to their needs, and help bring them up to speed so that they can become an even more important resource and move up the pyramid.

These are positive gains for women, but discrimination persists. In 1955, women earned 63.9 cents for every dollar earned by men. Today, women's earnings are still only 64 cents for every dollar earned by men, according to the National Commission on Working Women. And, according to a survey of the executive recruiting firm Korn/Ferry International, only 29 of 1,362 senior executives in positions just under the rank of chief executive at the nation's largest companies are women.

Barriers to progress

Women who tried to enter managerial ranks before the 1964 Civil Rights Act faced bigger problems than they do today: they didn't have Title VII precedents or pay equity. But, even though the law is on their side, women face more subtle forms of discrimination than they did in the past. "Managers and CEOs have grown up with a common pattern of social relations. They're all from the same schools, these heads of corporations. They talk to one another and they know a lot about business, but they have a dangerous tendency to stick too close to one another," says Felice Schwartz. One of the biggest barriers to women at top management levels is what E. Pendleton James, former head of personnel for the Reagan White House and now head of his own executive recruiting firm, E. Pendleton James and Associates, calls "BOGSAT"; a "bunch of guys sitting around a table" making decisions.

Sarah Hardesty and Nehama Jacobs, authors of *Success and Betrayal: The Crisis of Women in Corporate America* (Watt, 1986), report that a number of former CEOs candidly agree that this BOGSAT dynamic exists. A former CEO of Phelps Dodge International, now a senior vice-president with executive recruiters Haley Associates, says, "Women seldom enter the ranks of contention for top-management promotions because the 'old boy' frame of reference excludes them." A 1986 University of Michigan study confirms that of 800 promotions to vice-president or higher positions at medium to large corporations, only 2.6 percent went to women.

The composite CEO was described in a recent study by the University of California in Los Angeles, "The Executive Profile: A Survey of Corporate Leaders in the Eighties." The survey focused on top executives' business careers, education, cultural backgrounds, and personal lives in order to create a more accurate portrait of them. The composite CEO is a 51-year-old white male, typically a first child, born in 1933. He spent most of his childhood in a mid-sized Midwestern city. Ninety-four percent of the executives are married. The CEO's wife, like his mother before her, does not work outside the home. His business associates are nearly all white, male, and married. He is Protestant, although a growing number of his peers are Catholic and Jewish. Politically, he is conservative and a registered Republican.

When Jane Evans first joined Butterick/Vogue in 1974, it was the first time she was faced with the issue of gender in the workplace. She was already used to working with men from her previous positions in business (she was a CEO at age 25), but the men at American Can, Butterick's parent company, weren't used to women executives. "I began to notice the little things. There wasn't the same comfort level at meetings. I was always seated next to the highest-ranking executive; doors were always opened for me; and the men were overly courteous to me and to each other in my presence." They would avoid swearing in front of her and apologized if they did. She remembers with a laugh, "Sometimes I felt like letting loose with a string of four-letter words myself just to get this whole issue out of the way."

Tara Roth Madden, author of *Women vs. Women: The Uncivil Business War* (AMACOM, 1987) and a former corporate manager, says a number of traditional behaviors are "built in." She explains, "Men take us to lunch, they hold the door, and they pay the bills. They do everything if you expect them to. But a lot of men are now having difficulties knowing what women expect these days."

Women shouldn't start out working relations without being sensitive to the very real cultural differences between men and women, according to Madden. For example, "Women shouldn't go to the restroom with other women to compare hairspray and clothing, because it just doesn't look professional."

Madden's solution to "unhealthy" competitiveness among female coworkers is "trial distancing." She asks women to "stop being friends with their peers and secretaries," and to talk only about work during work hours. She compares trial distancing to trial separations in marriages or parental "tough love" for teenagers with behavioral problems.

Men quite often aren't aware of their own discriminatory behavior, according to Lisa Hicks, senior associate for Catalyst. A report published by Catalyst cited a number of examples. One male supervisor hesitated to offer a single woman manager opportunities to travel with him because he anticipated the discomfort they might experience—either because of sexual tension or their respective spouses' misgivings. In another instance, a man was hesitant to give a woman honest and constructive criticism—crucial to improving her professional skills—because he feared she would react emotionally to negative feedback. Yet another sex-related barrier reared its head when a male supervisor decided not to offer a mid-level woman executive a relocation opportunity that would advance her career, on the assumption that her family priorities take precedence. Hicks explains that these men honestly believe they are reacting sensitively toward women, but are actually preventing women from making their own choices.

According to Dr. Hazel J. Rozema and John W. Gray, consultants on male/female communications who taught a course on the topic at the University of Arkansas in Little Rock, there are many sex-related myths in the public mind. The following surprising findings were drawn from their 1985-1986 survey of 400 bankers and small business managers in that state:

1. Men actually talk more than women. Women are more likely to ask questions, while men are more likely to answer questions.
2. In same-sex conversations, interruptions are fairly evenly distributed. However, in mixed-sex conversations, men interrupt women more often than vice versa.
3. Female managers are no more emotionally open or dramatic than male managers.
4. Women are touched more than men in most contexts. Men touch women to guide them through hallways, to help them on with their coats, or help them into a car.
5. Male trainees initiate more interaction with trainers than females do.

The "pink-collar" prison?

Dr. Daniel Levinson, a professor of psychology at Yale University, says the 1970s' active movement toward equality for women is slowing down in the 1980s. In recent research on the stages of women's lives, he has found that, although most women today expect to work outside the home, the great majority regard their domestic responsibilities as their first priority. The professor offers some noteworthy opinions based on his interviews with 45 women between the ages 35 and 45. According to his observations, most women still enter traditionally "feminine" positions, such as nursing, teaching, and social work. Women managers hold mostly staff, not line, positions. And when women *do* reach top executive positions, they are often pigeonholed into certain departments to perform "women's work."

Levinson also found that, contrary to logical expectations, many of the successful businesswomen he interviewed did not have long-term goals. This is a major mistake, he believes, because having a "vision" and definite goals are the keys to success. Florence Bonner, executive director of the Albany, New York-based Center for Women in Government, explains, "I think that occupational upward mobility depends on individuals being able to assess where their skills are needed, and being able to shop between those places and figure out how they can get the best out of the environment both in terms of work and [quality of] living."

Ilene Gordon, a vice-president at the Packaging Corporation of America, says more than 20 percent of all managers in American industry are women, yet they still are underrepresented in the manufacturing sector, including the paper and steel industries. She believes women usually are placed in such departments as customer service and data processing because they don't have the educational credentials and dedication to assume "profit responsibility."

Manufacturing is a good option for women with science and math backgrounds, according to Gordon, because it offers great opportunities to move into operating positions—the surest path to the very top management jobs. Five years ago, less than 15 percent of all college women enrolled in engineering or math programs. Today, however, 33 percent graduate with these degrees.

In fact, in 1985, women earned 30 percent of all medical degrees, up from 13 percent in 1975; 21 percent of degrees in dentistry, up from 3 percent; and 38 percent in law, up from 15 percent a decade earlier. In the fall of 1985, only 10 percent of women entering college planned to major in education, while 28 percent chose business, making it the most popular major for both sexes, according to a report in *The New York Times*.

Finding qualified women for manufacturing line management jobs is no longer the dilemma it once was, according to Gordon. She feels, however, that women must become more dedicated to their jobs, and claims she was able to win her present position not only because of her degrees in mathematics and statistics from M.I.T., but also because she was willing to dedicate herself primarily to her job. "My job comes first, then my family, and then myself," she says. "If you want to make it in this field and obtain a management position, you must be totally committed to the job. The problem with many women is that they won't commit themselves, and this hurts the chances for future generations."

Gordon's normal workday is from 8:30 a.m. to 8:30 p.m. She is with her children in the early morning, late evenings (sometimes), and weekends. Following the birth of her first child, she returned to work after three months; after her second was born, she returned in one month. "I feel my two children are handling my husband's and my hectic schedules just fine. You have to keep in tune with this business, or you'll be pushed out."

Dropping out

Futurist John Naisbitt has predicted that a woman will be president of the United States before there is a female CEO at IBM. A recent cover story in *Fortune*, "Women Bailing Out," was illustrated with a photograph of a woman sitting at home with her child. "Women may drop out to have children, to change careers, or start their own businesses. But by going into business for herself, a woman sacrifices the rewards and the challenges of the corporation," says Catalyst's Schwartz. She thinks women should simply "hang in there," because "we're on the threshold of a lot more flexibility."

Both men and women experience a "dangerous period" in their mid-career years (usually between ages 36 to 43), according to Barbara Kovach, dean of University College at Rutgers University and author of the article "The Derailment of Fast-Track Managers" (*Organizational Dynamics*, Autumn 1986). Kovach told *Management Review* in an interview that during this period, employees on the "fast track" are in danger of derailing or plateauing. But this slowdown in the climb up the corporate hierarchy happens to women for different reasons than it happens to men.

Kovach says men must learn to be *more* flexible during this period to survive in the corporation by fitting in with senior management. They have to let go of some of the very characteristics that put them on the corporate fast track in the first place: assertiveness, high energy, initiative. Women, on the other hand, are generally *already* flexible, says Kovach. "The women have to be more achievement-oriented. Because of cultural expectation, the men will always work toward what they are supposed to achieve—men have more of a tendency to hang in there, because they have to. Women have less tendency to 'gut it out' and keep that long-term goal in sight.

Women opt out about this time because they want to spend time with small children, or they want to 'run their own shows.'"

Why promote women?

Why should corporations be concerned about the problems of advancement faced by woman managers? According to Montgomery Securities' Evans, women bring a tremendous amount of balance to the workplace. In her experience, men treat each other better with women around: "There's less masculine game-playing." Evans adds, "Women tend to view things differently and are more sensitive and approachable by employees on a personal level. We also can be good friends with men who've never had that kind of relationship with women, and thus help broaden their horizons." She says women look at marketing issues differently and often get more enthusiastic about ideas or concepts.

Evans' job is to review companies in the $25- to $250-million range as candidates for LBOs [leveraged buyouts]. She was recruited from her position as the CEO of Monet Jewelers by Montgomery to be a senior partner. "I was recruited because the managing partner at Montgomery Securities Fund wanted someone with a strong consumer retail/soft goods marketing background," explains Evans. She sees herself as a "consensus manager," but says the buck stops here. Evans tries hard to listen to coworkers' ideas and to change plans based on others' input: "I give my employees the decision-making power." A vice-president at Butterick—the one who led the walkout attempt—later told an interviewer Evans was the best boss he ever had, because she made them all feel important. Her bosses, who have been mostly men, have sometimes questioned whether she was tough enough, Evans says, but she has retained her even-tempered manner, explaining, "I'm not a screamer or a fighter. I just try to work things out."

Bernadette Kenny, a senior consultant for Lee Hecht Harrison, a New York-based outplacement firm, believes women will enter management ranks in small- and medium-sized companies, not huge multinational corporations. They will fill more local and service-related roles, according to Kenny. She supports Marilyn Loden's ideas in the book *Feminine Leadership* (Times Books, 1985). Kenny says Loden's ideas on developing a strong leadership style while retaining a strong sense of personal, feminine style are credible, and will encourage women to be themselves.

It is to management's advantage to provide—and publicize—equal opportunities for both men and women. Otherwise, executives may alienate talented female managers. And while women add diversity to predominantly male institutions, as pointed out by Evans, Kenny, Loden, and others, they also may help foster more creative, people-oriented working environments. There is an increasingly strong economic incentive for hiring and promoting qualified female managers as well: In the 1990s corporations will face a dwindling supply of college graduates from which to recruit managers.

Women already outnumber men at 52 percent of the nation's colleges and universities, and are entering business, engineering, and law schools in greater numbers. It stands to reason that they will be a growing percentage of the workforce in the near future, and that companies will need to offer an attractive working environment to compete for top management trainees and entry-level people.

What companies can do

To bring about any meaningful decline in discrimination against women in hiring and career advancement, companies must adjust not only structurally, but also attitudinally. Managers, from the top down, must examine such harmful organizational practices and problems as tokenism, performance double standards, and sex-related discriminatory practices, and take immediate steps to eliminate them. Good performance evaluations, according to Schwartz, are essential: "Performance appraisals must be thoughtful. They must ... help make them aware of how to translate their abilities. Women, especially, need to find out how to be more valuable to corporations, and managers can help them."

Women shouldn't be afraid to act naturally simply because they have entered a more male-dominated environment, says Leonard Chusmir, an associate professor at Florida University's College of Business Administration. "The number one thing is to treat women as individuals, not women. Although there are some male characteristics that are helpful the higher up you go, essentially the worst thing a woman can do is to be a male clone," he maintains.

Chusmir adds, "An essential step is to break down the informal, unstructured barriers to women that exist both inside and outside the organization." His suggestions for managers:

1. Establish an organizational climate in which men accept women as colleagues. Top-level managers should act to minimize the effects of sex stereotypes and prejudices about women and make a concerted effort to promote them.
2. Encourage decision making by women and give them more autonomy, feedback, and opportunities to use their skills.
3. Provide training and education for women with the necessary qualifications to make them managerial candidates.
4. Organize programs that allow flexible working hours and provide childcare facilities or information on outside programs.

5. Work to break down the informal, unstructured barriers to women that exist both inside and outside the organization, such as the "old boys' network."
6. Encourage women to act as role models, mentors, and confidants for other women.

Strong support needed

Strong support systems—both at home and on the job—are crucial for women to reach the pinnacles of corporate and public-sector management. Says Evans, "I was blessed with great support, feedback, and encouragement in the early stages of my career. My early management training, when I was right out of college in 1965, was also in a great environment. I really didn't feel any culture shock." The chairman of the first company where she worked after college was a firm believer in putting women in positions of power. "They even called him the 'queenmaker,'" recalls Evans, "because so many women became managers in his organization, and because he believed in having women market products for women."

This LBO specialist says it also takes an extensive support system on the home front to be able to progress through the managerial ranks. "I'm very fortunate in having a helpful husband, a son who understands that sometimes my job comes first, and live-in help," she reports. Evans is indeed lucky; although many more men these days help with domestic chores, "women are still putting in more than full-time work" at home, according to Women in Government's Bonner. She says women in business are being pulled in so many directions by family and job obligations that it is often very difficult for them to "stay in one piece."

Many of America's most successful women managers have adopted nontraditional lifestyles to deal with their frenzied schedules and frequent travels. According to an article in *Business Week*, Ellen Marram, a 40-year-old Harvard Business School graduate who earns almost $250,000 a year at Nabisco's Grocery Products Division, married a laywer last year. She works 65-hour weeks, not counting two hours of commuting each day from her Manhattan apartment to the company's Parsippany, New Jersey headquarters. The couple doesn't do much grocery shopping; they eat takeout Chinese food a lot. But a more typical lifestyle may be that of the working mother, single or married. When *Management Review* asked Lee Hecht Harrison's Kenny how she balances her career and home life, she replied, "I read on the train home to relax. But I come home to two small children, so as soon as I walk in the door I'm too busy to think about work."

Bonner says organizations like the Center for Women in Government, American Women's Economic Development Corporation, or Catalyst provide much-needed support because they bring a wide variety of talented female managers together and make it easier to cope with working life's pressures. Schwartz of Catalyst says, "The major challenge is to recognize that we're used to thinking of white males as the leaders. The whole system is set up so that the white male moves up automatically. He is identified earlier, and he's part of this succession planning." She believes there must be special efforts taken to recognize and identify able and talented women.

This year Catalyst honored several leading corporations for their outstanding programs in recruiting, retaining, and developing good female managers. The winners include:

1. *The Equitable Financial Companies,* for its collaboration with the Women's Business Resource Group on a policy action agenda. The organizations work together to identify and address the career and work-related needs of women, including salary and career progress as well as work and family supports.

2. *Connecticut Consortium for Child Care,* a group of 11 corporations that have created a unique childcare referral service to help parents learn about and locate adequate, affordable options.

3. *IBM,* for developing its national network of more than 200 community-based childcare referral organizations for IBM employees.

4. *Mobil Corporation,* for its senior management development program for women and minorities. The program identifies high-potential employees and ensures that they have the opportunities and exposure necessary to advance to their fullest potential.

In another progressive effort, Corning Glass has gathered 150 top managers together and is laying out the most comprehensive plan to identify and develop women managers that has ever been launched, according to Schwartz.

Corporations offering daycare programs, flexible work schedules, and nonsexist management training and development programs will breed a more confident and loyal group of women.

Too many women drop out of the corporate world today because they become disillusioned. They see only a few token women at the top, but no real effort to bring gender equity to the workplace. After years of hard work, they get tired of knocking their heads against the "glass ceiling." They "derail," reach a plateau, or start their own businesses. In fact, the entrepreneurial boom has been driven by women, according to Steve Solomon, author of *Small Business USA* (Crown Publishers, 1986). "Self-employment among women has been increasing three times faster than total self-employment growth. By the early 1980s, women represented about one-third of all self-employed, up from one-quarter in 1975," Solomon reports.

Women must be able to picture themselves in major corporations' boardrooms and executive suites in order to reach them. But for that to happen, management also must help them assess their abilities and focus their energies. In the next ten years U.S. corporations will be in need of well-trained and qualified individuals. If women believe they have a fair chance to move up the ranks with the same opportunities as their male colleagues, perhaps they will stay in corporations long enough to reach the highest levels.

Age Bias in the Workplace

Robert P. Hey

He had toiled 31 years for a large manufacturing company in the Northeast. The children had just finished college; at 56 he looked forward to six more years of earnings to make retirement possible at 62.

But it was not to be. Out of the blue came an early-retirement offer that this man, who asked not to be named, could hardly refuse. His corporation, like many others across the United States, decided to trim its payroll; his job, it said, would be abolished in a few months. The company offered half-pay retirement for the next four years, provided he not work elsewhere.

He didn't know how he could afford those terms. But he was afraid that the alternative would be no job and no retirement pay. He wondered: Was he being discriminated against because of his age?

This is a typical case for thousands of older American workers. In the 1980s, many have been offered similar early-retirement plans; employment experts say these one-time incentives-to-retire will occur more frequently in the near future.

They are "growing in favor among employers," says Burton Fretz, a Washington lawyer who monitors age discrimination, "because it's a way of reducing the work force. At the same time, it's a really tricky area," because these offers can mask age discrimination. Mr. Fretz is executive director of the National Senior Citizens Law Center.

Many workers have been content with the offers: "There are a lot of people who are very happy with this" trend, says Rosalie

Silberman, vice-chairman of the Equal Employment Opportunity Commission (EEOC). "I hope that they will be heard from."

But many others are mightily unhappy, feeling they have been discriminated against because of age. Increasingly they are being heard from: They are filing charges with the EEOC, whose mandate includes protecting Americans against age discrimination in employment, and going to court. They are complaining to organizations of older Americans, like the 28 million-member American Association of Retired Persons (AARP). And they are fuming to members of Congress.

These one-time incentives are not to be confused with the early-retirement options. No one criticizes these permanent programs, which enable employees to reach decisions about retirement age by planning ahead for years.

Age discrimination is "one of the hottest policy issues that we are looking at now," Mrs. Silberman says.

As a society "we need to do more everywhere" to combat age injustice, says Jack Carlson, AARP's executive director. Seven million organization members, all of whom are at least 50, are actively employed.

Fretz says "if you judge by the number of charges filed with the EEOC, [age discrimination on the job] seems to be a growing prob-

Figure 1. Number of age discrimination cases filed with the Equal Employment Opportunity Commission (in thousands).

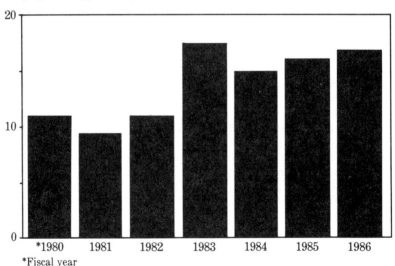

Source: Equal Employment Opportunity Commission.

lem. The number of these charges has tripled since 1980." Fretz says he personally believes "the problem is a considerable one."

He cites several reasons for inequity:

1. Because of economic pressures many companies are scaling down. "When they do that, they tend to look at higher salaries," which are generally earned by longtime employees, who are older.
2. Age discrimination in society is still pervasive, because of hoary stereotypes that falsely assert older workers are less capable than younger ones.
3. Many young entrepreneurs run small companies; often they prefer people their own age around them.
4. There is a "growing awareness" among older workers that they can fight back against injustice, by contacting the EEOC or filing suit.

Early-retirement offers are the cutting edge of the age-discrimination issue. Individual cases vary; the EEOC and various courts have decided cases both for and against employees.

But in the broadest sense neither America's people nor its legal system has yet decided whether these one-time offers, and many other actions involving older workers, are legal or not. Job discrimination against the elderly "is a developing area," Silberman says. "In age [the law] is all over the lot."

Laws exist that are designed to prevent discrimination; the keystone is the federal Age Discrimination in Employment Act. But this "act is ... still in the toddler stage," Michèle Pollak, an AARP legislative representative, says. Experts agree that many more court cases, and legal decisions, are needed before society can tell precisely which actions in the workplace are permissible, and which are not.

During 1987, the American Management Association surveyed its member businesses: It found that 45 percent of the more than 1,100 that responded had instituted "significant reductions" in the number of employees in the preceding 18 months. "We found," says project director Eric Greenberg, "that early-retirement incentives were the most popular" way to decrease the staff.

Moreover, American businesses expect to offer more early-retirement incentive plans to employees, as international competition remains keen and signs multiply that an economic downturn is possible in the US in the near future.

In the same survey, Mr. Greenberg found that 44 percent of the responding companies expect to make future early-retirement offers to managerial-level employees. Further, 31 percent of companies expect to make similar offers to their hourly workers.

One-time incentives to retire are attracting much skepticism from older workers, their advocates, and members of Congress. Particularly at issue are waivers. Employees who decide to accept retirement incentives must almost invariably sign a waiver of all future rights to bring age-discrimination suits.

But that brings questions. Is an individual retirement incentive fair to older workers, or discriminatory? Is there any way for a would-be retiree to tell at the time he's required to sign the waivers? Are the waivers enforceable? And should the EEOC supervise them to make sure the programs are not unjust?

"There is no way in the world . . . that we could supervise each and every waiver," EEOC's Silberman says flatly. To do so, Clarence Thomas, EEOC's blunt-spoken chairman, says, would require a larger budget and bigger staff. "We're here to carry out the responsibility of this agency," he says. "But I'm not going to tell you that we can do everything that a committee staffer or an interest group dreams up, without new resources. It's as simple as that."

Besides, Silberman says, "implicit in the criticism . . . is the [implication] that older workers are not able to take care of themselves and make decisions in their own best interests." She says that's an implication older Americans "generally find insulting."

AARP's Ms. Pollak has a quite different perspective. She says incentive programs, which can require a decision within a few weeks or even days, can be "so sophisticated that . . . there's no evidence of discrimination" for months or years. Sometimes even if a program is discriminatory "the evidence of the discrimination is just not there" at the time workers are given the retirement option.

AARP does not like waivers. But it says that if firms do want to ask employees to sign them, then the EEOC should supervise them to make certain that they are valid, that no discrimination exists. Pollak stresses that AARP is certainly not against early-retirement programs per se. But, she says, "like every other employment practice, these programs should not discriminate."

Sometimes, she says, it turns out that companies have reduced their payroll by letting higher-salaried, older workers go, and hiring instead younger, cheaper employees to do virtually the same work.

Further, she says, some employers are "basically indicating in a nice way that if employees don't sign [a waiver] . . . they're not going to get their pension. . . ." Such a tactic, she says, is "blatantly illegal."

Pollak says that EEOC supervision of waivers would send employers a powerful message. It would tell companies that their early-retirement plans must be nondiscriminatory. But if waivers are unsupervised, "the message is: 'Go ahead and do whatever you want.'"

Over vigorous opposition from Congress and advocates for

older Americans, the EEOC decided it would not supervise the waivers. But Congress had other ideas.

As part of the frantic pre-Christmas package of major bills [in 1987], Congress suspended for fiscal year 1988 the EEOC's rule that signaled employers that they could require employees to sign unsupervised waivers to retire early. This action sent the EEOC its own message: that some members of Congress are dubious about how zealous the EEOC is on behalf of older workers.

Equally dubious is AARP, which says that EEOC in these circumstances too often sides with business at the expense of the older workers that they are supposed to protect. "I'd like to know what the last [court] case was that they brought on behalf of employees on an early-incentive program," AARP's Pollak says. "They haven't brought any that we know of."

All this criticism bothers EEOC chairman Thomas. "We continue to fight, to pursue the age area," he says, "and this kind of a rear-guard action [the congressional prohibition] is incredible to me." In the short run, no one is certain what effect the forbidding of unsupervised waivers for a year will have, although it likely will make companies think twice about the content and implications of their incentives.

Congressional committees are virtually certain to examine the issue this year. But whether Congress will take any sweeping action, or decide simply to forbid unsupervised waivers for a second year, is anyone's guess.

In the long run it may not much matter, EEOC's Silberman says. She notes the changing US demography with its lower birthrates, and the many forecasts that in a very few years the American economy will be in need of more workers, not fewer: "We may very well have early recruitment instead of early retirement."

On that point AARP's Pollak agrees. "Employers that are looking to get rid of older employees now," she warns, "and think that is good labor policy, are very shortsighted."

But that is small consolation to those Americans now in their 50s and 60s who feel they are the victims of age discrimination in the workplace. They are expected to continue to file charges with the EEOC, and to sue in state and federal courts. "The number of charges will keep going up," EEOC's Silberman forecasts. Most of them are of subtle discrimination, and thus "are relatively difficult for us to deal with." Silberman says, however, that the EEOC frequently still receives clear-cut cases of "let's get the old guy out."

While the EEOC negotiates and the courts adjudicate, employers, older Americans, advocacy groups, and Congress will be watching. What else they will do, if anything, depends on how the EEOC and the courts themselves act.

Responses to the Career Plateau

Ellen K. Harvey and John R. Schultz

John had enjoyed a successful career, advancing up the organizational ladder on a regular basis, even a bit faster than most. This year John had been anticipating his next promotion to GS-14. The competition was heavy, but John had been optimistic; after all, his ratings had been as high as ever.

But when the selections were announced, John didn't get the promotion. For the first time in his career, he had failed to advance. When he went to his supervisor for post-selection counseling, it was a difficult session for both of them.

"It's not fair," John said. "I mean, I don't think anyone works any harder around here, do they?"

"No, and you do very good work," his supervisor replied. "The problem is that others are doing a good job, too, and the competition for the openings we have is tough. The organization is just not growing the way it used to."

As John walked out of the office, his supervisor felt badly. She also wondered if she would be able to motivate him to keep performing now that he faced the possibility that he would not progress in his career the way he wanted to.

Organizations are being forced to deal with situations like John's with increasing frequency. It's a multi-dimensional problem called "plateauing." Plateauing can be demeaning for the individuals undergoing it, and it can cause real difficulties for the organizations in which these employees work. However, it is a problem that can be managed if we understand why it happens and devise strategies to cope with it. This article will address some causes of career plateauing and how organizations can deal with it. By understand-

Reprinted with permission from *The Bureaucrat*, Fall 1987.

ing the modern working environment and how to motivate employees, managers can help them deal with plateauing and still maintain their effectiveness on the job.

Understanding plateauing

Plateauing is that point in an employee's career beyond which further promotion is unlikely, at least within the same organization. Career plateauing can occur at either an organizational level or a personal level. At the organizational level, plateauing means that an employee can perform well at higher levels jobs, but the scarcity of openings makes promotion unlikely. At the personal level, it is the employee who stops his/her own advancement. He/she may lack technical, managerial, or career skills, or simply the desire to achieve a higher level position.

Combination of factors   Although we commonly view plateauing as a sudden, unexpected development, such as a missed promotion, it really results from a combination of demographic, organizational, and psychological factors. Understanding these factors is the first step in dealing with plateauing.

As Dr. Judith Bardwick points out in "SMR Forum: Plateauing and Productivity" (*Sloan Management Review*, Spring 1983), the pyramidal structure of organizations makes plateauing inevitable. Since the highest executive level consists of less than one percent of an organization's employees, nearly all executive, technical, and professional people will become plateaued before they reach retirement age. Dr. Bardwick says that plateauing will become an increasingly difficult problem as the baby boom generation matures.

In 1982 a *Wall Street Journal* article by Earl C. Gottschalk, Jr., reported that the population aged 35-44 would increase by 42 percent between 1980 and 1990, while the number of middle management jobs for which this group would compete would increase only 19 percent.

That prediction was made before organizations began to streamline their mid-management ranks in order to cut costs and remain competitive in a world market. We suspect that the 19 percent figure reported in the *Journal* is even lower today.

At the same time that middle management opportunities are decreasing, many baby boomers are entering the stages in their lives in which they may naturally begin to question a number of things about themselves and their career aspirations anyway. This questioning process has been described by Gail Sheehy and Daniel Levinson.

Mid-life transition   In his book *The Seasons of a Man's Life* (Knopf, 1979), Levinson says that between the ages of roughly 32 and 40 we go through a process in which we make a few key choices about how we want to live our lives. We have a sense of urgency to get serious about our long-range plans and invest heavily in our work, family, community, solitary interests, friendships, and so on. Then, we enter what Levinson calls "the mid-life transition."

During this period we tend to make some judgment about our relative success or failure in reaching the goals we have set for ourselves. Levinson says that in mid-life we often identify a key event that, if it comes out favorably, assures us of success in our own minds. An unfavorable outcome can lead to a profound sense of failure not only in our work but also with ourselves as people. For many people that key event is the attainment of a particular position or grade level.

Gail Sheehy, in her book *Passages: Predictable Crises of Adult Life* (Bantam Books/Dutton, 1976) writes about the ages of 35 to 45 as being the "deadline decade," a crossroads offering us both opportunities and dangers. Here we can rework the narrow identity by which we have defined ourselves in the first half of our lives.

Competing goals   While a mid-life transition may not make us plateau, it often causes us to assess the importance of career vs. other life priorities. Some people emerge recommitted to work and upward advancement; others consciously focus on other interests.

Furthermore, researchers such as Daniel Yankelovich and John Immerwahr report in their article "Putting the Work Ethic to Work" (*Society*, Jan.–Feb. 1984), that the way employees view work and their relationship to their employers is changing. They note that the contract that used to exist between labor and management was based on money as the only major work motivator. In exchange for receiving enough compensation to live a material "good life," workers abdicated discretion and control over their jobs.

Demand for freedom   However, today's employees want to exercise discretion over their work. The evolution of our society from an industrial to an information and service orientation, and the concomitant increase in the work force's education level, have led to a general demand for greater freedom over how work is to be done. At the same time, employees expect their careers to give them more than just monetary compensation. They view careers as a means of self-development and fulfillment.

A final contributing factor to the career plateau is that millions of Americans, regardless of their ages, may at some time begin to feel that they are simply in the wrong career. They may suffer stress, dissatisfaction, or burnout from the pressures they have endured. Or, they may simply want a new challenge. Such a realization may be prompted by a life transition phase or by an unsatisfactory performance rating, but it could occur at any time.

Effect of plateau on work

Plateauing may cause agonizing self-questioning, in which employees blame themselves for what has happened. Dr. Bardwick points out that Americans, more than any other culture, fuse work and personal merit. Consequently, when career progress stops or work ceases to be challenging and interesting, employees begin to question their personal worth.

One of the common myths about plateaued employees, however, is that they necessarily lack motivation and stop producing. According to Dr. Janet Near, one of the few researchers to study the problem empirically, that is not the case.[1] Some plateaued employees work fewer hours per week, are absent more frequently, and are less likely to describe their health as excellent. But there is no direct link between plateauing and productivity. Many employees continue to produce at high levels. The emerging challenge for managers and organizations is to maintain the level and quality of work in these plateaued employees.

Types of employees in organizations   To face this emerging challenge, managers and organizations need to understand the types of employees in organizations. Researchers at Columbia University (Joseph P. Carnazza, Thomas P. Ference, Abraham Korman, and James A. F. Stoner) have described four main types: stars, learners, solid citizens (plateaued and still productive), and problem employees (plateaued and unproductive).[2] The researchers categorize the four types of employees according to current performance and likelihood of future promotion. A modified version of their model is shown in Figure 1.

Current performance	Low ———————————————— High Likelihood of promotion	
High	Solid citizens	Stars
Low	Problem employees	Learners

Figure 1. Types of employees.

The number of employees in any one of these categories will vary from organization to organization. But as a general rule the number of stars and the number of problem employees in any organization will be small. The number of learners will reflect whether the organization is growing, and consequently undertaking an active recruiting process, or is in a period of no or low growth where recruiting efforts are leaner.

Solid citizens, according to Judith Bardwick, probably comprise the largest group in organizations, performing up to 80 percent of the work. But most organizations' human resource dollars—not to mention management attention—go to the rising stars and the problem employees, the smallest groups. Few organizational dollars and relatively little attention are devoted to the solid citizens, even though they form the backbone of most organizations both in terms of numbers and amount of work accomplished.

The risk we run by continuing to devote large amounts of time and money to a relatively small segment of the population is that we ignore the vast population of solid citizens, thereby enhancing the likelihood that they will later become problem employees.

Motivating plateaued employees

Fortunately, there are a number of organizational interventions that can serve to motivate solid citizens and reduce that risk. The interventions are such things as effective use of performance appraisals, retraining, lateral transfers, job rotations, mentoring, use of negative sanctions, and altering hiring practices.

Performance appraisals   While most organizations give some sort of formal performance appraisals, they are not always as effective as they might be in motivating staff. Effective performance appraisals are always constructive rather than critical. By focusing first on what the individual does well and then proceeding to the areas that need improvement, constructive appraisals honestly tell employees where they stand. Dr. Bardwick notes that unless employees receive accurate feedback and information, it is likely that incorrect self-evaluations and expectations will occur. Employees who are insecure may undervalue their competence; others may exaggerate their competence and be particularly traumatized if they later become plateaued.

Ference, Stoner, and Warren caution that long-term problems can be created by managers who avoid the short-term unpleasantness of giving a negative appraisal.[3] Failure to give appropriate negative feedback can allow possibly correctable behavior to become entrenched habit.

Moreover, feedback on performance must take place more often than the traditional annual assessment conducted by many organizations. According to Carnazza, Korman, Ference, and Stoner, on-going feedback about specific tasks, as well as overall performance, yields higher levels of performance from employees, particularly plateaued "solid citizens."

Retraining   Currently, retraining is the most common corporate response to plateauing. Dr. Bardwick reports that organizations typically offer in-house education or tuition benefits so employees can acquire skills and knowledge related to their present jobs. Retraining and skill upgrading is recommended to ensure that performance does not slip because a worker's skills have become obsolete.

Retraining sends a positive signal to employees that the organization is still willing to invest in them. It may also provide the spark many employees need to re-interest them in their work, because it provides a means of self-improvement, which is becoming an increasingly important career element.

Retraining is usually provided on a limited basis, serving only to enhance the employees' present skills and knowledge. Almost no corporations make it feasible for individuals to be retrained in order to pursue a second career.

Symbolic rewards   Increasing the number of awards ceremonies or the number of awards granted conveys the message that, despite the large size of the organization, individuals are noticed and their contributions are valued. Researchers have found that receiving accolades and plaudits is very important to employees. Carnazza, Korman, Ference, and Stoner believe awards that recognize employees' accomplishments are likely to increase performance.

There is virtually no limit to how creative organizations can be in rewarding employees. Employee recognition days, letters of commendation, and public praise cost organizations very little and go a long way in developing employee camaraderie and company spirit.

Lateral transfer, job rotation, or job enrichment   Sometimes a change in the physical or mental makeup of the work itself can benefit both the individual and the organization. Such changes offer the possibility of stimulating an employee's work by introducing a new level of challenge. A job change will also signify to the employee that the organization recognizes him/her and has confidence that he/she can master a new set of skills. Dr. Bardwick notes that what an organization initially loses by transferring or rotating an employee (his/her expertise at the old job) will be recaptured by the employee's enthusiasm for the new work.

The organization must be careful, however, of the message it sends to employees who are being transferred or rotated. Job changes of this nature can signify to an employee that he/she is being considered for a promotion. If no promotion possibility exists at this time, that message should be conveyed so that the employee's expectations will not be dashed later.

Mentoring   Mid-career is often a good time for employees to begin giving back to the organization part of what they have reaped from it. One of the best ways to do that is to begin coaching or training younger employees. Plateaued solid citizens particularly may take a special interest in teaching new employees. Management can encourage the establishment of mentoring relationships either informally or formally through the development of a mentoring program.

Since the mentor relationship can be quite influential in shaping new hires' beliefs about the organization and its work practices, close attention should be paid to assigning mentors to new employees. Obviously employees with a "sour grapes" attitude would not make good mentors.

Employees, on the other hand, who know the organization well, who have reached a satisfactory level of achievement, are continuing to produce, and are interested in such a relationship, would likely make excellent mentors and would enjoy showing new employees the ropes.

Altering hiring practices   This constitutes perhaps one of the most controversial interventions. Bardwick suggests that organizations hire employees who do not regard career success as a primary life goal. She says that these people, if plateaued, would be less likely to interpret the plateau as a core failure in their lives and would consequently adjust to the phenomenon with far fewer problems.

She goes on to say that it can be in the organization's best interest to have "competent, dependable (and also plateaued) employees who derive their most important gratifications from interest outside the job and who have expectations that match current and future realities."

This kind of recruiting objective might represent a considerable change for organizations that typically feel the best employees are those most likely to progress up the hierarchy as far as possible. But that feeling is based on traditional work motives that are changing, and that kind of worker is the very kind who might be most disappointed if progress slows.

Use of negative sanctions   This usually involves firing unproductive employees or taking some form of job action. Negative sanctions are commonly levied against unproductive employees but should be viewed as an organizational last resort. Negative sanctions do not remedy the problem of organizational plateauing, and they serve to raise the stress level of both the individual involved and other employees around him/her.

If negative sanctions are unavoidable, positive outplacement may be the best route to take. That way the employee is at least helped to find another job. Such outplacement could include helping the employee find suitable retraining for changing careers.

Summary   It is important for organizations to understand that dealing with the motivational challenges in today's workplace will require a high degree of sophistication. All of the interventions discussed, though, are good human resource practices and will go a long way toward helping organizations deal with the plateaued employee.

Notes

1. Near, Janet P., "A Discriminant Analysis of Plateaued versus Non-Plateaued Managers," *Journal of Vocational Behavior*, 1985, Vol. 26, 177–188.

2. Carnazza, Joseph P., Thomas P. Ference, Abraham Korman, and James A. F. Stoner, "Plateaued and Non-Plateaued Managers: Factors in Job Performance," *Journal of Management*, Vol. 7, No. 2, 1981, 7–25.

3. Ference, Thomas P., James A. F. Stoner, and E. Kirby Warren, "Managing the Career Plateau," *Academy of Management Review*, October 1977, 602–612.

PART 2

Employee Performance, Motivation, and Training

Evaluating the '80s Employee

Robert W. Goddard

Most managers are flying blind in their evaluation of people. Few have asked two critical questions: How accurate is our appraisal system? Is it a dependable measure of present worth and future potential?

The answers, in most cases, are resounding "Nos!" Most of us haven't any idea what performance appraisal is doing for—or to—our organizations. And, as employees are challenging the employment-at-will prerogatives formerly enjoyed by management, there is sharp attention on the entire appraisal process.

Researchers and the courts have found that the majority of appraisal systems now in use contain the seeds of their own destruction. These systems allow—even encourage—subjectivity and discrimination. They are expected to serve several different functions. They are the primary, and frequently the only, means of determining differences in bonuses, pay increases and choices between individuals for training, promotion and the like.

These appraisal systems preclude comparability by ensuring that performers in different jobs will be evaluated on different criteria. They promote summary ratings that are not needed and can actually be counter-productive. They attempt to evaluate performance that is differently perceived. Research studies indicate that only 40 percent of superiors and subordinates agree on more than one-half of a subordinate's job duties.

Even more alarming, there are many *non-performance* variables that influence or correlate with performance ratings, such as current salary, hierarchical status, business function, occupation,

Reprinted from *Management World*, April 1985, with permission from AMS, Trevose, PA 19047. Copyright 1985 AMS.

sex, race, length of service, appraisal purpose and method, rater training, frequency of appraisal, and the personalities and relationship of the boss and subordinate.

For example, researchers have found the following flaws:

1. Job tenure frequently correlates with performance ratings
2. Mean ratings of managers and executives are typically higher than those of non-supervisory personnel
3. Rating differences between sexes and races are not justified by valid performance differences
4. Those whose salaries are above the midpoint of their salary range usually receive higher average ratings than those below
5. Ratings which are discussed with subordinates will be higher than those which need not be discussed
6. Significant rating differences often exist between corporate business functions (for example, those in finance rating themselves more highly than those in manufacturing).

Today the courts are scrutinizing—and penalizing—this kind of discrimination. Since the enactment of Title VII of the 1964 Civil Rights Act, various court challenges have sought to clarify which employment practices the act encompasses.

Over time, the definitional process has gradually come to include performance appraisal systems, where they operate to discriminate against any individual. Performance appraisals now are viewed as a selection device and hence subject to the Equal Employment Opportunity Commission's (EEOC) *Uniform Guidelines on Employee Selection Procedures.* As a result, employers soon may have to defend the adequacy of their existing performance appraisal systems in light of the act's prohibition against discriminatory employment practices.

To date, some major companies have had their appraisal systems subject to penalty. General Motors was condemned by a court because the promotional process to salaried jobs reinforced prejudices and totally lacked objective standards. U.S. Steel, Bethlehem Steel, Union Carbide, and Procter & Gamble have been found guilty of using subjectivity in promotion practices.

International Paper Co. was unable to justify certain appraisal practices because the rating instrument was not based on an analysis of the job. Western Electric has been ordered to increase the number of female supervisors and to set goals and timetables for better pay and promotions. Court officials estimate the suit will cost the company more than $10 million.

In the 21 years since Title VII became law, managers have modified personnel practices to meet new legal requirements. But the majority have yet to recognize and accept fully the fact that the law expects rewards to be distributed fairly and *only* on the basis of an employee's contributions to the organization.

The law now states that all requirements and procedures used to measure performance, determine placement, plan transfers, or promote people must be valid, job related, and not used to create a disparate impact on any group of employees. The following characteristics are essential.

1. Performance standards, objectives, and criteria for measuring or verifying performance must be established in advance of any evaluation.
2. Factors unrelated to the job must be eliminated from the assessment.
3. Priorities or weights (if any) assigned to different factors should be established in advance, used in the same way for all persons, and communicated to employees.
4. Any subjective results that will be included in performance appraisals, that is, factors that cannot be easily quantified or measured objectively, should be spelled out along with the basis for evaluating them.
5. A written form should be used at least annually. This should include expected results; appraisal standards or criteria; weight attached to the outcome; manager's rating; employee strengths; areas needing development; agreed-upon development objectives; space for employee comments; and signatures of both manager and employee.
6. A formal appraisal interview should be conducted by the supervisor with each employee at least annually.

Two extremes

Despite the present situation with performance appraisals, selection, promotion, transfer, training, retention, and compensation decisions continue to be based on them. Managers, continually faced with the possibility of charges of discrimination, must find ways which not only will satisfy the enforcement agencies and the courts, but also provide an accurate performance measure on which to base personnel decisions.

It's a tall, but not impossible, order. Over 20 years ago, behavioral scientist Douglas McGregor observed, "It is probably safe to say that we can discriminate between the outstandingly good, the satisfactory and the unsatisfactory performers. When, however, we attempt to use the results of appraisal to make discriminations much finer than this, we are quite probably deluding ourselves."

After many valiant, but unsuccessful, attempts to devise the perfect "do-it-all" appraisal system, most professionals now agree that appraisal methods should be adapted to the current, inadequate state of the art. Dr. Nathan Winstanley, management consultant and former compensation research manager of Xerox Corp., believes that error would be minimized if administrative distinctions were restricted to three categories only, such as the bottom five percent (poor), the top five percent (outstanding) and all others in between (competent). "Since most of the research indicates you can probably identify only the two extremes," he says, "simplify and use a three-point rating scale."

James Young, management consultant and former director of human resource development for CIBA-GEIGY Corp., believes that performance appraisal should be a tool for development rather than administration. "Performance appraisals," he says, "are primarily communication mechanisms and procedures used by the boss and subordinate to achieve the performance and rewards both desire."

Managers, in other words, should be counselors, not judges. Their appraisals should concentrate on ability, motivation, and training needs rather than on results achieved. "By moving away from our legalistic preoccupation with the design and administration of systems and toward the essential performance dynamic," Young suggests, "we will stop being part of the appraisal problem and begin to be part of the solution."

Today, many organizations are moving in these directions. Typical is an appraisal system developed by management consultant Jack Stone. The system starts with the identification of all major job elements. "Products" are then defined for each element. Each product is rated in terms of six factors: results, timeliness, quality and completeness, manner of performance, and workdays applied. Point values are assigned from five to one, covering the qualitative range from "outstanding" to "unsatisfactory." The points are summed and averaged, and a final numerical value for each job element is computed. Ratings for all job elements are then summarized for an overall performance rating of the individual.

There are three rating categories: marginal, satisfactory, and excellent (the unsatisfactory and outstanding levels are implied). Production standards are specific, simple, and objective. The following are standards for satisfactory performance:

1. *Results*—goals met; some important issues and certain identified problems resolved in routine ways
2. *Timeliness*—product or service produced on time
3. *Quality and completeness*—product or service responsive, accurate, grammatically correct, complete, and consistent with policy and procedures
4. *Manner of performance*—mature, professional and with a positive attitude; employee accepted constructive criticism
5. *Method of performance*—product developed with standard operating procedures
6. *Workdays applied*—within plan.

This type of appraisal instrument has several advantages over more complex systems. It is comprehensive and concise. It defines acceptable standards of production. It measures output rather than activities. It minimizes error, bias, and leniency by restricting choice. It improves accuracy and fairness by requiring *constant* evaluation. It identifies specific areas of performance that need improvement.

General Electric, by comparison, threw out traditional performance appraisal and devised a less formal, more frequent appraisal system with a participative approach. The program resulted from an in-house study in which selected managers were asked to work

---

Appraisal advice

As managers, most of us are locked into an appraisal system over which we have little or no control. But there are steps we can take to ensure that our employee appraisals, regardless of format, are as objective and productive as possible.

1. Provide every evaluator with clear, written instructions or formal training on how to conduct performance appraisals.
2. Make sure everyone understands that you are interested in performance evaluation (definable output) *only*, and that personal bias and prejudice will not be tolerated in any appraisal.
3. Inform supervisors that satisfactory performance—standards met—is not a poor rating; it is the company goal. Most organizations don't need many high achievers to survive and grow, but they do need performers who meet acceptable production standards.
4. Don't put much weight on such subjective criteria as the employee's initiative, drive, integrity, loyalty, cooperation, and so on. Unless these traits or work habits are part of the job description (and they rarely are), they have no place in a performance appraisal.
5. Ask employees to rate themselves prior to the formal appraisal, and, if possible, to rate their superiors. It's a good way to foster a healthy dialogue between employee and manager.
6. Use multiple appraisers, if practical. It enhances the overall quality and reliability of assessment.
7. Conduct frequent appraisals. Annual or semi-annual evaluations lead to a low probability of behavior change.
8. At the end of the appraisal discussion, establish a written agreement on performance improvements to be made. These commitments become objectives for the next evaluation and provide a mechanism for coaching and regular feedback.
9. Review your appraisal system to see just what performance it is measuring. It will help you determine how and where to best use the results.

with their subordinates in preparing a set of goals for improving job performance. Subordinates were encouraged to exert as much influence as possible on the formulation of the final list of goals, which were reviewed and approved by the manager.

The results of the GE study indicate that employees who fully participate in the appraisal process achieve a much greater percentage of their goals than those in the more traditional annual review and criticism. The key is whether or not goals are set. In many appraisal discussions, GE managers mentioned areas of performance where improvement was needed; and those managers who went on to develop specific plans and objectives had a much higher rate of success than those who identified performance improvement areas but did not develop specific goals.

These findings suggest that comprehensive annual performance appraisals are of questionable value; coaching should be a daily, not a yearly, activity; goal setting, not criticism, should be used to improve performance; and that separate appraisals should be held for different purposes. The appraisal system finally adopted at GE differs from traditional appraisal programs in that it involves more frequent discussions of performance, no summary judgments or ratings, separately held salary discussions, and emphasis on mutual goal setting and problem solving.

What is the long-term outlook for performance appraisal? Dr. Edward Lawler, professor of business administration at the University of Southern California, predicts it will be *the* human resource issue of the future. Already, changes in philosophy and practice are under way, with the theory that individuals differ in many ways, that these differences affect behavior on the job, and that both employers and employees will benefit from developing and using such distinctive personal differences in making personnel decisions. Backing up this view, the U.S. Supreme Court has supported a lower-court decision that states in part: "To the extent that EEOC guidelines conflict with well-grounded expert opinion and accepted professional standards, they need not be controlling."

Until the forces affecting the future of performance appraisal run their course, many managements will proceed with much more care and caution. Organizations are expected to increase their appraisal training and research, and reduce their dependence on questionable finite rating discriminations for administrative use. Some will abandon traditional appraisal, while others will use it only for employee development where summary ratings are not required.

Certainly, until great advances are made in this area, human limitations will continue to foster low validity and reliability. While the practical, legal and ethical implications of all this are disturbing, they also offer hope for establishing appraisal systems that expand and enhance the capabilities of companies and individuals.

Characteristics of a High Quality Performance Appraisal System

The following is a list of characteristics that agencies may want to consider in attempting to develop and implement performance appraisal systems and processes that will be effective in improving individual and organizational effectiveness.

1. As much time is spent on the process by which performance appraisal is implemented as on the technical design of the system.

2. The process should make clear what objectives and values the performance appraisal system is designed to achieve, and resolve potential ambiguities and conflicts.

3. The system must have top management support, not only in words but deeds. Since employees will take the process no more seriously than they see their supervisors taking it, top management needs to serve as the role model through active involvement.

4. Managers and supervisors need to see the process of setting standards, providing feedback, evaluating performance, and reinforcing improvement as the essence of their jobs. They must be willing to spend a substantial amount of time in making performance appraisal serve as a management tool.

"Some Characteristics of a High Quality Performance Appraisal System and Process," prepared by the Special Programs Consulting Division, Office of Personnel Management. Reprinted with permission from the Winter 1980–81 issue of *The Bureaucrat*.

5. Higher levels of management must make sure that subordinate managers and supervisors have enough time to make performance appraisal work.

6. Adequate financial and staff resources are made available for the design, implementation, evaluation, and refinement processes.

7. Diagnostic work is undertaken to determine what approaches to setting standards (e.g., MBO, WPPR, BARS, critical incident, job analysis) are most appropriate for different categories of jobs in the agency.

8. Diagnostic work is undertaken to assess the attitudes of managers and employees toward performance appraisal and its uses, in order to determine degrees of acceptance and to identify possible needed modifications.

9. The agency provides meaningful opportunities for involvement of line managers, field supervisors, unions, and employees in the process, so that performance appraisal is not viewed as a personnel system forced on the rest of the agency.

10. The agency has a meaningful and active goal planning process to which individual performance plans can be linked.

11. The agency gives high priority to designing and implementing a rigorous evaluation process, designed to assess whether the performance appraisal process is contributing to improved organizational effectiveness and achieving other objectives, such as equity, fairness, and acceptance.

12. Expert assistance is obtained to help insure that the system meets the psychometric tests of reliability, validity, discriminability, freedom from bias, and so forth, in order to make the system as fair as possible and defensible against legal challenge.

13. The agency gives high priority to providing adequate training for all managers and supervisors, including refresher courses, covering such topics as: setting performance standards, understanding motivation, setting goals, providing counseling and feedback, and conducting the appraisal interview.

14. The agency provides resources for follow-up assistance to line managers from its training/personnel, management analysis units, to help them work more effectively with the performance appraisal system.

15.   Where lack of trust and a fearful organizational climate exist, the agency mounts a major team-building effort to avoid defensive, counterproductive "game playing" with the system.

16.   The system procedures strongly encourage periodic progress review and problem-solving meetings between supervisors and their subordinates. The system should also insure periodic revisions and modifications of individual performance plans so that they remain dynamic documents reflecting actual changes in job requirements.

17.   The system provides for clear and perceived linkages between performance appraisal and organizational compensation and reward systems. The system must succeed in the eyes of employees in being one which rewards good performers and takes appropriate corrective actions with poor performers. The agency also systematically links cash award programs as well as non-monetary rewards (such as developmental opportunities, more interesting work assignments, etc.) to the performance appraisal system.

18.   The agency takes as many actions as possible to insure the objectivity and equity of its system, such as:

a.   Ensuring that higher-level reviews of performance standards exist for comparable work.
b.   Providing for independent or higher-level review of appraisal ratings, to insure inter-rater consistency and avoid leniency-severity tendencies on the part of individual rating officials. Also to insure that the system discriminates between actual levels of performance and avoids everyone being rated "satisfactory."
c.   Providing appropriate mechanisms for considering individual complaints about the system.

19.   The agency maintains an open-minded and experimental approach to performance appraisal, with a willingness to change and modify the system and process to make it a living and dynamic management tool.

How to Motivate and Retain Employees in a Depressed Economy

_____ Maxine M. Wade

My business career began in September 1979 when I joined John Deere Waterloo Tractor Works after graduating from Oklahoma State University with a major in accounting and organizational administration. I was graduated from the university with honors, was voted one of the top ten seniors by the Business College, and was mature, settled, and had prior industrial experience. I chose John Deere for employment because, as a strong, prosperous company, it would give me many opportunities for advancement. My main goal was to become a manager and be a vital part of the decision-making and planning function. I felt that with my qualifications and choice of company it would happen.

Everything started as planned. I had been with John Deere only a year and a half when I received a promotion: to direct the forecasting function at the newly organized John Deere Component Works. My job was to develop a method of forecasting thousands of parts and to supervise several employees. My career was heading in the direction I wanted, and I felt confident I could meet any challenge set before me.

Then a series of business events took place which changed my prosperous, growing company. In 1980, President Jimmy Carter placed an embargo on the export of grain to the Soviet Union. The grain markets started to decline, interest rates rose, and the farmers in the Midwest felt squeezed financially. To help them through what they thought would be a short-term slump, the farmers postponed agricultural equipment purchases. My "green giant" began to weaken.

By 1981, John Deere had laid off 7,000 of its 50,000 hourly employees and had frozen salaries and promotions for office workers. In the short run the salary freeze did not hamper my ambitions and desires to perform because money was not a primary need. As years passed and the opportunities for advancement dwindled, however, I became frustrated. I had set goals for my career and had worked hard to develop myself to reach them, but now I could not achieve them. I felt torn. I needed to be a leader and to develop and manage others, so I turned to outside organizations for fulfillment. This outlet didn't satisfy me because my conscience kept telling me that these outside activities would not help me achieve my main goal—to become a manager. I grew discouraged, began struggling to maintain self-confidence and motivation, and eventually began searching for other employment.

This story is not unique to me or to John Deere. The 1980s continue to be an era of depression for many businesses, as illustrated by the proliferation of failing and financially constrained companies. This loss of jobs, the continual combination of positions, and the elimination of administrative layers in an organizational hierarchy affect the ability of companies to motivate and retain valued employees.

After talking with others in my position and experiencing the emotional and psychological stress caused by the current economy and by my struggle for self-actualization, I have concluded that a company must address three major employee needs in order to motivate and retain employees in a depressed economy: the employee's needs for freedom, for job meaningfulness, and for career development. There are three ways to meet these employee needs: through a cafeteria benefits plan; job enrichment; and a coaching, sponsoring, mentoring management development program.

What is a cafeteria benefits plan?

You might say today's employees have been "spoiled" by working for companies that could afford to give them generous benefit packages. They have experienced many paid vacation days and holidays; the opportunity to further their education (even during working hours if necessary) with company reimbursement; the ability to participate in civic organizations during the day; the luxury of drug, dental, and eye coverage; and company-paid hospital and medical doctor visits.

These benefits and freedoms are valuable to an employee. If a company becomes constrained financially but can maintain this same level of freedom, it will help motivate and retain its good employees. For example, recently I was offered a job that would have fulfilled many wishes. I would have been supervising an office of clerical employees, working with customers on benefit packages, directing the accounting function for the benefit packages, occupying my own office, and directing my secretary. I did not accept the position, however, mainly because I couldn't give up the financial freedom and benefits I enjoy at John Deere.

John Deere continually tries to motivate and help its employees. At present, it is in the first stages of implementing a cafeteria benefits plan, which will save the company money and provide an excellent set of benefits for all employees. In a cafeteria plan, employees choose the benefits *they* want or need rather than accepting an inflexible plan established by the company in which all employees receive the same benefits regardless of need. There are three types of cafeteria plans: core cafeteria, buffet, and alternative dinners.

An example of the core cafeteria plan is shown in Figure 1.[1] Under this plan a company requires an employee to take a minimum level of coverage called the core, which may consist of $5,000 of group life insurance, a short-term disability income plan, one week of vacation, and a minimum level of hospital and medical coverage. The core will vary from company to company, but a corporation usually requires this minimum level of benefits.

Figure 1 also shows several elements surrounding the core. They represent choices of additional life insurance, more vacation, better health insurance, dependent health insurance, long-term disability, dental coverage, or any other items in the plan. An employee is given a specific amount of money—an allowance—to spend for any benefit in the company's plan. If he doesn't want additional benefits, he may simply receive cash. If he wants more benefits than

Figure 1. The core cafeteria plan.

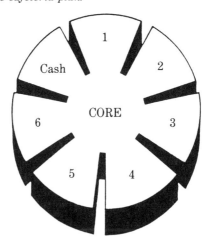

Contributory benefit options

he can afford with his allowance, he can purchase the additional ones through payroll deduction. The payroll deduction feature, called contributory benefit options, is depicted as the outside rim of the core cafeteria in Figure 1.

The buffet plan is shown in Figure 2. Under the buffet plan, employees start with benefits offered by the company before the cafeteria plan was introduced. This concept is depicted by the center portion of the figure. Employees have the option of maintaining an existing level of life, disability, hospital/medical, and vacation benefits or choosing fewer benefits, such as less vacation. By choosing fewer benefits, the employee receives credits he can accumulate to purchase other benefits, such as dental coverage.

As in the core cafeteria plan, a minimum benefit level exists which the employee cannot go below. The buffet also includes an option to buy additional benefits through payroll deduction.

The alternative dinners plan is illustrated in Figure 3. This plan does not provide as much freedom for employees as the other two plans. In an alternative dinners plan, the employer designs a set of benefit packages targeted to meet the needs of certain groups of employees. The company determines the target group, and the employee may choose only one package.

Implementing a cafeteria plan

To implement a cafeteria plan, a company should establish an area in its personnel department that would be responsible for surveying

Figure 2. The buffet plan.

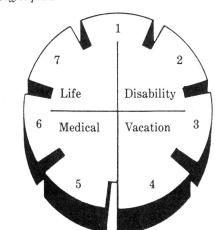

Contributory benefit options

Figure 3. The alternative dinners plan. Packages may be developed for the following groups: (A) Employee with nonworking spouse and no children; (B) Single employee; (C) Single parent; (D) Employee with a working spouse and no children; (E) Employee with a working spouse and children; (F) Employee with a nonworking spouse and children.

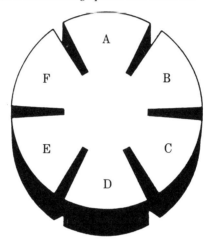

Contributory benefit options

the employees, planning the benefit package based on the survey, performing cost-benefit comparisons, and administering the plan.

For example, a benefit administration group should send a survey to all employees, asking them to respond to several questions:

1. Which benefits currently being offered need to be improved and why?
2. What additional benefits would you like?
3. Name the five benefits that are most important to you in the order of their importance.

The benefit administration area then would tabulate and evaluate the responses. Those benefits perceived to be most important to the majority of the employees should be selected for further analysis. Cost-efficiency comparisons should be made, and the six preferred cost-effective benefits should become a part of the benefit package.

For example, if a company selects the core cafeteria plan, it would give each employee either a stated amount of "allowance" for the benefits or cash. The benefit administration group then would keep a file on each employee, maintaining records on which benefits the employee purchases. The employee could change his benefit coverage once a year during his anniversary month. If he spends all his allowance but would like more coverage, the amount could be deducted through payroll.

Once a benefit program is implemented, the benefit administration area should keep on top of employee needs by sending annual surveys to the workers and updating the program based on their findings. The survey also should solicit feedback about the current cafeteria benefits plan.

Job enrichment

After satisfying employees in the benefits area, a company must deal with their desire for achievement or the feeling of meaningfulness in their jobs. Job enrichment is one method. It involves changes in tasks—increased opportunities for responsibility, personal achievement, feedback, growth, and advancement. To be meaningful, a job should contain three main ingredients: skill variety, task identity, and task significance.

Skill variety is the degree to which employees use a variety of talents and abilities on the job. Employees usually find a job more meaningful when they are challenged. They become frustrated if they believe they have talents and abilities that can't be used in their job and soon may stop performing. If their tasks are increased, however, workers will use some of their current abilities and develop additional ones, which can make even insignificant jobs more meaningful.

Some employees also prefer to do a "whole job" from beginning to end, thus allowing them to see an identifiable outcome. When employees have the opportunity to do a whole task or service, they consider their job more meaningful than when they are responsible for only a small portion. For example, assembling a whole toaster is more rewarding than simply soldering electrical wires.

Employees need to feel their jobs are important to the company. For example, when I was in the forecasting area at John Deere Component Works we were responsible for providing the tonnage forecasts for the company. This forecast determines the amount of labor and material needed in the future and is the basis for the company's budgets and all long-term planning. I perceived my job as being important, and thus it became more meaningful to me.

Freedom to influence the way his work is done is another employee need. By prescribing procedures to be used in fulfilling a schedule and then allowing the worker to set his own schedule, an employer gives him a sense of responsibility toward the outcome of his efforts. For example, if an individual working on an assembly line were allowed to schedule the workload and pace of the assembly belt in a specified production requirement, that worker would feel responsible and work very hard to achieve the production level.

The last step in achieving job enrichment involves employee

participation in planning, directing, and controlling the work; receiving adequate feedback; and experiencing opportunities for advancement and personal growth. If an employee receives feedback, he usually will be motivated to better his performance or to maintain the high quality. Gaining feedback even may become a challenge or a game.

The employee also must have opportunity for advancement and personal growth to stay motivated. I had an experience in which I worked very hard for the company and received only positive feedback about my performance. My career seemed to be moving in the direction I wanted, but, then through a layoff and termination process, I was forced to move into a different department. The manager of the area commented that, "If you're 'good,' your name will rise to the top like Mark's and Jane's, and eventually you will have a chance for promotion."

This comment was discouraging because I already had given 100+% to the company, but, instead of being rewarded, I was asked to start over. This experience demonstrated to me that feedback is not enough to keep an individual satisfied. He also needs opportunity for advancement and personal growth.

Does job enrichment work?

To allow the job enrichment concept to work, a company must make major changes in an employee's duties, sometimes even a restructuring. Minor changes have little impact. Department managers should be responsible for this program, but first the personnel department will have to train them in the concept of job enrichment and provide support. Before implementing job enrichment, you should discuss the ramifications with each employee. For example, managers should ask:

1. Would you like increased responsibility in your current task?
2. Do you feel your job is important to the company?
3. Are you able to use your talents in this job?
4. Do you find this job challenging?
5. Do you find this job rewarding?
6. Would you like your job changed in any way?
7. What would you like to be doing in the next three to five years?

By discussing these points with employees, a manager can tell if an individual and a job are candidates for job enrichment. This step is important because some employees do not want more responsibility or challenges. They like their job just the way it is now, and a company should respect that desire. When individuals want meaningful changes, however, their manager should work with them and the personnel department to restructure their jobs accordingly.

Once the job has been restructured, the manager should consult with the employee semiannually to verify the results.

Becoming a Vince Lombardi

Highly motivated employees also need a chance for advancement in order to maintain their momentum and satisfy their need for career development. If a company cannot afford to promote as many employees as planned, it can reduce the adverse impact of stifled advancements by establishing a management development program based on coaching/counseling, sponsoring, and mentoring. This type of program will show motivated employees that the company cares about their future and recognizes their potential.

Managers are supposed to develop their subordinates—to coach them.[2] Today's managers, however, seem more concerned with work details and deadlines rather than with developing their people so they can do the work efficiently and effectively. Ideally, managers should set challenging tasks for their subordinates, tell employees exactly what is expected of them and monitor their progress toward each goal, counsel workers throughout all projects, and appraise them regularly and objectively, using positive feedback and positive reinforcement. Managers also need to train subordinates to fill in during their absence and ready subordinates for promotion.

If managers actually "manage people" rather than "manage things," companies will have a steady supply of good employees who are ready to assume broader responsibilities.

After a company prepares its coaches, it should develop good sponsors. Sponsors match people and jobs in all areas of an organization. For example, sponsors get individuals' names placed onto promotion lists, get people assigned to task forces or committees and called into meetings, tell managers names of employees with potential for special or existing openings, apply subtle pressure to get proteges considered or placed, tell proteges how to get desired assignments and positions, say good things about their proteges, and actively seek promotional opportunities for their proteges.[3] Sponsors don't need to be at the top of the corporate ladder, but they must be knowledgeable about openings and new programs.

Are mentors important?

A mentor is the most significant stage in management development. The mentor relationship is much deeper than coach or sponsor. A coach counsels the employee in performing his current responsibilities, a sponsor serves as the employee's press agent, but a mentor is a trusted counselor and guide.

There are four stages in a mentor-protege relationship: initiation, protege, breakup, and lasting friendship.[4]

The mentor and protege find each other in the initiation stage.

The mentor usually is eight to 15 years older than the protege, powerful within the organization, very knowledgeable, and willing to share his expertise with others. The protege usually is 22 to 39 years old, but occasionally a woman may be older if she has delayed entering the business world. A mentor usually seeks a protege who has worked for the company for several years and has demonstrated high skills and abilities, who appears to have a high level of managerial abilities, and who is willing to learn and to take direction. This stage lasts six months to a year, which allows mentor and protege to get acquainted, build trust, and set the stage for openness.

In the protege stage, the mentor instructs, encourages, supports, and advises the protege. The mentor provides opportunities for the protege to make key decisions and shelters him or her from criticism, but the protege is not yet recognized for his own efforts. This stage lasts two to five years.

When the protege wants his own work recognized, he will initiate the move into the breakup stage and the mentor and the protege separate. If the mentor can accept the protege as a peer or even a superior, the relationship will continue to the final stage—lasting friendship!

Some companies employ a formal mentoring program where new staff members are paired with senior members for a prescribed length of time. The program's goals have been set and optional or required activities established. This type of program reduces "entry shock," introduces new employees to the inner workings of the organization, and helps their career advancement. From the other perspective, these programs help management spot new talent and identify senior employees who have the ability to groom workers, plus they seem to instill loyalty and commitment to the organization.

How to score

Companies should keep several points in mind when setting up a management development program. Coaching should be made available to all employees. Department managers/supervisors would be responsible for coaching the employees who report to them. Semiannually, both the employees and the coaches would complete a coaching evaluation form on which each individual would rank the counseling effort from 1 (poor) to 10 (excellent) based on the following skills: provides challenging work, gives feedback, communicates clear goals, provides adequate training. This report would be given directly to the personnel department.

The personnel department would analyze the forms. If an employee's ranking of the counseling effort differed from the coach's by four or more points, the discrepancy would be investigated and corrective action taken. In addition, divisional management would receive a quarterly report showing the rankings for each manager/

supervisor and would be responsible for periodically commending or reprimanding subordinates by memo or phone for their coaching abilities.

Before such a program can be implemented, each manager/supervisor should attend a coaching training class. Many managers and supervisors are promoted because of technical competence, not managerial ability, so they need proper managerial training to succeed.

Sponsor/mentor sectors of the management development program should apply only to those individuals requesting such development. In fact, if implemented as part of a company's cafeteria plan in which an employee is required to spend some of his benefit allowance to enter the program, it will attract only those who are sincere about career development, and it will help eliminate the reliance on politics for recognition and advancement.

Sponsors and mentors should be manager ranks and higher who have volunteered. Those individuals who want to be sponsors or mentors should be instructed as to the goals and objectives of the program and should receive a list of suggested activities. They, too, will be evaluated—on a merit review form that reports sponsor/mentor efforts—and should be recognized by their superiors.

Although some of these suggestions may sound difficult to implement, businesses must motivate and retain their employees to avoid the expense of dissatisfaction and turnover. Cafeteria benefit plans give employees freedom to choose the benefits which best fit their individual needs and desires. Internal job enrichment programs help employees develop a sense of pride and meaningfulness in their work and loyalty to the company. Management development programs can satisfy employees' needs for power or development, especially if promotions aren't imminent. Through these satisfying, enriching techniques, financially constrained companies of the 1980s can safeguard their most valuable asset—their employees.

Notes

1. Figures 1, 2, and 3 are from "Flexible Benefits Are a Key to Better Employee Relations," by A. Cole, Jr., *Personnel Journal*, January 1983, p. 49.
2. C. Atkinson, "Management Development Roles: Coach, Sponsor, and Mentor," *Personnel Journal*, November 1980, pp. 918-921.
3. *Ibid.*
4. David Marshall Hunt and Carol Michael, "Mentorship: A Career Training and Development Tool," *Academy Management Review*, July 1983, pp. 476-485.

How to Reward the '80s Employee

Robert W. Goddard

The reward jitters are besieging increasing numbers of companies. Surveys report a growing mismatch between employee values and existing reward systems. Employees who work primarily for self-development have a very different set of needs and expectations from those who work for material success and an increasing standard of living. Managers have to figure out how to tap these diverse cultural values to improve productivity.

One approach is to revise financial and nonmonetary rewards so they are more directly geared to actual effort rather than just time served; and to supplement financial incentives with psychic rewards that enhance effort.

Another approach is to offer a range of employee benefits that match the changed realities of the new lifestyles that abound today. Improved benefits won't generate higher productivity, but they do satisfy a growing employee desire for personal security, and they vastly improve a company's competitive edge in the recruiting process.

To reveal the fundamental changes in job values that are transforming the workplace, the nonprofit Public Agenda Foundation interviewed a national random sample of 845 jobholders. Their findings indicate an impressive shift in attitudes toward work; from work as a means of survival toward work as a means of enhancing self-development and self-expression. Specifically, employees say their productivity is improved by the following factors:

Reprinted from *Management World*, January 1986, with permission from AMS, Trevose, PA 19047. Copyright 1986 AMS.

1. Good chance for advancement (67%)
2. Good pay (67%)
3. Job enables them to develop abilities (61%)
4. Pay tied to performance (59%)
5. Recognition for good work (58%)
6. Job requires creativity (55%)
7. Job allows them to think for themselves (54%)
8. Interesting work (54%)
9. Challenging job (53%)
10. A great deal of responsibility (50%)
11. Good fringe benefits (45%)
12. Fair treatment in workload (42%).

Today's organizations are responding to this new yearning for a more humane workplace. The financial and psychological reward system that rules the workplace is being restructured—in some cases, dramatically. In the large companies, a variety of innovative rewards serves to meet these employee needs. The following are examples of what many of the *Fortune* 500 companies are now offering.

Toppling pyramids

Companies are inverting their hierarchical pyramids and moving accountability to where the work takes place. Allstate, Honeywell, Lockheed, General Dynamics, Westinghouse, and more than 500 other companies are using quality circles (QCs) to identify, analyze, and solve production problems. Honeywell alone has more than 9,000 QC teams. Ford, General Electric (GE), General Motors (GM), Continental Group, and dozens more have formed quality-of-worklife committees to examine anything in the organization that can be improved.

General Foods and Kaiser Aluminum involve employees, from top to bottom, in productivity improvement through departmental, divisional, or plant meetings; work groups; informal discussions; and joint labor-management committees. Planning, wherever appropriate, is done by a committee selected by employees and managers.

Intel Corporation provides extra conference rooms for informal problem solving among different disciplines. Texas Instruments and Tupperware insist that work teams set their own objectives.

Lincoln National Corporation has integrated the fragmented functions of work into human-structured whole jobs, or "core dimensions," that incorporate a significant task, varied skills and activities, autonomy, feedback, and a recognizable outcome. The company has also set up a "total involvement" program in which all levels of employees doing the same job or within the same unit meet weekly or biweekly to talk about what they do and how to do it better.

A networking management system that provides lateral and horizontal, multidirectional, and overlapping linkages of people has been established at Intel. Workers may have several bosses; functions such as purchasing and quality control are the responsibility of a committee or council, not a hierarchical staff; there are no offices, only partitions separating workspace; the company is operated by a triune of top executives—an outside person, a long-range planner, and an inside administrator; and employees are encour-

---

Rewards and strategy

Strategic planning is a splendid management tool, but plans often fail because the planning process stops too soon. The missing ingredient is a good employee reward system that makes a clear link between performance and payoff.

Strategy guides management decisions, but the reward system reinforces the strategy and makes it work. Self-interest is a prime motivator for employees. Use the reward system to tell them that rewards depend upon contributions to strategic goals; don't give free rides or allow dead wood.

The reward system must be a part of the planning process, whether your objectives are in operations, marketing, technology, or finance. It should be tailored to the special needs of the task, though all successful reward systems share certain characteristics that bridge the gap between plan and action.

Avoid undesired tradeoffs   Incentive systems that consider only a single yardstick for rewarding employees may backfire. For example, a strategy designed to attract new users for a product or service can fall apart if ambitious sales personnel neglect current customers in their zeal to acquire new ones. Similarly, a goal of lower production costs can divert attention from quality standards or result in maintenance cutbacks that increase equipment downtime.

Make goals explicit   Successful reward systems express clear, measurable performance goals within a timeframe for accomplishment. A 10 percent increase in dollar sales volume by year's end is a crystal-clear goal. On the other hand, a goal of "more-careful machine operators" is ill-defined and vague in its purpose and method of measurement. A more practical goal would be a five percent reduction in the cost of production waste over a six-month period.

Targets that are specific, realistic, and have a clear purpose increase the chances that strategic plans will result in action. Productivity at all levels is improved when employees understand the

aged to challenge superiors and are expected to participate in discussions as equals, though decisions are ultimately the responsibility of top managers.

A better self

IBM currently spends approximately $500 million annually on employee training and education, and some 300 of the nation's largest companies operate remedial courses in basic math and English for entry-level workers.

Universities that teach employees needed skills have been created by Dana Corporation, Walt Disney Productions, and McDon-

---

results expected, believe they are achievable, and know how they serve the organization's master plan. Goal setting with subordinates is a sterling opportunity for you to talk about possible future projects and opportunities, as well as about current goals.

Link rewards to long-term strategy   Successful reward systems steer an organization toward the future while satisfying its current needs. Reinforce behavior that enhances both short- and long-term bottom lines. To accomplish this, evaluate employees' behavior in terms of both present and potential future contributions; they are not necessarily the same. For example, a profit-conscious sales manager can be a star in the short run, but may be devastated by a planned growth strategy that will temporarily reduce profits. When current targets are explicit, measurement of short-term performance is straightforward. However, some digging is usually needed to predict the effects of certain kinds of behaviors and attitudes on future projects. Foresight is at the core of successful strategy.

Make rewards visible   A good incentive system gets maximum mileage from rewards by bringing them out of the closet. The reward system is a splendid role model for other employees. It reveals the behaviors that are valued in the organization and the kinds of rewards given for outstanding performance. Whatever form the reward takes—money, stock options, promotion, or praise—it must be valued and visible. The type of subordinates you want to encourage will quickly realize what they have to do to get recognition and rewards in the organization.

The characteristics of a good reward system are quite straightforward. You need careful planning to weave the connection between performance and reward into the strategic fabric of your organization. Once this is done, you will have created a strategy-supportive culture that can indeed yield handsome payoffs.

By Dr. Janet Barnard, assistant professor, College of Business, Rochester Institute of Technology, Rochester, New York.

ald's. Harmon International allows employees who exceed an agreed-upon daily production quota to go home early; those who can't leave can attend a company-operated school to study a variety of subjects.

Employees at Gulf Oil, IBM, GE, Xerox, TRW, and GM have access to career-planning programs to help them select meaningful goals for their lives and determine and accomplish career objectives. More than 9,000 managers and professionals have used the service at GE.

Employee development is promoted by Tektronix through fully funded outside study, on-site credit courses, job posting, internal promotion, career workshops, career counseling, flextime, child care, and a handbook that describes job opportunities and the educational requirements and potential earnings of specific positions.

Bonuses for improved productivity are provided by DeSoto, Northrop, TRW, Midland-Ross and Dana Corporation. Nucor Corporation uses a group-incentive system that includes supervisors and maintenance personnel. Beech Aircraft hands out monetary rewards and citations. Crompton Company uses a three-day, 12-hour work schedule along with incentive wages. Each employee at McDonald's earns an extra dollar if one of them has a $300 hour. Each employee earns two dollars if the restaurant has a record day.

Herman Miller, through its Scanlon Plan, rewards employees for cost-saving suggestions and pays a bonus to everyone involved in surpassing a departmental or corporate performance goal. In the last three years, bonuses have totaled more than $14 million at the company.

Some companies are even experimenting with "pay-for-knowledge" salary systems under which managers are paid for their ability and know-how—for what they *can* do rather than what they actually do. This system is based on the theory that for motivation and commitment to grow and for management succession to succeed, both performance and potential should be rewarded.

Personal touch

Every employee at Mars, Inc., including the president, gets a weekly 10 percent bonus if he or she comes to work on time each day that week.

IBM, Tupperware, McDonald's and other top performers actively pursue endless excuses to give out rewards, showering pins, buttons, badges, citations, medals, and prizes on employees at every opportunity. IBM sets quotas that almost all salespeople can meet, and sponsors a One Hundred Percent Club that fosters achievement by making the perceived possibility of winning something very high.

Everyone from the president on down at Disney wears a name tag with only his or her first name on it. The chairman of IBM answers all complaints that come to him from any employee; the chairman and president of Delta airlines do the same.

The chief executive officer of RMI, a subsidiary of U.S. Steel and National Distillers, spends much of his time riding around the factory in a golf cart, waving to and joking with his employees, listening to them, and calling them all by their first names. In the last three years, his close collaboration with workers and unions has helped reduce grievances from 300 to 20 a year and boosted productivity almost 80 percent, with virtually no investment spending.

Spreading power

Digital Equipment Corporation (DEC), 3M, Emerson Electric, Exxon, and other giants have employee task forces with real power to resolve all kinds of issues. These groups are small, voluntary, temporary, and composed of diverse specialists pulled together rapidly to solve and manage thorny problems.

Massive project teams are used at GM, IBM, Boeing, and Bechtel to design and develop complex products and systems, tackle strategic issues, or perform developmental research. These project teams and project centers may operate for several years, but usually are disbanded when the task is accomplished.

General Foods has reorganized one plant into independent work units. Employees are grouped into teams of six to 17. Each team selects a supervisor, and at the beginning of each shift, decides how to meet production quotas, assigns jobs, and provides the opportunity to air grievances. Each worker is trained to do virtually every job in the plant. The teams operate semiautonomously, and team leaders are responsible for hiring replacements and disciplining malingerers. Plant management makes a point of sending shop-floor employees rather than executives to meetings on local problems and safety.

Another growing trend is guaranteed employment security. Employers are finding that employees who feel secure in their jobs are more productive, and that the benefits of stable employment outweigh the financial gains of layoffs. Full employment policies are in effect at Lincoln Electric, Bell Laboratories, 3M, Polaroid, Texaco, Wyeth Laboratories, Ford, GM, Chrysler, Rand, Xerox, and others. Although unions have been pressing the issue in recent years, many companies recognized and implemented the concept long ago.

In the past 30 years, despite recessions and momentous shifts in products and technology, no IBM employee has been laid off. Job-secure companies use reduced workweeks, temporary help, labor redeployment, retraining programs, and strict hiring controls to avoid layoffs and overhiring.

Benefit potpourri

A flexible-compensation policy is designed to give employees many options as their needs change. Computerization enables TRW and American Can to offer a "cafeteria of compensation." Employees can decide to have a certain combination of salary, pension, health benefits, insurance, flextime, job sharing, vacation arrangements, and job objectives.

Nearly 25 percent of *Fortune* 500 companies offer employees a choice of work hours. More than 500 companies, including Exxon, Chase Manhattan, Johnson & Johnson, and Mobil Oil, have in-house fitness centers and programs managed by full-time directors.

DEC, Xerox, Hallmark, and Pitney Bowes use an adoption-assistance plan to cover part of the expenses incurred by an employee who adopts a child. Benefits for handicapped children are offered by IBM and Eastman Kodak.

Tandem Computers provides employee stock options, Friday-afternoon beer parties, a company swimming pool, and a required sabbatical leave every four years. Engineers at Hewlett-Packard have free access to the company's stock of electrical and mechanical supplies and are actually encouraged to take items home for their personal (and, hopefully, educationally innovative) use.

Another innovation is the tax-reduction stock-ownership plan under which companies are setting up a tax-qualified trust for employees and contributing employer stock equal in value to 10 percent of the amount taken as an investment tax credit.

Some firms are establishing sick-leave pools in which a portion of each employee's sick leave is pooled to be used by those who need it. Others are experimenting with anniversary and vacation bonuses, employee legal services, child care, extended vacations, student loans and scholarships, group automobile insurance, split days, work sharing, summer work hours, retirement planning and counseling, and floating schedules. Each of these ideas is indicative of the innovative thinking that will lead employee benefits in entirely new directions in the next 10 years.

These and other company programs and policies represent a revolutionary change in the reward system that governs the workplace. It is innovative, humanistic, pragmatic, and tied directly to current employee values. It is a movement with a valuable message for those who are wise enough to accept it.

Employee Attitude Surveys: What Managers Should Know

Ned Rosen

Managers who use employee attitude surveys and have unrealistic expectations end up getting burned. Such managers walk away from the experience blaming their misfortune on the survey concept rather than on the inadequacies of the particular survey used. The end result, unfortunately, can be serious damage to the organization.

I have found over the years that executives contemplating attitude surveys raise a set of questions that human resource professionals can anticipate when their superiors come to them for help. But remember: Conducting a survey is not a simple project you can assign safely to intelligent amateurs. Your qualified professional guidance can ensure that the survey reaps full value. Consider the following 15 questions and their answers as a strategically useful primer.

Q. Why do employers conduct attitude surveys? What are the organizational objectives?

A. Surveys are conducted

1. To assess the organization's internal employee relations climate and monitor the trends.
2. To identify emerging or existing attitudinal issues before they become explosive.
3. To provide feedback to managers on how well they are balancing their various managerial and supervisory responsibilities.

4. To build a data base that can inform the organization of the content and processes of selecting, developing, and training managers.
5. To assist in the design and modification of personnel policies, management systems, and decision-making processes, thereby improving overall organizational effectiveness.
6. To assess progress during periods of change.
7. To identify the parts of the organization that are experiencing pain and need help.
8. To provide a safety valve for excess "steam."

Q. Is it possible to achieve these objectives with a single survey?

A. While some can be achieved with a single survey—such as the second, fifth, and eighth items above—a repeated measurement program on a regularly scheduled basis offers far more potential. You can build several objectives into one survey program if you administer surveys periodically over a significant period of time.

You should consider an attitude survey program as part of an overall and continuing process both to clarify issues and stimulate innovative strategies for working together. It is *not* a popularity contest, a happiness exercise, or a route to instant cures. It *is* a useful organizational tool.

Q. Won't we just stir up a hornet's nest or artificially create attitudes that aren't real?

A. The first question any management considering using a survey must answer is, "Are we prepared to do an effective job of feedback and follow-through when the findings are in?" Whether the results are good or bad, management must share them with the employees and must address the problems with confidence.

The effective use of attitude surveys requires top management participation in framing the program's objectives and commitment to following through on results.

And as far as being afraid of arousing sleeping dogs, remember: they usually only appear to be sleeping. Employees have attitudes all the time. Systematically measuring them and then visibly trying to deal with problems is the healthy way to manage.

Q. Aren't attitude measures soft? Shouldn't we be more concerned with productivity measures and getting the work done?

A. Employee attitudes are a direct reflection of frustration levels. When frustration is sufficiently serious, a variety of disruptive behavioral consequences occur. Some people become hostile, thereby disturbing the peace or even sabotaging work processes. Others become discouraged, leading to reduced motivation and teamwork, lower standards of performance, absenteeism, and general lack of enthusiasm. Still others develop stress-related health problems— such as alcoholism—that bear on the cost of doing business.

A well-administered attitude survey program, while not as hard as an accountant's cost-control system, offers a practical strategy for controlling important elements of the human costs in running an organization. There is not question that those human costs are closely tied to organizational effectiveness.

Q. Should we use another firm's questionnaire or develop our own?

A. The advantages of building your own survey instrument far outweigh the advantages of using a questionnaire borrowed or bought from outside. A tailored questionnaire has a much better chance of capturing local issues, incorporating local lingo, and developing management and employee ownership of the process.

Building a tailor-made questionnaire includes steps that ensure communication about the program, enhance the response rate, and help prepare everyone for what is coming later. Assuming you use a participative process, building your own questionnaire improves the organizational climate.

Q. Should we make comparisons with other organizations?

A. The advantages of such comparisons are overrated and don't match the advantages of building your own questionnaire. Moreover, attitudinal data are highly susceptible to environmental differences, subtle language differences, the state of the economy, political considerations, union activity, organization structure and size, and wage and salary influences. Unless you're quite confident that these and other factors are equivalent across the organizations you're comparing and that the comparison data are quite recent, the results are likely to be misleading.

Specialists in psychological measurement almost always recommend establishing *local norms.* Organizations are far better off establishing their own baseline data for comparison purposes rather than relying on chancy external norms. Just as in golf, "par" varies from course to course and hole to hole.

Q. Should we hire an outside consultant?

A. Most medium to large organizations have people inside with enough background and interest in this type of program to take a major role in its administration. Normally all they need is a task force and an experienced external consultant to provide guidance on the process and technical input at crucial junctures. But it may be best, depending on local circumstances, to have the data, once collected, statistically processed externally. You need to consider the degree of trust between employees and management, availability of computers and software, and time constraints.

Q. Isn't it easy to develop a questionnaire?
A. Questionnaire construction requires professional input. It also requires pretesting on a representative sample to get the bugs out. Assembling a questionnaire from collections of items—or by lifting items out of other questionnaires used elsewhere—probably will waste some of the survey's potential value.

Qualified professionals in this field have item-writing skills and extensive training in psychological measurement and statistical methods necessary for good results. They also bring valuable concepts and knowledge of the literature to the task.

Q. Should we use a single-item measurement strategy?
A. Single items are inherently unreliable measurement devices when applied to complex issues such as employee morale, motivation, stress, and managerial effectiveness. Psychological measurement specialists advise using some scaling techniques to combine several items into reliable indexes. This has the dual advantage of better quality data and reduced interpretation complexity.

Measurement reliability is important if you are planning to use the data for decision-making purposes and for testing trends. Single items, *if properly worded* and preceded by others that influence summary judgments, can be useful.

Q. How long must a questionnaire be to provide reliable data?
A. That depends on how many fundamental dimensions you plan to measure and how many special, local issues you plan to cover. Rather than worry about number of questions, it is more important to be concerned with how much time the average employee needs to complete the questionnaire. A good target is 45 minutes. Most high-school graduates can handle 100 to 150 items in that time frame, depending on question complexity and format.

Q. Should we have separate questionnaires for different employee categories?
A. A well-constructed questionnaire will have a substantial section relevant to all employees and subsections for special interest categories.

Q. What is the best approach for sampling our organization?
A. This question involves complex issues and raises other questions you have to answer first.

You must know the purposes of the survey, the degree of accuracy required, the size and composition of the population, the likely strategy—mail versus group meetings, for example—for collecting data, and time and cost factors. If you want a good feedback process, you should sample intact organizational units rather than individuals. If sampling is necessary, see a competent consultant for advice before making sampling decisions. But keep in mind that it often is more effective to include entire populations, or large intact segments, than to use samples.

Q. What response rate can we expect?

A. Employee attitude surveys *can* produce anywhere from 25 to 90 percent or even higher response rates. Obviously, the bigger the percentage of returns, the more confidence one has in the data. Response rate is influenced by factors such as the following:

1. The existing-employee relations climate
2. The questionnaire's length and interest value
3. Whether employees believe the questionnaire allows them to express themselves on what *they* consider important issues
4. The amount of confidence employees have that management will do something about the results
5. Fear of reprisals from managers
6. A belief that some "secret way" exists for managers to find out what specific individuals said about them
7. How the questionnaire is administered, such as group meetings versus through the mail
8. The amount of support and encouragement managers and supervisors provide
9. The effectiveness of publicity both before and during the survey data collection period
10. The posture of relevant trade unions.

You can minimize nonresponse by using appropriate, participative practices in designing and administering the program.

Q. Just how much diagnostic value is there in attitudinal data? Are the interpretations self-evident?

A. Attitudinal data are social data and, as such, are susceptible to a variety of human foibles: halo effect, general negativism, temporary mind-sets, and group-think.

Employee surveys, then, typically reveal more at a group level of analysis than along other lines. In other words, because of the strong social and group influences on work-related attitudes, analyses based on individual differences such as age, sex, pay level, and other demographics will explain only a limited amount of variation in data patterns.

Survey designers can squeeze out modest diagnostic value if

they anticipate the comparisons they need to make in such areas as job categories and occupational definitions. The major diagnostic value of survey data lies in comparisons of organizational units such as departments and divisions. And given the strong influence of group attitudes, the analysis needs to get down to the primary work-group level to produce maximally valuable information.

While properly constructed attitude survey indices are capable of showing which units or groups in an organization are different from others, the data in and of themselves are not capable of explaining the reasons for the differences. The possible explanations are numerous. You'll need some form of follow-up to understand the data patterns.

Generally speaking, employee attitude survey data take on maximal meaning only when the various work groups involved discuss the data. A large percentage of the survey's potential value to an organization is lost without a planned feedback and discussion process. You can't fully interpret the data if you take it out of context and if local factors known only to the participants play a major role. In some cases you'll need a trained neutral as a group facilitator in order to unlock the process.

Q. How do we develop useful linkages between the survey process, the survey data, and the design and conduct of training courses for supervisors and managers?

A. Both the survey's content and the process involved should be linked with training and development.

1. You must carefully select and design the questionnaire items—especially those dealing with perceived managerial behavior and work-group task procedures—with due regard for the organization's culture and staffing patterns.
2. Managers and supervisors need to take ownership of the process so they will perceive face validity in the data.
3. You need to conduct useful comparisons and sophisticated analyses on the data to identify relationships and potential linkages to training.
4. The nature of the data received by individual managers on their own operations normally arouses their interest and leads many of them to seek help with their problems. This sets the stage for follow-up workshops and links to existing training courses or for the design of new ones to meet the better-defined needs that emerge from this process.
5. Staff responsible for training and developing managers and supervisors should receive periodic updates on what the survey data imply about managerial behavior and its consequences. You should encourage them to use this information in their work and teach them how to do so.

Employee Recognition Programs

Five key elements of a successful recognition program

Successful recognition programs share five key elements, according to O.C. Tanner Co.: a recognition symbol, an attractive means of display, a meaningful presentation, effective promotion, and review and updating.

Recognition symbols   The first step is to develop an attractive symbol of service, which usually involves the company logo. By using the logo, an organization establishes the symbolic focus of a recognition program and gives it continuity.

Display options   The second element is an attractive accessory or gift that gives the symbol of service mobility and utility. Whether it's jewelry, knives, pens, key chains, or desk accessories, it's important to get the service symbol out where it will be used and recognized by other employees. Even a leaf shredder can be imbued with meaning if it has the company symbol on it.

Meaningful presentations   Management puts the symbolic worth into the award when it is presented. By carefully structuring who presents the award and when and how it is presented, management can make the award worth many times its dollar value. It is essential that the manager sincerely express appreciation and cite personal accomplishments.

Reprinted with permission from "Today's Employees Choose Their Own Recognition Award," by Abby Brown from the August 1986 issue of *Personnel Administrator*, copyright, 1986, The American Society for Personnel Administration, Alexandria, VA.

Program promotion   A recognition program will only be as important to the employee as it is to the company that sponsors it. An announcement/selection brochure describing the program and the kinds of awards that will be given is the cornerstone of effective promotion. Company bulletin boards, house organs and personal letters also serve effectively to generate employee interest.

How to determine if you need a service award program

Chances are, you already suspect that your company might benefit from a service award program.

You have an underlying, "gut" feeling that management/employee relations . . . or employee commitment . . . or dedication to company goals . . . can be improved. But you can't quite put your finger on the problem or how to solve it.

To find out how accurate that feeling is, take this short quiz.

1. Does your company have a **systematic** way of letting people know that you value their contributions?
    Yes _____   No _____
2. Does your company publicly single out those people who do something right, rather than those who do something wrong?
    Yes _____   No _____
3. Has your company established one, or at most two, fundamental attributes (e.g. pride of workmanship, dedication to customer needs) to be best at—and continually reinforced that goal?
    Yes _____   No _____
4. Does management believe your company's assets are primarily its machines, product or money, rather than its people?
    Yes _____   No _____
5. Do you encourage performance competition among workers in a way that is non-threatening?
    Yes _____   No _____
6. Do you offer rewards that are strictly monetary (salaries, bonuses) and fail to provide symbolic awards as well?
    Yes _____   No _____
7. Is management as totally committed to its people and their well-being as they wish their employees to be towards the company and its goals?
    Yes _____   No _____
8. Is top management visibly involved in the recognition of employee achievement **at all levels**?
    Yes _____   No _____
9. Does management recognize and reward only the few very top performers, and ignore the remaining 80 or 90 percent?
    Yes _____   No _____
10. Has management tried various incentive programs in the past, and given them up because they "just don't seem to work?"
    Yes _____   No _____

Review and updating As employee tastes and values change, and as companies shift their own directions, recognition programs also need to be modified. Periodic evaluation keeps a program fresh and exciting to the employees. New accessories and gifts, new promotional efforts, and new ways of presenting awards, all keep the excitement building.

Scoring: Check your answers and assign the number of points shown for each answer, then add up your total points.

1.	Yes	2	-	No	0
2.	Yes	4	-	No	0
3.	Yes	2	-	No	0
4.	Yes	0	-	No	5
5.	Yes	3	-	No	0
6.	Yes	0	-	No	4
7.	Yes	4	-	No	0
8.	Yes	3	-	No	0
9.	Yes	0	-	No	2
10.	Yes	0	-	No	1

26-30: Your management understands the needs of its people and is actively pursuing a policy to fulfill those needs. Taking this quiz may point up one or two areas for improvement, but basically your workers know you care.

18-25: You've tried to institute some system of rewards, but management's lack of commitment has caused inconsistency and only sporadic positive reinforcement for workers. A renewed commitment will increase effectiveness.

9-17: Management's attitude toward any reward system is one of looking for a "quick fix" for a problem or of focusing only on a few very highly motivated individuals. This basic misunderstanding of how, and why, to institute an award program must be corrected at the management level, and the system revised to reflect this change.

0-8: People are a means to an end—to be used and discarded or ignored at management's discretion. Workers know it—and act accordingly. You've taken this quiz because you're ready to change things for the better. Let's get started!

Reprinted with permission from the pamphlet "A Simple Guide to Running a Service Award Program" published by Bulova, The American Watch Company.

How to Help Troubled Workers

J. B. Miles

Seemingly ordinary people, some of whom might even work for you, can pack a fairly bizarre range of personal baggage into their morning briefcases. Take Conrad. He's single, 32 years old, fluent in several programming languages, and working for a major Washington political organization. He's bright, talented, and ambitious. He's also a white-collar junkie, with a strong taste for cocaine.

Then there's Phil, 52, a programmer for a leading eastern insurance carrier. His short-range output is terrific, but his long-term assignments are spotty—inaccurate summaries, missing data. You suspect Phil might be an alcoholic.

Finally, there's Laurie, 23. She's a Stanford graduate, and this is her first job. She's catching on fast, but she's been absent from work seven times in the last six weeks. Is it her boyfriend, who once had a brush with the law for selling some kind of drug? Or is it her night classes in advanced programming languages?

That's only a small sampling of problems your employees—and you—could face. Other examples could include the recent divorcé who's now squiring around a major vendor's 25-year-old appointments secretary, and the accounts manager who's sometimes stoned on the drugs her doctor prescribed for tension.

If these folks only give you a slight case of the jitters, or if you think such a rogue's gallery operates only in other managers' backyards, think again. Research indicates that at any given time in the average workplace, one employee in five is preoccupied with a personal problem—at the expense of his or her job performance. And that's just the half of it.

There are three types of employee problems. First there are the relatively short-lived preoccupations, such as anxiety over a child's school behavior, a spat with a spouse, and other typical family crises. Then, there are problems due to an underlying personality disorder. These include chronic financial strain, travel phobia, credit-card abuse, sexual anxiety, and serious family stress.

Finally, there are those problems that are deeply embedded in the employee's personality, and these are more common than you may think. One in six employees suffers from a serious emotional disorder, one in 10 is an alcoholic, and one in 20 has a drug problem. (The latter represents a special problem; drug addicts may become suppliers to other employees to fund their addiction.) Estimates like these of the extent to which employees bring their problems to the workplace are relatively conservative. For example, the "Big 3" disorders just mentioned are diseases of denial—the sufferer goes to great lengths to deny or disguise them, not only from managers or fellow workers but from himself or herself, as well. Similarly, some employee maladies are just beginning to surface as real problems. Common varieties of depression, for example, used to be considered merely pesky symptoms of other problems—curable, much like the common cold, with a few aspirins and a few days' rest. Research now shows, however, that the manifestations of depression in the workplace are serious, extensive, and expensive; they affect not only the depressed individuals, but all co-workers, as well.

The cost of all this is astronomical. The direct cost to U.S. businesses of such employee ills as alcoholism and drug abuse alone is estimated to reach $75 billion annually, and it's heading steadily upward. This estimate does not account for the less tangible, but still serious, cost brought about by the reduced morale and efficiency of employees who are adversely affected by another's behavioral problems.

It doesn't take a great amount of astuteness to realize that even large corporations are hurt by employee problems. Managers should be concerned about these problems and act to mitigate them. It's smart business to help the troubled employee, especially the one who occupies a critical niche in your corporate framework.

For the most part, managers accept the responsibility of dealing with some of their employees' personal problems. But many are uncertain about how far they should go. They need to know more about limits of analyzing employee problems and assessing corrective steps. And in today's litigious and rights-conscious society, managers need to know a great deal more about such matters as their employees' right to privacy.

Harrison Trice, a researcher at the Cornell University School of Industrial and Labor Relations, Ithaca, NY, is outspoken about the manager's responsibility to intervene when an employee's performance is slipping because of personal problems. "Managers have to manage people, even if their job is to manage computers. And managing people means managing the job performer, especially those with problems," says Trice.

Terry York, director of the U.S. Information Agency's Advisory, Referral, and Counseling Service (ARCS) agrees: "I've heard managers say they're more interested in getting out their products than in dealing with human problems; they maintain they're not qualified to intervene in an employee's troubles. But you shouldn't be a manager unless you have people skills. Solving these kinds of problems goes with the turf."

York, Trice, and others consider the manager the front line when it comes to dealing with human problems. Ideally, the manager is a conduit, able to skillfully intercept and monitor the many signals given out by an employee who is having problems, and savvy enough to help determine the best approach for intervention— whether it's a quiet conversation, referral to an in-house consultative employee-assistance program, an up-the-line referral for discipline, a lateral transfer, or a recommendation for dismissal. Firing is always the last, and most expensive, resort.

Jim Talley, MIS/dp manager for the Washington-based Organization of American States, is responsible for computer operations and systems development for OAS' connections with 31 member nations. Talley, who describes himself as a "techie" constantly on the firing line, says he isn't qualified to handle many types of employee problems, and admits he usually tries to bypass and avoid such confrontations at all costs. But, he adds, "I do have to get involved in these problems, because they usually don't disappear by themselves. If I wait too long, they get worse, and then service to my clients suffers."

If you agree with Talley about your responsibility to intervene when your subordinates bring personal problems to work, you probably are still concerned about the limits of your responsibility. How, for example, do you intervene without becoming heavy-handed, or worse, getting in over your head into problems that might be much too complicated for you to handle?

A simple rule of thumb about management limits should be etched onto the brain of all who supervise others. Its application could save millions of hours of unnecessary headaches and millions of dollars in revenues lost because of poor time management. It can also reduce threats of legal action from employees who have had— or think they have had—their rights to privacy violated. The rule is this: The personal problems of employees are private until job performance deteriorates because of them. Sound simple? It is, but it's amazing how the pressures of a hectic production schedule mixed with a sincere desire to help someone can obscure this rule. Keeping the privacy rule firmly in mind helps the manager remember the necessary limits to what is his or her—and the company's—function when an employee is behaving or performing poorly. Forgetting it, the manager often gets drawn into problems not of his or her own making, and usually beyond his or her control.

In *How to Help a Troubled Employee* (Association Management, 1983), William Hoffer provides a tongue-in-cheek list of stages he says managers go through when dealing with employee problems:

1. "Praying for a miracle:" The manager ignores the problem— and the employee.
2. "Reason will prevail:" Characterized by a short series of heart-to-heart talks.
3. "Pleading:" Includes random begging, cajoling, threatening.
4. "Bleeding:" The manager disciplines, fires, forces to resign, transfers, or retires the employee.

If Hoffer's stages seem amusing or cute, think about them again. He's put his finger on some tendencies that, admit it or not, most of us have exhibited from time to time without achieving productive results. Chances are, such oversights have taken place at considerable cost to employers and to our own self-esteem as well.

A few do's and don'ts, sprinkled with a liberal dose of common sense, might help managers deal with employees' personal problems in a way that works for, rather than against, the corporation.

Do operate from a well-defined strategy for intervention that is endorsed by brass and top managers. If corporate strategy is absent or vague, develop stringent guidelines for your own behavior.

Do insist on full organizational support for your decisions. This is your right as a manager.

Do help your corporation clarify vague, unspecific, or ambiguous policies concerning troubled employees. If you are a front-line manager, you shouldn't be exposed to unnecessary risks resulting from poorly stated company policies, or from the whims, unwritten rules, or hidden agendas of your own superiors when it comes to managing subordinates with personal problems.

Do avoid the clinical approach. Given today's trend toward analyzing employee motivation and psychology in the workplace, managers can readily slip into the trap of defining and redefining the symptoms of everything from employee drug abuse to bed-wetting, without ever coming to terms with the need for specific action in particular cases.

Don't try to be the company shrink. It's not your job. Leave the diagnosis to the pros. All you have to do is keep your eye on the employee's performance. As Cornell's Trice says: "The manager never has to make a clinical diagnosis. It's his job to make a performance diagnosis."

Don't let yourself become the informal company guru on personnel policy. Chances are if you're a decent compassionate listener with a good record of employee problem-solving, you'll occasionally be called on by your bosses or peers to lend a helpful ear to other employees. This can be acceptable for a time, but it's not necessarily a good practice.

Don't become your employees' pal. You may have a terrific relationship with employees before or after work, but if they are having personal problems, you're not going to help by getting enmeshed in all the details. Pat Renfro, manager of personnel for the 1,400-member American Newspaper Publishers Association in Reston, VA, says it's human nature to give advice, "but if it doesn't work well, the employee feels let down, and will avoid further contact, or worse, become angry and hostile."

Don't allow yourself to actually enjoy the role of "confessor" to your troubled employee. Richard Orlando, a Cambridge, MA-based clinical psychologist and computer specialist, says some managers feel more powerful—and maybe feel a twinge of voyeurism—when their subordinates reveal some of the seamier details of their personal lives.

If you've got a case of managers' blues at this point, cheer up. There is a wealth of programs, counseling services, consultants, and useful literature to help you help your employees—without risking your own neck on the job.

Within the past 10 years, for example, the number of employee-assistance programs has grown from about 400 to more than 5,000. Usually company-sponsored or supported, they meet a variety of employee problems—everything from alcohol counseling and hospitalization to financial advice. And they work! Their organization and thrust vary from corporation to corporation, depending on the need and savvy of those who set them up and use them. Some of them are supported and staffed by company-paid professionals; others are available through a growing network of community services to smaller companies and businesses; still others are tiny pinpricks of light on the personnel horizon.

Few managers doubt the effectiveness and usefulness of employee-assistance programs, both in terms of cost-effectiveness for the organization and the help they give to the troubled worker. Although they differ slightly in function according to the organizations they serve, the most effective ones operate according to a general time-tested set of operating principles. These include:

Independence   Even in-house employee-assistance programs operate as separate units. They are staffed by qualified professionals whose judgment is respected by corporate brass and who serve as on-the-spot advisors to personnel managers and top decision-makers.

Confidentiality   The confidentiality of an employee who brings problems to an employee-assistance staffer is guaranteed. Once a manager refers an employee to such a program, the details of the problem belong to the helping professional and the individual.

Easy access   Nobody seeking help should have to jump through hoops to get it. And nobody using the services should continually have to explain where he or she is going and why. A fluid, easy system can be developed between the manager and employee. The most an employee should have to tell a supervisor about attendance at such a program should be: "I'm going to the personnel department this afternoon for one hour, and it is arranging for weekly sessions on Wednesdays at 2 p.m. for the next two months."

Performance-based referrals   An employee referral to an assistance program is always based on his or her work record. Ideally, the manager will make the referral, saying something like this: "Look, I think we're having a problem. Your job performance is not showing your usual high standards, you've been absent from work six times during the last seven weeks, and you've been in two arguments with your supervisors in the last month. If you're having some kind of personal problem, I don't need to know its details, but I'm going to refer you to our employee-assistance program."

Follow-up   The manager as a frontline observer and referral agent doesn't need to know all the details about the employee's problem. But some method of cross-checking between the employee-assistance staffers and the manager is needed to see if performance is being enhanced by treatment. Has the employee's attendance record improved? How about relationships with other employees? Are quality-of-work requirements, such as accuracy of data, deadlines, and so on, being satisfied?

Volunteer basis   Mary Joyce Pruden, director of a Corning, NY, employee-assistance program that serves, among other corporations, Ingersoll-Rand, Woodcliff Lake, NJ, and Corning Glass, Corning, NY, has developed what she calls a "constructive confrontation" technique. It lets a manager help the troubled employee recognize that a problem exists, based on performance-related evidence. But Pruden stresses that the final decision on the employee's participation in an assistance program belongs only to the employee. "The manager can help by strongly recommending the program as a helpful step the employee can take for his or her own benefit, but only that employee can decide to go."

Full management support   Obviously, no program, however well-designed, will work without the backing of its principal users. The major clients of employee-assistance programs are organizations that have come to recognize the validity and cost-effectiveness of helping troubled workers improve job performance. Managers know the company's balance sheet will also show improvement as a direct result.

It also pays to make use of national services and hot lines set up for particular problems. Your local chapter of Alcoholics Anonymous is one such service. And the national cocaine hot line (1-800-COCAINE) is another. Others can be found in the Yellow Pages.

Once you recognize the advisability of approaching an employee whose job performance is suffering from a personal problem, how do you make your move? Before you approach the individual, heed a few tips:

1. Don't delay the inevitable; it won't help you or your employee.
2. Don't analyze your employee's motivation—analyze job performance only.
3. Never apologize for your role as manager.
4. Avoid verbal overkill; don't argue about the record or get into a circular debate. Keep it short and simple.
5. Don't make observations about the employee's personal style or limitations that are not strictly related to work performance.
6. Don't take on the responsibility for your employee's poor performance.
7. Don't become a hero, a pal, or a confidant to your employee. Research shows that such relationships foster the unhealthy belief on the part of the employee that the manager is the only person who can help. And that can cause the employee to reject genuine help from professionals.
8. Don't be fooled by employee denials or downplaying of the record. Statements like: "There's really no problem," "You and I are both probably overreacting," "Yeah, my work has suffered a little over the last month or so, but I'll get back on track" are very common. People with personal problems affecting their work will usually go to great lengths to deny the underlying causes, even from themselves. And they will manipulate, cajole, beg, even threaten, to protect themselves from this information. Don't be fooled by such denials, and keep your sights on the employee's performance.

Your approach to the problem employee, as a rule, must be cautious and even-handed. The legal ramifications of a botched intervention can be severe for both you and your employer. Follow these common-sense precautions when intervening.

1. Document your intentions. It's always helpful, before entering a difficult situation, to jot down your objectives. You might include a timetable of the number of sessions you are willing to have with an individual before you recommend outside intervention.
2. Know your own limitations, and those of your role as manager. Remember, you aren't expected to save anybody. You are responsible for employee performance; the final decisions affecting an employee's success or failure on the job are that employee's responsibility, not yours.
3. Respect yourself and your employee enough to be absolutely clear about the performance level you expect.
4. Focus, firmness, and fairness are the best tools you have. Focus on the employee's work performance and the steps that can be taken to improve it. Keep any dialogue or confrontation centered on job performance. Help the employee devise his or her own strategy for improving performance.

Discipline vs. Punishment

Eric L. Harvey

Traditional approaches to discipline may just be the ultimate demonstration of our failure to apply what we believe about ourselves to the management of others. As professionals, we feel that we are responsible, mature, committed adults, and we expect to be treated that way. We expect to work in an environment of similarly committed individuals who also want to be treated as worthwhile contributors to the organization's mission. We expect to be recognized for our achievements and confronted with our lapses. And when problems do arise, we expect to be advised of the need for change in a way that maintains our self-esteem and reinforces our commitment to the organization and its goals.

Unfortunately, our traditional beliefs about discipline (and the organizational systems for maintaining it) not only fail to produce commitment, but frequently prevent it from arising. The system that could be the primary vehicle for generating genuine employee commitment to the organization and its goals too often becomes the primary barrier to achieving organizational objectives.

Discipline, as defined by the behavior and policies of many American organizations, means punishment. Often paralleling the criminal justice system, the discipline process these organizations use provides for increasingly serious sanctions as misbehavior mounts. Warnings and reprimands are followed by suspensions and probations, all in the hope that the individual will come to his or her senses and start performing properly. The employee errs and management determines the penalty that fits the crime, operating under the curious belief that by treating the individual progressively

Reprinted, by permission of the author, from *Management Review*, March 1987.

worse, he or she will become progressively better. When the criminal justice model for the discipline system is adopted, those who administer that system must eventually look on employees with problems as criminals.

Successful organizations no longer look upon "discipline" as something that a manager *does to* a poor performer when he or she misbehaves. Instead, these companies now approach discipline as something that must be *created.* They have abandoned traditional punitive measures, and in their place have developed systems that require acceptance of personal responsibility, individual decision-making, and true self-discipline. They have made the transition from the concept of "doing discipline" to the more constructive perspective of "being disciplined."

Discipline without punishment?

What these companies—among them Pennzoil, General Electric, Procter & Gamble, and the Bay Area Rapid Transit System—have discovered is that little of value comes out of the common belief that discipline and punishment go hand in hand. Rarely does a written warning build a better relationship between supervisor and subordinate. More rarely still does an employee return from three days without pay dedicated to excellence. What these organizations are doing is redefining discipline—changing from a traditional punishment orientation to a new orientation of building commitment.

The problem with the traditional approach, they have found, is not only with the administrative system itself. The more subtle problem lies in its goals and the expectations managers have of it. Under traditional "progressive discipline," when an employee breaks a rule or fails to meet expectations, management sees its responsibility as determining the appropriate amount of punishment, based on the nature and severity of the employee's offense. The organization's primary objective then becomes the enforcement of compliance; it willingly suffers all the side effects of a punitive approach that any line manager can relate in gory detail (and must live with daily).

Because most managers find the enforcement of discipline to be a distasteful task, other problems arise:

1. Managers are frequently reluctant to take appropriate disciplinary action until a problem becomes impossible to ignore. Then they may respond out of proportion to the most recent act, after having sanctioned previous misbehavior through their silence.
2. Managers of professional, highly educated individuals are reluctant to use a disciplinary system that they view as appropriate only for "blue-collar types."

3. Employees who do not meet organizational standards are absolved of personal responsibility simply by accepting their punishment. The employee then perceives the score to be settled—having paid the price, he or she owes nothing more to his employer. "The biggest problem with traditional approaches," according to Alan Bryant of General Electric, "is that we don't ask enough. We only ask the person to accept his warning or serve out his time. We rarely talk about individual responsibility or ask for a genuine commitment for the future."
4. It promotes adversarial, "we/they" relationships. Instead of concentrating on common goals, the supervisor and subordinate often become locked in battle. Only the past is discussed; action plans for the future are not requested or created.
5. Finally, everyone's a loser. The employee on the receiving end of a warning or suspension is an obvious loser. The manager who must perform the distasteful act also gets the short end of the stick. But it is the organization itself that loses the most. When people do things only because they must, the organization loses the benefits of individual commitment and acceptance of personal responsibility.

The basics of a commitment approach

The visible mechanics of a system whose goal is commitment rather than punishment are deceptively simple. Instead of using warnings and reprimands, the manager concentrates on identifying the specific discrepancy between actual and expected performance, and the good business reasons why the performance expectation must be met. He describes why meeting the standard is important, and concentrates on gaining the individual's agreement to change and perform properly in the future. The emphasis in this discussion is not on warning the employee of the future negative consequences that will follow another violation, but on reminding the individual that it is he or she—not the manager—who is responsible for proper performance and behavior. Apologies and guilt disappear.

If the problem continues or another arises, the discussions become more serious. The goal, however, never changes. The employee is continually reminded that he or she must accept personal responsibility for his or her performance and meeting the organization's standards. Even if the employee's reaction is hostile or defensive, the mature and adult explanation of the difference between what is expected and what is delivered and the communication of trust and individual responsibility by the manager doesn't change.

If these initial conversations are ultimately unsuccessful in bringing about a satisfactory resolution, as a final step the employee is suspended for a day, without the loss of pay. On this day, the employee is asked to consider his or her future and decide whether he or she is willing and able to meet the standards. The suspension from work reinforces the seriousness of the situation and the fact that his or her job is at risk; being paid for the day removes the usual hostility, and demonstrates management's honest desire to help the individual take responsibility and decide to meet the organization's expectations. Upon the worker's return from this "decision-making leave," he or she advises the supervisor of his or her decision—either to make the required change and stay, or to quit and find more satisfying work elsewhere. If problems continue, the individual then faces the logical consequence—termination.

Just as important as the formal levels of disciplinary action is the system's formal provision for recognizing good performance. Most individuals in an organization are never involved with the formal discipline process. Too often, though, their self-discipline and commitment go unrecognized. Therefore, a system whose goal is commitment rather than punishment provides specific means to recognize the fully acceptable performance of the great majority of the organization's members. The premise of this approach is the belief that the organization and its managers have the right to set reasonable and appropriate standards; that managers have the responsibility to point out performance discrepancies when they arise; and that only the individual can decide whether or not to perform properly and meet those standards and expectations. The burden of responsibility for appropriate performance, therefore, is placed cleanly on the shoulders of the employee, and not the organization and its managers.

Obviously, just renaming the steps of a traditional discipline system, or changing to a paid suspension, or exhorting supervisors to recognize good performance will have a negligible effect on bringing about true employee commitment and organizational change. What is required is a change in the organization's entire approach to performance management. If managers use new words but continue to behave in old ways, employees will see through the deception immediately. The impact of the change on the organization will be no more than that of putting a new Mercedes emblem on the hood of a rusty Pinto. What is required is a total organizational commitment to an entirely different approach to the issue of managing people, performance, and professionalism.

Making the change

General Electric's Alan Bryant describes the reasons for making the change to a commitment-oriented approach to discipline that he installed when he was manager of employee and community relations at GE's meter plant in Sommersworth, New Hampshire: "All employees—whether they be blue-collar workers or highly educated professionals—deserve to be treated as responsible adults, if this is the behavior that we as an organization actually expect of them."

Bryant recognizes that not everyone is ready for this change: "Certainly every organization has a very small population of employees who seem to hold the belief that they aren't really responsible for their own behavior, and that any performance discrepancies are caused by factors outside their control. However, whether or not they believe they are responsible, they are still held specifically accountable to maintain acceptable performance. While there may be some individuals who may not respond to a commitment-oriented approach, the organization will not compromise its performance, attendance, or conduct standards. By treating the employee as a responsible adult, we earn the right to expect a reciprocal response. If the individual fails to live up to his obligations, more serious consequences, including termination, will occur.

"With our approach," Bryant continues, "this occurs very rarely. When it does, however, management's response is much more defensible, both from a legal standpoint and in the perception of the manager who is responsible for taking the action."

Bryant today heads employee relations at GE's Nuclear Energy Business Operation, headquartered in San Jose, California, an organization of 5,500 employees with a heavy concentration of highly educated engineers and other professionals. "Even with professionals," he says, "managers are faced with performance that does not meet organizational standards. Traditional approaches to discipline, however, are perceived as inappropriate for a professional workforce. By installing a commitment-oriented performance management approach, we have developed a more effective system to deal with the few, but still significant, performance discrepancies that do occur. Managers of professionals now have the ability to identify, analyze, and discuss performance issues that are more subjective and less directly related to specific work rules and standards of conduct."

Other companies are also recognizing that commitment is the appropriate objective of an effective discipline system. "Our overall thrust in Procter & Gamble Soap Manufacturing is to move from a control to a commitment orientation," says personnel manager Jim Robinson, "and we emphasize the commitment element in everything we do."

"Pennzoil Products Company prides itself on quality products, quality service, and certainly quality employees," says Dan Duncan, manager of employee relations for the automotive products division, in describing the company's decision to change to an approach that focuses on individual responsibility. "To create and maintain our professional expectations, we needed to develop a more effective administrative system that also included strategies for recognizing and reinforcing good performance. Our performance management system now allows us to reinforce that commitment to our jobs and company regularly. An employee who has slipped for one reason or another also is given the opportunity to recommit to his or her job and to the Pennzoil image."

Duncan's statement pinpoints the essential elements of effective performance management—*recognition* and *confrontation*. When people perform well, their contributions and commitment are recognized. When problems arise, people are not punished for their misdeeds but are confronted, maturely and supportively, with the need to change by being formally reminded of their responsibility for their own behavior and performance.

Results

Organizations that have abandoned punishment and moved to a commitment orientation for their discipline system have gained more than significant decreases in the number of formal disciplinary discussions their managers must hold. "Employees are more at ease in offering ways to improve their jobs," says Jeff Rehwald, Pennzoil's manager of employee relations for the manufacturing division. "The supervisor feels more comfortable confronting employees using this approach. In addition, unions support the premise that employees are responsible for their own actions." Rehwald's statement highlights the primary beneficiaries of a commitment approach to discipline—managers, employees, and those who deal with unions, in addition to the organization itself. (See Figure 1.)

For managers, one of the biggest benefits is the formal transfer of responsibility to the employee. Through the training they receive, supervisors discover that their responsibility is no longer to "write up bad guys," but to reinforce good performance and let problem performers know the consequences of their decision not to meet the organization's expectations. In dealing with disciplinary lapses, they no longer have to "play the heavy," and can deal with difficult situations with skill and confidence. Another major benefit to managers is faster resolution of problem situations. Since they are no longer required to be punitive and judgmental, managers tend to confront problems earlier. With the change in emphasis from punishment to commitment, the tone and tenor of performance discussions also change. Immature, emotional, and inappropriate behaviors diminish when managers confront employees as mature adults.

For employees, the greatest benefit may be increased managerial attention toward the great majority of individuals who already are performing well. "A higher number of employees are receiving recognition for good performance," reports Larry Williams,

Figure 1:   The benefits of a commitment approach (© Performance Systems Corporation, 1986).

Employee's perspective	Supervisor's perspective	Organization's perspective
Recognizing good performance	Responsibility for behavior to employee	Commitment
Adult treatment	Encouraging problem solving	Consistency
Early problem identification	Minimizing formal discipline	Defensibility
Non-punitive system	Encouraging discretion	"Just cause" focus
Fairness	Building solid management skills	Operationalizing human resource beliefs
Recognizing improved performance		Proven results
Future orientation		

employee relations department manager of San Francisco's Bay Area Rapid Transit System. "Prior to implementing Positive Discipline, most of the attention was focused on 'getting' the poor performers through punishment, and little attention was paid to motivating the good workers." When problems arise, employees also benefit from the early identification of performance problems and adult treatment, as well as the nonpunitive series of formal disciplinary steps. The emphasis on commitment to the future, rather than punishment for the past, tends to build relationships of mutual respect between the individual and his or her supervisor. Finally, the great majority of employees benefit by knowing that others who don't share their level of commitment will be confronted with the need to improve. They will find far fewer instances of having to shoulder more than their fair share of the workload because someone else isn't pulling his or her weight.

For those involved in labor relations and dealing with outside, third-party challenges, an approach to discipline that concentrates on commitment makes the organization's actions easier to defend. Exposure to Equal Employment Opportunity and wrongful termination suits is reduced, since employees now commit to good performance and create their own action plans. All disciplinary action is fully and properly documented. With the new system's goal of solving problems rather than punishing offenders, less conflict with the union is experienced. Grievances decrease as unions focus on more substantive issues, instead of merely trying to regain a suspended worker's lost pay. Finally, when challenged in an outside arena, organizations find that their actions are far more defensible. "Our success in sustaining disciplinary action under appeal after implementing our new approach," according to Larry Williams, "has been almost 100 percent. Previously, we were not only losing many of our appeals outright, but others were reduced to a lower level of severity—for example, ten days' suspension reduced to five. All discipline is now nonpunitive, even to the point of our telling arbitrators who are hearing termination cases that if the discharge is not sustained, there should be no loss of pay by the employee if he or she is reinstated."

Moving toward commitment

Implementing a commitment approach to discipline is not a process to be taken lightly. It is not a fad or a quick fix; not a "program of the month"; not this year's version of transactional analysis or the next Theory Z. Most managers and employees are bright enough to recognize halfheartedness. They spot the lack of investment and learn to go through the necessary motions, all the time muttering, "This too shall pass." What we are dealing with here is not a fad or façade, but a crucial organizational issue—who shall remain a part of the "family" and who shall be separated from it? By whom and by what means will that decision be made?

While the result of implementing a commitment approach to discipline is a significant cultural change, few managements adopt such an approach because they seek a "new culture." What they want is to reduce the gap between the organization's publicly stated beliefs and values and the day-to-day behavior of its managers and supervisors. Ultimately, however, culture is what we are dealing with. It is through the discipline system that the organization's culture is revealed most directly to the individual.

Discipline is the arena in which the organization displays its most fundamental beliefs about people and professionalism. Accepting a commitment approach to discipline generates a discipline system that applies to all employees. As Dan Duncan of Pennzoil puts it, "It is our objective to incorporate this approach into the daily activities of *all* employees—from plant manager to laborer; from delivery driver to sales manager; from president of our division to a secretary in a field office."

To abandon punishment and move toward individual responsibility requires confronting skepticism and challenging the innate sense of comfort in a bureaucracy with "the way we've always done things." Resistance will occur, but according to Procter & Gamble's Robinson, "Most resistance goes away when people come to understand and internalize the concept." Still, some managers will complain that this commitment stuff sounds good in theory but isn't really applicable in the "real world." What the complainers fail to recognize is that it is the traditional approach to discipline, with its focus on punishment, that has *created* this "real world" about which they complain.

The approach of building commitment rather than settling for mere compliance has been proven to work in several hundred companies. They recognize that whatever the "real world" may be, it was created by management behaviors and beliefs, and therefore can be changed through different behaviors and beliefs. They realize that commitment can not be mandated—it must be built. By eliminating punishment, by recognizing good performance, by creating effective administrative systems that emphasize individual responsibility and decision making, commitment to high performance and achieving organizational goals is for them a workplace reality.

Who Can Plan?
You Can!

Patricia McLagan

"Professional development. Ho hum. Another list of things to do, rational steps to take, resolutions to make and break, theories that sound great—but in practice? On my job there's not much time; not much support. Besides, development happens anyway. I've been growing; taking some steps forward and some back. Learning has been part of my life, whether planned or not. When an opportunity has arisen, I've usually taken it. Who can plan, anyway? I don't even know what jobs will exist in five years. Plan for them? Develop systematically? I'm skeptical. I've been around."

The years have not been kind to the idea of professional development. Few in today's work force have active professional development agendas. Existing development plans are often separate from day-to-day life. They focus on the means—the course—rather than on the ends—the learning and performance impact. Even those fields providing continuing education credits or certification options often cannot equate certificates with increased competence. And the idea often prevails that "you can't teach an old dog new tricks."

Nevertheless, it is clear we need to develop at accelerated rates. Today, standing still means moving backwards, as information available in many fields doubles every six to ten years. As computers become more of a commodity, this information half-life will undoubtedly shrink further.

Yet, the idea of planned professional development still seems to lack spark. This is because we persist in an old view of professional development—a view that focuses on technical subject matter, teacher-centered development, task-focused performance criteria, lock-step career paths, and activity-based development plans.

We need to break out this old way of thinking. While it contains some truths, it isn't adequate for today's and tomorrow's developing professionals and professions. Furthermore, a new view could excite us about professional development again, allowing us to energize the forces around us to create the environment of risk, innovation, and personal growth individuals and organizations feel is crucial to their success as well as their survival.

What is professional development?

This seems like a simple question. How would you answer it?

The American Society for Training and Development (ASTD), the society representing "professional developers," offers a comprehensive definition stressing that professional development is an ongoing process enabling professionals to improve their performance. It is a benefit to the professional, the professional's organization, and the profession in which he or she works.

The definition describes what professional development is and includes. What about how we make it happen? I'd like to suggest five qualities of excellent professional development. As you read them, think about how your own professional development measures up to these criteria:

Excellent professional development uses both social processes and appropriate technology   During times of rapid change and evolution of professions, we can't wait until new ideas appear in courses and journals. By the time ideas are printed or packaged, they're already months or years old. Rather, timely development requires networking, contact with "grapevines," even direct "high-touch" contact with others through "high-tech" computer connections.

The challenge is to use other people as sources of late-breaking information and to use technology to help speed communication and help sort through the mountains of data and resources available for more formal development.

Excellent professional development anticipates the future and helps prepare us to shape and respond to it   It is increasingly difficult to predict the future based on the past. Where will technology take us? What will the increased average age of the work force mean for careers? Are organizations flattening, or are we moving toward entirely new forms of organization? What will be the balance between specialists and generalists?

In this environment it's difficult to know what to develop. We don't know what jobs will exist in the future. It won't be enough to just "fix" our past deficiencies. If we wait until the future to prepare for it, we'll be left behind. Millions are out of work today because they didn't develop skills ahead of time.

Professional development in the past was reactive. People developed to strengthen weaknesses and prepare for the next job or credential. In contrast, professional development today must be proactive. It must answer some new questions: "What new social, technical, and economic forces will affect my work as a professional?" "What competencies will be important, regardless of how work, careers, and jobs are organized?" "Since the future isn't predetermined, what role do I want to play—and can I play—to influence the forces affecting my field?"

The theme again is professional development as a dynamic process we as individuals must influence. Courses, degrees, tests, and credentials play a role, but they don't equal professional development. In true professional development, the profession itself benefits because each individual has accepted the challenge and responsibility of the statement "Count me in!"

Excellent professional development is a self-directed and high self-responsibility process Self-directed learning is in fashion these days. It parallels the participative management philosophies many companies are adopting or are trying to adopt. Is it a fad? What does self-direction mean for the developing professional? Does self-direction mean "anything goes"? How do we assure excellence and consistent standards of practice?

Before we answer these questions, let's consider the facts. We self-manage most of our own learning and change. Canadian Alan Tough's research indicates that individuals choose, plan, and implement about 70 percent of their own changes. Nonprofessional helpers—such as friends, the boss, and colleagues—direct about 20 percent. Professional helpers—such as teachers and therapists—play a key role in about 6 percent of our individual changes. TV, books, and other nonhuman resources guide the rest.

Self-managed learning is the most common and natural learning format. Still, it isn't the most efficient, respected, or effective. Honeywell Corporation's studies of managers' "professional development" in the early 1980s discovered a relevant phenomenon: although managers do most of their learning on the job, where either they or their colleagues manage the learning, it is often inefficient, overly painful, costly, and produces an aversion to risk.

Self-direction in professional development must be accompanied by self-responsibility. Think of professional development as a project. You are the project manager. You are in charge. But you must use good project management skills. This involves setting and committing to goals as well as finding and using the best resources for information, support, feedback, and skill building. Where there are standards of practice and codes of ethics, you take responsibility for understanding them, incorporating them in your work, and influencing changes when you feel changes are needed.

There is an essential tension between self-direction and professional standards, but the success and vitality of each depends on the strength of the other. Many professions have been strong on the standards side and weak on the self-responsibility side. Bureaucracy and atrophy are the inevitable results.

The challenge to each of us is to become strong and deliberate in our professional self-management while seeking and being open to help, ideas, and support. Self-direction doesn't mean isolation or hedonism. It means deliberately bringing all of our personal and organizational resources to bear for our own development.

Excellent professional development is efficient   Professional development uses resources. It requires time, energy, support from others, capital, and materials. If we treat professional development like an important program or project, the importance of effectiveness and efficiency is obvious.

Yet many of us tolerate massive waste in development. We sign up for the first course to come along. We learn through expensive trial and error on the job without having mechanisms to make that learning fully conscious. We read haphazardly even though search services exist to provide us with a broad array of articles and books that are targeted to our needs and interests. We draw on our immediate professional circles even though our profession's scope may be national and even global. We do all of this despite the availability of association and computer networks to put us in touch with colleagues beyond our daily geography.

Efficient professional development has two dimensions. First, it involves using the right resources and contacts from the start. This includes looking at the costs and benefits of development activities. Second, when we're efficient in professional development, we use good learning skills. We read effectively. We listen and participate with an open mind. We ask questions to discover other points of view. We also take advantage of opportunities as they arise, even if it means changing our action plans or modifying a timeline.

Excellent professional development is relevant to the individual's career stage   A key point throughout this article is that professional development *does not occur in spite of the individual.* Our own motivations, values, needs, and perspectives inevitably color our development goals and actions. I've suggested that this is desirable because the tension between the individual and the profession is a creative force benefiting everyone.

Part of this tension comes from the unique requirements of our career and life stage. Some psychologists claim that as we mature, we change our primary relationships to the world around us. For example, a common sequence of work-related roles is from student to apprentice to practitioner to helper to creator of legacies. The direction professional development takes will vary based on our current dominant role.

When we are *students*, we focus professional development on mastering a field's basic body of knowledge. When we become *apprentices*, we use professional development to help us apply the basics of the field. At this stage we try to understand how procedures and principles work in the "real world." We look to others to help us discover proven ways of doing things. We want to know whether we have done things right, and we look to our more experienced colleagues for feedback and critique.

After we have built a base of knowledge and are familiar with its applications, it becomes important to us to be full *practitioners*. In this stage we use more judgment in our work. The challenge to us as professionals is to create options for better ways of doing things. When we are full practitioners, professional development primarily occurs through creative problem solving with peers. We work hard to deepen our professional competencies and to broaden our ability to work effectively with others whose cooperation is important to our success.

Once we have built a solid base of technical skills and networks, we may enter the fourth career stage where our primary motivation is to *help others*—who are usually apprentices—grow and develop professionally. In some people's lexicon, this concern for helping others is off the mark or soft. But any profession's future strength depends on some of its experienced members helping new members through the student and apprentice stages. For people in the *helper* stage, professional development focuses on how to help others learn: how to coach, counsel, support, and affect other individuals' performance and development.

The fifth career stage, *creator of legacies*, may seem a bit grandiose, but many professionals are profoundly motivated and able to perform this role. Often it's a role that becomes primary later in life, although seeds may exist at all career stages. We want to leave our mark on the field itself. This may take the form of new theories, new ways of doing things, or new uses for old ideas. The legacy may be enhanced credibility and increased support from people not in the profession. Or it may take the form of better communication about old but valuable ideas and practices.

The legacy may have local, regional, national, or international scope. Professional development for people whose primary professional goal is legacy focuses on developing broader, more complex competencies: political skills, leadership, influence, or managing complex change. Someone at this stage may even begin to focus on philosophy and history to better understand the forces driving changes in human behavior and thinking patterns. Esoteric? I don't think so. In fact, I believe old views of professional development focusing primarily on the technical dimension and, thus, on the first three career stages, have actually retarded the overall development of many professional fields. We need strong "helping" and "legacy" skills.

Clearly, professional development must be relevant to an individual's career stage. But what sounds like a selfish requirement is also important for the overall good of the profession itself. A snapshot of a dynamic and adaptive profession inevitably shows people in all of the above career roles. Under a microscopic lens, that snapshot also shows that while each of us performs one dominant role, we are probably involved in several other roles as well. The implication for professional development is clear: Development plans and actions must help us competently perform our unique mix of career roles.

Professional development resources

Professional development today requires more than courses. In fact, the following are seven types of resources especially valuable for development use:

Performance models and diagnostic tools   A performance model describes the work, knowledge, and skill associated with professional excellence. A diagnostic tool is an assessment questionnaire or process to help individuals identify the knowledge and skills they will develop. Some professions have explicit models and assessment tools. In other professions, such models and assessments are implicit in the certification and licensing criteria and in standards for advanced degrees. It is becoming more important to make these models explicit, to be sure they anticipate future requirements, to continually update them, and to provide individual professions with self-diagnostic tools. Only when this happens will individuals be able to fully and deliberately direct their own development while assuring consistently high standards of practice throughout the field.

Information search services   Many services exist today to help us find books, articles, courses, subject matter experts, associations, and the like. All we need to do is decide what questions we want to answer and then translate our needs and interests into key words the computer can use to guide its search. Many professional associations (including ASTD) provide search services, often at reduced fees. Those who don't have services themselves can often tell us how to access them. Most libraries also have people who are skilled in information search and have access to the growing number of data bases available to help us find the learning resources we need.

Future scans and trend projection services   Every developing professional should have a working hypothesis about the future—or at least several future scenarios to guide professional development. But on what basis do we develop assumptions about the future? Some of our ability to forecast depends on an awareness of what is happening today. But we can also use formal trend analyses, demographic forecasts, scenarios based on pooled expert opinions, research done by futurists, projections prepared by professional associations, and more. An increasing number of futuring services exist. Whether their projections are right or wrong, they can provide information to help us become mentally prepared for change and anticipate new professional requirements. Many skills take time to develop. Anticipation can provide an increasingly important professional advantage for individuals. It is also a competitive advantage for the professional's organization.

Networks   In order to stay professionally current, it is vital to maintain regular contacts with people who are doing things in our professions. These include people who may be in the same career stage and are concerned with the same kinds of problems as well as those creating new ways of thinking and doing things. The best professional networking sources today are active memberships in professional associations and subgroups within them.

More and more professionals also are staying in touch via computer networks. Groups may set up their own or they may be sponsored by professional associations or private organizations. Several prominent technical companies have had computer-based technical skills networks since the 1960s.

Whether formal or informal, computer-based or face-to-face, real-time personal contact remains one of the best sources of professional development. The difference today is that networks transcend geography and, therefore, can be based truly on needs and interests.

Job aids   Job aids provide step-by-step guidance for professional problem solving and decision making. They are useful but aren't used frequently for professional development. Job aids may take the form of a checklist, a guide, a step-by-step video, a computer-based problem analysis, or a planning guide. They best reflect the processes highly competent professionals would use with a given problem or opportunity.

Job aids are most useful to us when we are in the early career stages or when we face a new role and don't have past experiences to draw on. They are also useful to guide us in dangerous or critical situations where step-by-step action must occur, such as when a pilot must complete all the actions on the preflight checklist or risk putting the takeoff in jeopardy.

Job aids are professional development tools because they help assure that our behavior meets standards of excellence. They also help train our thinking process so we are more likely to use high-quality logic and intuition in similar situations.

Direct learning experiences   This is the category most people equate with professional development. It includes courses, videos, computer-aided instruction, workshops, one-to-one coaching, audiotapes, books, or any experience *we or someone else has designed specifically to help us learn.*

Direct learning experiences are valuable for professional development *if* they help us "warp" our learning time. That is, one hour spent in a direct learning experience should produce significantly more learning than random day-to-day experience.

Direct learning experiences are costly. We must pay for the course or book or tape and spend time finding and acquiring or getting to it. There is also an opportunity cost. When we're in the workshop or listening to the audiotape, we aren't doing something else.

It is critical, therefore, to select direct learning experiences with care and to do everything we can to manage our use of these resources to achieve our professional development goals. And we have to do this in spite of poor teachers, bad examples, or classmates who may not want to learn.

"In process" learning   Day-to-day experiences certainly provide the most available learning options. Unfortunately, few of us fully exploit the learning potential of daily events. Those of us who *do* learn well as we work clearly approach our experiences with the intention to learn. We often help select our own projects and assignments. We have an agenda to learn and may even talk with others about it. We seek advice and support from experts, wherever they are. We often find our own mentors. We try things out, ask questions, and explore "what ifs." We ask for feedback and do deliberate self-critiques and "post mortems."

Of course, it may not always be possible to plan learning from day-to-day experiences. Sometimes we realize only after the fact that something we have experienced has development potential. In such cases, as experienced learners, we consciously draw lessons and generalizations from the experience to carry forward to the next challenge; we know the value largely will be lost if the learning is not deliberate.

Making professional development happen

"My head is spinning. It's too much to remember. Can you bring this all down to a few tips? I don't feel 'ho hum,' but I do feel, well, overwhelmed. Tell me what I can do."

Here are five actions each of us can take to launch a powerful professional development program:

Have a future vision Periodically spend some time answering the question, "What conditions and requirements will be prevalent in my field in five years, ten years, twenty years?" Read books and articles by futurists in your field. Call your professional association for references or information about future predictions. Identify and track relevant trends and issues yourself.

Identify against this backdrop what you'll need to be able to do and accomplish in the future. List the knowledge and skills you'll need in order to be a professional whose capabilities are in demand.

From time to time, write out your assumptions about the future and your list of target accomplishments, knowledge, and skills.

Know yourself Professional development is a personal experience with implications for the profession and for your organization. Thus it's important to know your own current level of knowledge and skill, your current level and types of professional and organizational contributions, and your own career stage. If there are self-evaluation tools or other career assessment programs available, use them to help you pinpoint your current strengths and development areas.

Ask people who have worked with you to tell you how they see your contributions, capabilities, and development needs. Others' opinions can provide valuable counterpoints and confirmations for your own self-analysis. Their opinions also may affect your options if they are in a position to refer you to other work, provide development resources, or influence your career in other ways.

Periodically list your major professional accomplishments, your competency strengths, and the knowledge and skills you want to develop. Think about your current career stage—student, apprentice, practitioner, helper, or creator of legacies—and the stages you want to move toward. Know yourself and you will be in a better position to recognize and create the professional development opportunities right for you.

Have a scanning system It is no longer enough to read your monthly professional journal or talk with colleagues over lunch about professional issues. Each of us needs a wide data network that goes beyond geography and cuts across a broad array of printed and media resources.

You can take major steps here by doing two things. First, identify the top professional challenges you will face in the next five years. Ask yourself and others "who else will be facing these issues or will have a useful perspective on this?" and "where are these people?" Then figure out a way to stay in touch with a representative sample. Your professional society may be one network source. You may want to set up or plug into a computer network. You may find five or ten people to contact periodically by phone, letter, or tape. The point is, use technology and networking channels to help broaden your network of professional development associates.

The second dimension of an effective scanning system is a periodic key-word search of the literature. Hundreds of data bases and several complete literature search services exist to help scan articles, papers, dissertations, courses, and books. A biannual or quarterly scan focusing on your key professional development interests and issues can help you reach beyond the constraints of subscriptions and pass-along reading. And such scans cost pennies in computer time.

Have an action plan and a vision of success   While we don't want to make the classic error of mistaking action for accomplishment, an annual action plan can help drive and manage professional development. A sample agenda and action plan are shown in the accompanying sidebar.

Plan formats may vary, but today's powerful professional development plans make all of our development goals and intentions concrete. Specifically, consider answering these questions in writing: What future conditions and requirements will have a major impact on my professional development? What are the major topics and issues to track in my scanning system? What scanning actions will I take, and when will I take them? What is my major current career stage? What do I want to be able to accomplish in five years? What competencies do I want to develop and strengthen this year? What specific, formal development action will I take off the job, and when will I take it? What projects, assignments, or actions will I take to further my development on the job?

When the plan is complete, talk to yourself until it becomes part of you. Close your eyes and imagine the year is over and you have moved to a new level of professional competence. Whether you write down your plan or not, envision what you will be able to accomplish or do more effectively because you took deliberate development steps. Then be prepared to modify your plan during the year if your goals change or if better development options emerge.

Professional development agenda and action plan

1. These future *conditions* and *requirements* will have a major impact on my professional development:

2. These are the *topics* and *issues* to track in my scanning system:

3. These are the *scanning actions* (networking, literature searches) I will take:

4. For the next year, this is the rank ordering of roles that describes my *career stage:*
   _____ student _____ apprentice _____ practitioner
   _____ helper _____ creator of legacies

5. These are the three to five major professional *accomplishments* I would like to achieve within the next five years:

6. These are the *knowledge and skills* I want to strengthen or develop this year:

7. These are the formal, off-the-job development actions I will take this year:

8. These are the development actions I will take on the job:

Develop your learning skills   Our ability to learn affects the quality of our professional development. Yet many of us use learning skills that were barely adequate for high school and college success. This must change.

We must continually improve our ability to listen, concentrate, read, think, explore ideas with openness and not defensiveness, take notes, and generate creative ideas. We must become adept at learning in groups, from computers, from mentors, from individuals with experience and knowledge to share, and from ourselves. We must sharpen our ability to think critically while recognizing and controlling our own biases and blind spots.

These learning skills are key tools for professional development. They set limits on what we can accomplish. Books and courses are available to help refine these critical skills. Find them and use them.

Conclusion

Professional development is an important personal, organizational, and economic process. During times of rapid change, it is also a key business and social success factor. Professional development plays a major role, for example, in Japan's long-term economic strategy. This makes sense. Countries, organizations, and individuals who are adept at professional development will undoubtedly prosper in the future. Fortunately, knowledge and skill are not consumable resources. They can be shared and expanded without taking away from one to give to another. As we develop we create, not deplete, wealth.

But it does take time to develop the capability we need to perform various career roles. Planned professional development can help accelerate our learning curves. It can help us develop and sustain the capacity and energy to contribute and prosper, whatever our chosen field or career stage.

Nine Ways to Make Training Pay Off on the Job

Ruth Colvin Clark

Ever observe a group of trainees a month or two after they emerged from your training program? Are the skills they learned in class being used on the job? Does your organization have a workable system for following up on its training efforts to see whether they result in better performance in the real world of the workplace?

Even after an excellent class, training frequently fails to pay off in behavioral changes on the job. Trainees go back to work and do it the way they've always done it instead of the way you taught them to do it. The phenomenon is called transfer failure. It happens because skills do not transfer automatically into job performance. In other words, the fact that you have learned how to do something a certain way doesn't necessarily mean you'll do it that way. Since the point of job-related training is to improve performance on the job, transfer failure obviously defeats the whole purpose.

Why does training—solid, effective training—fail to transfer? There are a number of reasons. Here are nine typical situations and some tips on how the problems could have been avoided.

1. Rocking the boat A supervisor in the documentation services department previewed a training program on structured writing techniques. The program taught an unusual method for formatting written material. The supervisor liked the approach and sent four of his writers to the course. They came back to work and designed a new policy manual using the techniques they had learned. When the department manager saw the result, she promptly vetoed it on grounds that its unique appearance would draw criticism from other managers in the organization. The supervisor pointed out the advantages of the new method, but the department head was adamant. "We haven't turned out anything like that before," she said. "Things have been going smoothly up to now. Let's not rock the boat."

Solution The supervisor just discovered—too late—that his own department manager, as well as other managers and supervisors should have previewed the course with him. Front-end consultation and approval by all interested parties would have prevented tail-end failure.

Management advisory committees can be formed to set policy and to help review training courses while they're still in the development stage—or before they are purchased. If a proposed program is scrapped due to lack of management commitment, better it should happen early, before a lot of dollars are invested.

2. Mismatching courses and needs The manager of a data processing center met a training vendor who demonstrated a very impressive course on prototyping. The DP manager asked the training department to send all employees to the course. However, the techniques applied only to about 25% of the employees who were building new applications. The other 75% were working on maintenance projects that did not require the use of prototyping techniques.

Solution Match courses to needs systematically. Curricula that reflect the ideas of one or several line managers, working independently and sporadically, tend to be fragmented and counterproductive. Training should flow from two primary sources: (1) a validated analysis of current job tasks and the skills required to perform them and (2) a model of the future technological directions of the organization, agreed upon by upper management.

To conduct a job analysis, first identify all major tasks and required skills. Then ask a sample of the employees currently in the job (and their supervisors) to rate the importance and complexity of each skill as well as their current proficiency in it. Concurrently, ask top managers to rate the same skills on the basis of their importance in meeting departmental objectives. Training priorities should be based on skills perceived as high in importance by managers and rated low in competency by employees and their supervisors.

This job analysis will only identify *current* skill needs. In any rapidly evolving technological environment you also will need to identify new technological applications to supplement the job analysis. Finally, the people in charge of training should have access to top management's strategic plans for the future so that appropriate training will be in place when needed.

3. Supervisory slipups The organization offers classes on time management and other generic skills. These programs are in heavy demand, and supervisors sign up their subordinates months ahead of time. When a given employee's turn finally arrives, the supervisor sometimes has forgotten why the individual was supposed to go to that particular class in the first place. Small wonder that supervisors rarely take the time to discuss the training with their people, either before or after the class. Supervisors are counting exclusively on the training department to improve their employees' skills.

Solution Ultimately it is the supervisor who must be responsible for the work performance of his or her employees. Training is one tool supervisors have to improve that performance. They need to recognize that training only teaches people to do things they don't know how to do: There is no point in sending anybody to a training program unless he lacks a particular skill required by the job.

Instead of abdicating all responsibility to the training department, supervisors can increase the impact of training dramatically by: (1) conducting brief pre- and post-course discussions with employees where they agree on how the skills learned in the program will be applied on the job and (2) making specific follow-up assignments after the employee returns to be sure that the skills are applied. This is especially important when employees are attending nontechnical training (time management, interpersonal skills, etc.), where the transfer challenge tends to be most difficult.

Busy supervisors will not do these things without a push. The training department should help them by teaching them *how* to handle those pre- and post-course activities. In addition, second-level managers should be persuaded to include planning and implementation of employee training as part of the supervisor's formal job responsibility, to be evaluated in regular performance appraisals. In other words, supervisors must be taught how to play their crucial role in training and they must be held accountable for playing it.

4. Losing track of what training employees need In the data processing department, supervisors typically have responsibility for 10 to 20 employees at different job levels working on various project teams. In constructing their training plans, supervisors generally refer to the training catalog and use their best judgment to assign training to individuals based on their recent performance. But because the supervisors are dealing with a lot of employees who work on varied assignments that involve a large number of different skills, it's difficult to be consistent and accurate in determining each employee's training needs.

Solution   Help supervisors assess and track employees' skills by providing an automated records system. A variety of such systems are available to run on either micro or mainframe hardware. They can be programmed to list all job-related skills and provide for a competency rating agreed upon by employee and supervisor. When the individual competency ratings are matched against recommended competencies for the particular job, discrepancies are flagged and training options matched to the job skills are generated automatically. These computer programs help supervisors make systematic training plans based on both the requirements of the job and individual assessments of employee skills.

5. Lack of a "critical mass"   Employees of a sales and product-support division were sent to a course on conducting and participating in meetings. But their attendance was staggered over a one-year period. By the time the last of them had attended the class, 10 months had slipped by since the first students had gone. Division supervisors found it very difficult to implement the techniques in real meetings.

Solution   Train intact work groups. Peer group support is a major factor in determining whether newly learned skills will transfer to the job. People are much more likely to do things the new way if everybody in the work group (or at least almost everybody) is trying to do them that way at the same time. When you train only a few people at a time from any particular group, you never develop a "critical mass" of commitment to the new skills. Without that critical mass, the status quo tends to defeat change. Furthermore, if people aren't called upon to use new skills immediately after they learn them, the skills tend to atrophy.

Whenever possible, train entire working groups at the same time. If it isn't practical to train an entire team, try setting up interdepartmental or even intercompany support networks. User groups have been formed around various computer-software applications. Why not set up user groups for other types of training as well?

6. No help applying skills back on the job   During the structured writing class mentioned earlier, most students did very well on the practice exercises they were given—but they had the instructor's help. When they returned to their jobs, the instructor wasn't there. Many had trouble applying the new techniques to actual work assignments. After a few attempts, some became discouraged and reverted to their previous writing styles.

Solution   Extend training beyond the classroom. If an intact work group is learning an important new skill, follow-up training is essential to transferring the skill. Require program graduates to work on a regular project assignment using the techniques they learned. The instructor or someone competent in the new skills should provide follow-up consultation, visiting the trainees and helping them apply the techniques to their unique job assignments. Or, as an alternative, give the graduates an assignment to work on for two weeks on the job. Then schedule transfer sessions where they meet as a group with the instructor, compare results and discuss problems.

7. The external instructor is gone   That writing class was taught by an outside consultant, and it was not feasible to arrange for her to follow up after the class.

Solution   To ensure continuing consultation beyond the classroom, consider using internal instructors—or supplementing a consultant's classroom training with an internal expert who can serve the follow-up functions. This may mean asking the consultant to spend extra time with the person who will serve as your internal expert.

8. Training as a "day off"   The training department teaches a variety of courses on supervisory effectiveness. Trainees are required to show up for class, but they aren't evaluated on their performance in the course or back on the job. Practice exercises are voluntary and many trainees choose to skip them. Most of the supervisors listen politely in class. Some ask a few questions. But rarely does anyone invest much effort in acquiring the new skills. A day in training is generally regarded as an opportunity to kick back and drink coffee.

Solution   Build accountability into your training. Competency-based training is built on specific, job-related objectives. Learners must be held accountable for reaching these objectives. Instructors should send a summary of course objectives and the trainee's performance in class to the trainee's supervisor. The organization should demand that all training courses be instructionally valid, i.e., each course should prove that people who take it and invest reasonable effort will attain the objectives.

If the course is just plain ineffective, the issue of transfer to the workplace becomes irrelevant. Likewise, if learners are not held responsible for investing effort in their own training, even the best instruction will not generate maximum benefits. Accountability in training should address both of these problems.

9. Training is not available when needed   Many organizations rely heavily on classroom training, scheduling courses on some fixed timetable (e.g., quarterly) or when there is sufficient enrollment to justify teaching the class. This means that people may be on waiting lists for several months. Knowing this, supervisors will send employees to courses as the classes become available, even though the employees will not be needing the skills in the near future.

Solution   Consider self-instructional training. When live classes are scheduled on a body-count basis, there is often a lack of coordination between the timing of the training and the opportunity to apply the skills on the job. Self-instructional courses delivered by workbooks, video or computer-based training provide access to information when it's needed.

Course Title _____ Dates Attended _____

Company Division (please circle):
  Sales   Manufacturing   Customer Service
  Data Processing   Other _____

Course Objective _____
        (Section above completed by training department.)

....

A. At the end of this course, to what degree did you feel that you achieved the objective stated above?

Very little		Moderately		Very much
1	2	3	4	5

If you circled below 3 on question A, stop here and return the questionnaire. Otherwise, continue.

B. Since completing this course, how *often* have you used the skills you learned in class on your job assignments?

Rarely never		Occasionally (monthly)		Frequently (daily)
1	2	3	4	5

C. As a result of this course, how much improvement have you experienced in completing your job assignments?

Little/no improvement		Some improvement		Major improvement
1	2	3	4	5

If you answered question B or C with a 3 or greater, then go on to questions D and E. If you answered question B or C with less than a 3, then go on to question F.

Figure 1.   Training follow-up survey.

The drawback to self-instructional courses is that even when they're well-designed (and a lot of them aren't), they demand a high degree of motivation from the learner. There is no instructor to answer to; learners often start the courses but fail to complete them. An obvious alternative is to build or buy self-instructional courses and supplement them with live tutors to help trainees, give them regular feedback, and measure and report their progress.

All of these "solutions" demand a greater investment of time and resources—both finite quantities—on the part of the training department. You may want to consider offering fewer courses, but investing more effort to enhance transfer: Rather than offering six new courses next year, concentrate on one or two critical programs

---

D. Describe at least three typical ways that you have used the skills you learned in class and how your job performance has improved as a result.

E. Place a check next to each reason below that might explain why you have applied the skills you learned to your job assignments:
    _____ My supervisor discussed with me how my new skills would be used on my job assignments.
    _____ My supervisor required me to use the new skills.
    _____ I received help from others in my work area.
    _____ I was given necessary time and/or tools to apply the skills.
    _____ I received training at the right time to provide me with the skills when I needed them on the job.
    _____ The skills I learned applied directly to my job assignment.
    _____ Other: Please list other factors that helped you apply these skills to your job assignments.

F. Place a check next to each reason below that could explain why you have not been successful in applying skills learned to your job assignments:
    _____ My supervisor did not require me to use the skills.
    _____ My supervisor did not agree with the skills I learned.
    _____ My supervisor was not aware of what skills I learned.
    _____ I was not given time/tools to implement the skills on the job.
    _____ There was no one to help me implement the skills in my work area.
    _____ The skills did not seem to apply to my job assignment.
    _____ My job assignment changed so these skills did not apply.
    _____ The training was not timed right for my job assignment.
    _____ Other: Please describe other reasons you did not apply the skills to your job assignments:

---

but build in the pre-course planning and post-course follow-up that will help ensure transfer to the job.

Measure your training transfer quotient

Figure 1 is a generic survey you could adapt to your own training situation. Send the questionnaire to everyone who has completed a given course within the past six months. (Or, randomly select 100 employees who have completed the course.) Even a 50% response rate will give you a good indication of whether the training transferred to the job. Administer the survey anonymously to ensure honest feedback.

Scoring: Add up the number of responses of "3" or above to both question B and question C (i.e., one person who checks "3" to question C and "4" to question B counts as two responses). Divide by twice the total number of questionnaires returned, and multiply by 100. A score of 80% or better probably means that the skills you're teaching are transferring adequately to the workplace. A score of less than 70% suggests that you need to make some changes.

PART 3

Employee
Issues

Privacy Rights: Whose Life Is It, Anyway?

Employee privacy is a growing concern. Since George Orwell raised the specter of Big Brother with his *1984*,[1] computer technology, court rulings, government intrusion and the right of business and industry to know more about the people they employ—all have eroded the American worker's sense that his/her life is a private matter.

Businesses face a three-pronged dilemma. First, information from employees is necessary to make decisions for initial hiring, promotion, training, security, compensation and benefits, retirement, disciplinary actions, termination and job opportunities. Second, businesses are bombarded with requests from other companies for information on their present or past employees for reference checks, credit checks, security checks and/or medical records. Third, employees expect their privacy to be protected. This expectation is reinforced by company policies and the norms of society.

Thus, businesses face a balancing act: protecting employee privacy, running their own business, and keeping good relations with other organizations. Court decisions many times hinge on business necessity and public good vs. employee expectations of privacy. What legal rights to privacy do employees have in the public and private sectors, and what safeguards do businesses need to take to protect their employees' privacy?

Business necessity and public good vs. employee expectations

Businesses collecting data on their employees are using polygraphs, honesty paper and pencil tests, psychological tests, voice analyzers,

Information gathering techniques

Electronic supervision
Polygraph test
Voice analyzer test
Personal strip searches
Surveillance by private investigator
Searches of desk, purse, briefcase, and other containers
Genetic testing
Urinalysis test
Monitoring of urinalysis testing
Blood test
Monitoring of mail
Electronic eavesdropping on telephone lines
Chest X-rays
Training reports
Performance appraisals
Audiometrix test
Ophthalmologic test
Work station monitored by use of one-way mirrors
Pre-employment interviewing screening about geography history
   (where reared, locations in which employee has lived), sex, age,
   race, etc.
Work station videotaped
Subordinates' meetings taped
Finger printing
Locker searches
Release of medical records to third party
Behavioral profile

fingerprint analysis, handwriting analysis, medical records, genetic testing, behavioral profiles and electronic tracking devices. Other more traditional techniques of collecting data include performance appraisals, disciplinary reports, training tests, interviews and applications. All those techniques plus those portrayed in the accompanying sidebar are present in the work environment. Businesses claim the information gathered is necessary for legitimate business decision making.

The critical issue of breached privacy hinges, then, on the business necessity and employee's expectation of privacy. How is the information used after it is collected? Can the company operate efficiently and effectively without this information? Should this information have a date of expiration denoting when it will be purged from the files? Who should have access to this information? What effects will the release of this information have upon the employee?

In *Bratt vs. International Business Machines Corp.* (1986) the United States Court of Appeals for the First Circuit ruled that a limited claim for invasion of privacy is warranted against both the employer and the physician under contract to the employer. After appointment with IBM, Bratt received a medical examination from the "local examining physician." This physician subsequently contacted Bratt's supervisor and told her that Bratt was paranoid and should see a psychiatrist immediately. Bratt's supervisor then told other supervisors, as well as issuing a memorandum to other supervisors telling them of Bratt's mental problems. The claim against the supervisor's invasion of Bratt's privacy was dismissed. However, the appellate court found IBM violated Bratt's privacy when the company doctor released information to management about Bratt's condition. Lawyers summarized the ruling of the court as follows:

In balancing the degree of intrusion upon Bratt's privacy against IBM's legitimate business interest, the court found that the company's policy of protecting the confidentiality of its employee's medical information permitted Bratt an expectation of privacy.[2]

In *Eddy vs. Texaco, Inc.* (1986) the invasion of privacy claims were not upheld by the court. In this case Eddy's employer informed Eddy's co-workers that he had psychiatric problems and had been committed to a hospital for evaluation. In deciding the case the court stated that the information on Eddy's health was part of his employment medical record and that this information was a legitimate concern of Eddy's supervisor. The court did not feel that an unreasonable intrusion had been made on Eddy's privacy since only a limited number of his co-workers had been informed. The court felt that this case with such limited disclosure did not amount to "publicity" great enough for invasion of privacy.[3]

In considering the public good, one federal court regards protecting public health as more important than protecting the privacy interests of the individual. An interesting statement for justifying this position was that an employee willingly divulging sensitive information to the employer constituted a dilution of the employee's privacy interests.[4]

However, employees may feel that divulging sensitive information is necessary to obtain and/or keep a job. According to William Petrocelli, an authority on invasion of privacy, "Privacy is a luxury—far down the list of priorities that is headed by the need to earn a living wage."[5] This does not mean that individuals do not care about their privacy; it means that when their job hinges on their willingness to release information, they will give the information. The stark fact is that many people have no choice but to accept a job on any terms the employer wants to offer.[6]

If substantial evidence of adverse effects to the employee exists, the U.S. Supreme Court has ruled that a governmental agency cannot compel the employer to release sensitive information.[7] Thus, even though the employee may have diluted privacy interests, evidence of adverse effects can stop disclosure. Considering health and safety, however, managers should be aware that as long as the agency has reasonable safeguards to protect privacy, they must release information if the need is related to health and safety.

According to Adler, Parson and Zolke, releases of information can go beyond the need for health and safety needs.

Most courts have held that there is no infringement of privacy when ordinary sensibilities are not offended. So long as there is not a flagrant breach of decency and propriety, the courts will recognize that no individual can expect complete noninterference from the society in which he or she lives. Accordingly, information regarding salary, business connections, age, experience, education and criminal convictions will not constitute an unwarranted intrusion into an individual's right to privacy.[8]

With businesses needing information to run and with third parties requesting information on their employees, managers should be aware of the legal rights employees have to privacy.

Legal rights to privacy
A judicially approved definition of the right to privacy is: "It is the right to be free from the unwarranted appropriation of one's personality, the publicizing of one's private affairs with which the public has no legitimate concern, or the wrongful intrusion into one's private activities, in such a manner as to outrage or cause mental suffering, shame or humiliation to a person of ordinary sensibilities."[9]

Even with this broad definition of the right to privacy, there is no general explicit constitutional right to privacy. The U.S. Constitution does not specifically mention the right to privacy. However, the roots of that right may be found in the First, Third, Fourth, Fifth and Ninth Amendments, as well as in the concept of liberty guaranteed by the first section of the 14th Amendment.

Between 1957 and 1967 the Supreme Court began mandating steps to handle problems of privacy. With *Griswold vs. Connecticut*, Justice Douglas spoke of "zones of privacy" created by "various guarantees" of the Bill of Rights, citing the First, Third, Fourth and Ninth Amendments.

From 1890 to 1950 technological innovations such as the telephone, dictograph recorder and instantaneous photography prompted a majority of the states to adopt the common law principle of an individual right to privacy. After the Privacy Act of 1974,[10] which pertains to public employees only, eight states (California, Connecticut, Maine, Michigan, North Carolina, Oregon, Pennsylvania and Wisconsin) passed legislation for employees to inspect their own personnel files. As summarized by Duffy, Michigan's statute is the most detailed:

Employees may, upon written request, examine and copy personnel records at a reasonable time and place. (The term *personnel records* appears to be broadly defined, although the act specifically excludes certain reference letters, comparative evaluations, medical reports, and investigative or grievance files maintained separately.) Employees may request that information in their personnel files be amended or corrected. If the request is denied, they may file dissenting statements that are to be kept in a file with the disputed information. If the employer maintains investigative files, employees must be notified of their existence at the end of the investigation or after two years. Investigative files must be destroyed if no action is taken.[11]

Most states' privacy statutes provide the following privacy rights for employees:

1. Allow the employee to inspect his/her personnel file
2. Allow the employee to be informed of the existence of his/her personnel file
3. Allow the employee to correct what he/she considers to be inaccuracy in his/her personnel file.

At present there is no uniform code established to clarify matters for the courts and to help direct personnel administrators in their decisions. At present many personnel administrators may be risking liability suits for negligence in the way personnel files are being maintained. This possibility has already been established in a federal court.[12] Since there is neither a uniform law regarding invasion of privacy nor a privacy law for the private sector, managers need to be proactive and set privacy guidelines for their organization.

Recommendations to help safeguard privacy

The following general and specific recommendations should be considered by managers to safeguard employee privacy and to help protect the organization from liability.

General recommendations

1. Set up guidelines and policies to protect information in the organization. These guidelines and policies should cover types of data to be sought; methods of obtaining data; retention and dissemination of information; employee access to information; third-party access to information; and mishandling of information.
2. Inform employees of these information handling policies.
3. Become thoroughly familiar with state statutes regarding privacy.

4. Become familiar with the Privacy Act of 1974 covering the public sector.
5. Become familiar with the Fair Credit Reporting Act of 1971 permitting an individual to review his or her credit files. This act affects reference checking when an investigative report is prepared on a prospective employee. The applicant must be allowed to see the information collected.
6. Become familiar with the Freedom of Information Act allowing individuals access to information that a federal agency uses in making decisions.
7. Become familiar with the Family Educational Rights and Privacy Act permitting post-secondary students access to their educational records and letters of recommendations written about them. Release of some data is allowed only with written consent of the student.
8. Monitor legislation currently under consideration.

Specific recommendations

1. Avoid fraudulent, secretive or unfair means of collecting data. Collect information when possible directly from subject.
2. Do not maintain secret files on individuals. Inform subjects of what information is stored on them, the purpose for which it was collected, how it is to be used, and how long it will be kept.
3. Collect only information about individuals that is relevant to specific decisions. Substantiate the job-relatedness of information gathering.
4. Maintain records of individuals or organizations that have regular access or request information on a *need-to-know* basis. Determine the nature, date and purpose of access to the information in advance on a basis of *need*.
5. Verify with the subject if information collected and stored is correct. Incorrect or discriminatory data should be purged from the files.
6. Permit employees to review their files, correct, erase, or amend inaccurate, obsolete or irrelevant information. Accept an individual's statement of dispute and allow that statement to be accessed and transferred with other related data.
7. Release to outside parties only "directory information" such as position and dates of employment unless the employee gives written consent to the release of additional data or unless a subpeona is issued. Verify that the third party is a properly identified individual who has a legitimate right to the information.

8. Gain assurance that the information being released will be used only for the purposes set forth prior to its release. Have parties check off purpose of information and sign forms.
9. Store information regarding access to information for five years or the life of the record, whichever is longer.
10. Secure the system from any reasonably foreseeable threat to its security.[13]

Notes

1. Cook, Suzanne, "Invasion of Privacy: A 1984 Syndrome," *Industrial Management*, Vol. 28, No. 5, September-October 1986, pp. 18-21.
2. *Resource*, May 1986, p. 15, and No. 85-1545 (1st Circuit, March 6, 1986) U.S. Court of Appeals.
3. *Resource*, May 1986, p. 15, and No. 62086 (OK, S. Ct. Feb. 25, 1986).
4. *United States vs. Allis-Chalmers Corp.*, 498 F. Supp. 1027 (E. D. Wis. 1980).
5. Petrocelli, Williams. *Low Profile— How to Avoid the Privacy Invaders.* New York: McGraw-Hill Book Co., 1981, p. 112.
6. Petrocelli, pp. 111-112.
7. See *Detroit Edison Co. vs. National Labor Relations Board*, 440 U.S. 301 (1979).
8. Adler, Philip, Jr., Parsons, Charles K. and Zolke, Scott B., "Employee Privacy: Legal and Research Developments and Implications for Personnel Administration," *Sloan Management Review*, Winter 1985, p. 17.
9. Petrocelli, p. 4.
10. 5 U.S.C. Sect. 552(a).
11. See Duffy, D.J., "Privacy vs. Disclosure: Balancing Employee and Employer Rights," *Employee Relations Law Journal*, 7(1982), pp. 594-609, and Michigan Comp. Laws Ann. 423, 501.
12. See *Bulkin vs. Western Kraft East, Inc.*, 442 F. Supp. 437 (E. D. Pa. 1976).
13. Cook, p. 21.

AIDS in the Workplace: Public Personnel Management and the Law

_____ Robert H. Elliott and Thomas M. Wilson

The fear of AIDS has reached a level of hysteria in the United States—so much so that the fear of contracting this incurable disease has pervaded workplace settings. Newspapers have indicated that a majority of individuals polled favored quarantine for persons with AIDS or somehow prohibiting such individuals from having sex.[1] And we are now witnessing employers using AIDS tests to screen job applicants, and firing employees diagnosed as having AIDS. In short, what was once a purely medical phenomenon has, in a relatively short period of time, become a major social concern, and, more importantly for us, is gradually transforming the way we think about public administration in general and employee rights in particular.

Medical evidence regarding AIDS

AIDS is defined by the CDC as "a disease, at least moderately predictive of a defect in cell-mediated immunity, occurring in a person with no known cause for diminished resistance to that disease."[2] In other words, the immune system of an AIDS victim is gradually destroyed by the AIDS virus (variously called HTLV III, LAV, or HIV) and is unable to resist any number of "opportunistic" fatal diseases.

The HTLV III virus reacts differently in different individuals, and the visible symptoms of an AIDS victim vary considerably; however, there appear to be enough commonalities among AIDS sufferers to classify them into three categories according to severity of symptoms. Category one contains those individuals who have been exposed to the HTLV III virus, carry antibodies in their blood-

Reprinted with permission from _Public Personnel Management_, Vol. 16, No. 3 (Fall 1987).

stream, and can be considered to be carriers of AIDS; yet, they display no real symptoms of this disease. Category two contains those individuals who have a milder form of AIDS—sometimes referred to as ARC (AIDS-related complex). These individuals will have symptoms such as weight loss, persistent fatigue, swollen lymph nodes, night sweating, and some decreased effectiveness of the immune system. The last category is composed of individuals with the most severe form of AIDS. In these individuals the immune system is significantly weakened, and they have contracted any of various opportunistic infections.[3] Medical evidence suggests that the disease can be spread only through sexual contact or by direct introduction into the bloodstream. If this evidence is correct, it would appear that there is little cause for alarm regarding the transmission of AIDS through casual contact associated with most working environments. AIDS is, according to most physicians, a difficult disease to contract. According to a Commerce Clearing House report, "There have been no cases where the virus has spread through casual contact with an AIDS patient. The virus has never been spread via sweat, saliva, casual contact or through the air."[4]

In 1985, the CDC issued recommended guidelines for preventing the transmission of AIDS in the workplace. In these guidelines, AIDS was described as a "blood-borne, sexually transmitted disease that is not spread by casual contact... The kind of nonsexual person-to-person contact that generally occurs among workers and clients or consumers in the workplace does not pose a risk for transmission of HTLV-III/LAV."[5] Fear of contracting the AIDS virus on the job from activities such as using a telephone, eating at a cafeteria table, sharing a drinking fountain, sharing a rest room, or washing in the same sink used by an AIDS victim, based on the best available medical evidence, appears to be irrational.[6]

The CDC has also issued guidelines dealing with the prevention of the transmission of AIDS for workers who might be in more personal contact with AIDS victims, such as health care workers (nurses, physicians, dentists, blood bank technologists, paramedics, etc.) and personal service workers (hairdressers, barbers, manicurists, etc.). In these guidelines the CDC indicates that the risk of transmission is still very low, except in situations where there might be the likelihood of the accidental exchange of blood. Under circumstances where blood exchange is possible, normal medical precautions such as sterilization of instruments, good hygiene, protective clothing such as gloves and masks, and educational awareness are essential.[7]

The legal aspects of AIDS

Since AIDS is a debilitating disease with a high potential for affecting job performance, employers must consider the legal factors regarding AIDS victims in the workforce. We are still in the initial stages of arriving at explicit legal precedents regarding conflicts between employer concerns and the rights of AIDS victims; however, there are some important federal laws, state and local laws and ordinances, court cases, and legal opinions which are laying the groundwork for the treatment of AIDS-related questions in the workforce.

The most important legislation affecting AIDS victims may well be federal, state and local laws dealing with handicap discrimination. If AIDS is determined to be a handicap, then employers will be prohibited from discriminating against AIDS sufferers solely on the basis of that disease, provided, of course, that the employee can perform the job in question. At the federal level, Section 503 of the Vocational Rehabilitation Act of 1973 prohibits handicap discrimination by employers receiving federal contracts, and Section 504 prohibits discrimination against the handicapped by employers receiving federal funds in their operations.

Most states have some form of handicap laws and some have already acted to define AIDS as a protected handicap. A common definition of a handicapped person, at the state level, is one who "has a physical or mental impairment which substantially limits one or more of such person's life activities."[8] Florida, Maine, Massachusetts, New Jersey, and New York have already acted on the basis of their handicap statutes to protect AIDS victims from discrimination. Two other states, California and Wisconsin, have passed legislation protecting AIDS victims against some forms of employment discrimination. At the local level, the District of Columbia, Los Angeles, West Hollywood, and San Francisco have all passed ordinances protecting AIDS victims from employment discrimination.[9]

How the courts will consider AIDS under various handicap statutes remains one of the most important questions to be answered. Most of the sources consulted in this research agreed that the probabilities are high that the courts will consider AIDS victims to fall into the handicapped category.

In a recent Florida case, a county budget analyst with AIDS, Todd Shuttleworth, was dismissed because he was considered to pose a risk for co-workers who came into contact with him.[10] The Florida Commission on Human Relations ruled that Mr. Shuttleworth was a victim of handicap discrimination, since AIDS was a handicap under the Commission's definition of that term. The Commission also noted that employers could only discriminate based on handicap if the absence of the disability is a bona fide occupational qualification (BFOQ) necessary to perform the job.[11] This lawsuit was recently settled out of court, with the State of Florida agreeing to pay Mr. Shuttleworth $196,000 in back pay, medical bills, attorney's fees, and reinstatement of his health and life insurance. Broward County, Florida, also agreed to treat Mr. Shuttleworth and

other employees with AIDS as being handicapped under the Rehabilitation Act of 1973.[12] Recently, in a federal district court case, a
retarded child with Hepatitis B (a virus considered to be similar
to—albeit non life-threatening—and more contagious than AIDS)
could not be forced to attend school in a separate classroom.[13]

   In the only major departure from the tendency to consider
AIDS as a protected handicap, the U.S. Department of Justice issued an opinion memorandum on the application of Section 504 of
the Rehabilitation Act to persons with AIDS. Section 504, as was
indicated earlier, applies to discrimination in any program that receives federal financial assistance. In this memorandum the U.S
Justice Department stated:

> After carefully examining these difficult questions, we have concluded
> that section 504 prohibits discrimination based on the disabling effects of
> AIDS and related conditions may have on their victims. *By contrast, we
> have concluded that an individual's (real or perceived) ability to transmit
> the disease to others is not a handicap within the meaning of the statute
> and, therefore, that discrimination on this basis does not fall within section
> 504* (emphasis added).[14]

In other words, AIDS is a protected handicap, but firing someone
based on the real or perceived fear that the individual will transmit
the AIDS virus is not discrimination under the statute. According to
the Justice Department, "Congress, in enacting section 504, gave no
indication that it intended to disturb the venerable body of federal
and state law giving public health officials broad powers to prevent
the spread of *communicable diseases*" (emphasis added).[15]

   This opinion seems to ignore the government's own guidelines
indicating that AIDS cannot be spread by casual contact. The
American Civil Liberties Union, the American Medical Association,
and a number of civil rights groups have denounced the Department's opinion.

   With the exception of the Justice Department memorandum,
most evidence leads to the assumption that AIDS is likely to be
treated as a handicap, and that employers will be prohibited from
discriminating against AIDS victims because of that handicap. Indeed, in a case decided on March 3, 1987, the United States Supreme
Court quite likely established a precedent for such a defense. The
case concerns a school teacher, Gene Arline, who was dismissed
from her position after suffering three relapses of tuberculosis,
which had been in remission for 20 years. Following denial of relief
in state administrative proceedings, she brought suit under Section
504 of the Rehabilitation Act. The Supreme Court held that a person
with contagious tuberculosis may be considered a "handicapped individual" under Section 504, and that Arline was handicapped by
the disease and therefore protected. A crucial issue is that of conta-

giousness, and the court refused to draw a line between the contagious effects of a disease and the "disease's physical effects on a claimant." The Court stated, "It would be unfair to allow an employer to seize upon the distinction between the effects of a disease on others and the effects of a disease on a patient and use that distinction to justify discriminatory treatment."

In a footnote, however, the Court stated it would not reach the "questions about whether a carrier of a contagious disease such as AIDS could be considered to have a physical impairment, or whether such a person could be considered, solely on the basis of contagiousness, a handicapped person as defined by the Act." Thus, the Court's opinion is that since impairment and contagion result from the same cause, contagion is not sufficient grounds for dismissal. In approaching the issue of whether Arline was "otherwise qualified," the Court agreed with the amicus curiae brief of the American Medical Association that an "individualized inquiry" should be conducted, based on: (1) the nature of the risk (how the disease is transmitted); (2) the duration of the risk (how long the carrier is infectious); (3) the severity of the risk (what is the potential harm to third parties); and (4) the probabilities the disease will be transmitted and cause varying degrees of harm.

The *Arline* case has clear and direct relevance to the question of whether AIDS sufferers are protected by the Rehabilitation Act, and it also seems clear that the Supreme Court has set a precedent that the contagiousness of the disease (and fear of contagion) is not in itself sufficient grounds for dismissal from employment.

Personnel management concerns regarding AIDS in the public sector workforce

Public personnel professionals cannot afford to react to the AIDS threat on the basis of rumor or hysteria. In many instances the jurisdiction's personnel department will be expected to serve as an information vehicle to educate management regarding AIDS-related workplace issues. Important legal consequences may flow from any personnel-related decision regarding an employee or job applicant who is discovered to have AIDS, or infection with the AIDS virus. It is, therefore, important for personnel specialists to become familiar with the epidemiological facts as well as the legal considerations associated with this disease. The following will cover several important steps in the overall personnel process where important legal considerations may arise concerning AIDS.

The most relevant legal point any employer must determine is the extent to which AIDS victims are covered under that jurisdiction's handicap legislation. Normally, employers may discriminate against a handicapped person only if the person cannot perform the job in question, and if it is impossible for the employer to make reasonable accommodations for the handicapped individual.

Pre-employment inquiries Because of historical discrimination, many kinds of questions asked of applicants prior to making a hiring decision have come under close legal scrutiny. Questions about race, sex, religion, pregnancy, child care arrangements, or any other question which might serve as a pretext for discrimination, or which might be considered an invasion of privacy, will place on the employer a very heavy burden to demonstrate their job relatedness. The courts have imposed this heavy burden on employers because of the suspicion that the employer is simply using such questions as a mechanism to screen out potential applicants, then denying them employment for other reasons. If AIDS is considered to be a handicap under applicable federal, state, or local laws, then the applicants should not be asked if they have AIDS or if they have tested positive for the AIDS virus as a pre-employment inquiry.

Of course, no employer can be forced to hire any individual who cannot perform the job. Therefore, employers might reasonably ask all applicants if they are capable of working a full eight-hour day, or if they know of any reason why they cannot perform the duties of the job (assuming here that the applicant has been made fully knowledgeable of the job's essential elements). If, later on, the employee with AIDS cannot perform the job, the employer may have some basis for discharge. However, the employer cannot use any false answers as a pretext for discrimination against AIDS victims.[16]

In most positions in the workforce casual contact does not appear to be a concern of sufficient magnitude to justify pre-employment inquiries regarding the disease. However, there are circumstances where questions regarding the applicant's exposure to the disease may be justified. If the job involves invasive medical procedures, such as with some health care positions involving injections, surgical preparations, surgery, dentistry, etc., some pre-employment screening questions may be legally defensible.

Pre-employment AIDS testing Remember that the most commonly used AIDS test, the ELISA test, has been criticized for its high error rate and that this test reveals only the presence or absence of AIDS antibodies. In short, it cannot predict if a person who tests positive for exposure to the virus will eventually succumb to the diseases characteristic of AIDS. Since it was developed for use by blood banks, it is a very conservative test; that is, it has a high false positive rate (people who test positive but who do not actually have AIDS antibodies in their bloodstream)—which was necessary in screening blood donors. However, this high false positive rate (according to some estimates as many as 80% of all positive tests are false positives) makes it a very suspicious vehicle to be used as an employment screening mechanism.[17] In fact, a second ELISA test is usually recommended if the first test is positive, and this should be followed by the more precise Western Blot test in order to verify the original results. If AIDS is considered a handicap, then any action taken by employers against applicants based on test results would probably be considered handicap discrimination—again, assuming that the applicant can perform the job in question.[18] Summing up the predictive value of the AIDS antibody tests, an article in the International Personnel Management Association's newsletter concluded that "there appears to be, at this time, little evidence in general to support the utility of screening for the virus for the purpose of detecting potential AIDS victims among applicants and employees."[19]

Termination of AIDS victims   Suppose an employee within your organization has informed his supervisor that he has just been diagnosed with AIDS. What response should management make? Can the organization legally dismiss the employee? *Should* the organization dismiss the employee?

These are very important questions for both the organization and the employee diagnosed with AIDS. If there are relevant handicap statutes, and if AIDS is considered to be a handicap under those statutes, then it would be unwise for the employer to terminate the individual based solely on that handicap.

The normal reasons for termination of employment revolve around poor quality of job performance, threat or danger posed to fellow employees, or budget/financial contingencies. If the AIDS victim cannot perform the essential duties of the job in question, and if this is well-documented, then the employee can be terminated based on his or her inability to perform, not on the basis of AIDS. Given the medical community's consensus that the disease cannot be spread through casual contact, it is unlikely that the threat or danger of infection posed to fellow employees would constitute a valid excuse for termination. Although increased absenteeism and increased medical benefits costs to the employer are likely results of this disease, it is unlikely that either of these conditions will serve as an acceptable rationale for termination of employees diagnosed with AIDS.

When an employee reports that he or she is a victim of AIDS, the employee is likely to be under severe emotional pressures. There is concern about being fired, about responses of family, friends, and co-workers, and, of course, about the tragic reality of impending death. If the organization has no policy concerning individuals with catastrophic illnesses and accidents where guidelines are already established, then supervisors should never act alone in such a situation. Some authorities advise against having an "AIDS policy" as such, and prefer dealing with AIDS on a case-by-case approach.[20] Other individuals in the chain of command with a legitimate need to know about this situation should be involved. Attorneys, if available, should be consulted. The information about AIDS, as with all confidential medical information about an employee, should be held in strict confidence, involving, as was indicated, only individuals with a legitimate need to know. If the employee can perform the job satisfactorily, it is recommended that the employee not be terminated, and that the employer make arrangements for reasonable accommodations with the employee who has AIDS—as should be the case with any other handicapped employee. Employers should document their handling of the employee's situation in case any questions arise in the future.[21]

Employers should rely on the latest medical information, which now indicates that since AIDS cannot be transmitted through casual contact, AIDS victims can maintain a fairly normal career as long as they are able to continue working. One important point for any employer to remember is that there is a significantly greater danger for the sufferer of AIDS to contract diseases from fellow workers than there is for fellow workers to contract AIDS.

Dealing with co-workers' concerns   Any employer dealing with a worker who has AIDS may feel trapped between conflicting laws. On the one hand, employers, through common law long recognized by the courts, have an obligation to provide a safe working environment for their employees. On the other hand, the employer, if AIDS is to be considered a handicap, has a responsibility not to discriminate and to make reasonable accommodations to AIDS victims in the workplace.

One of the most difficult problems an employer may face has been labeled "AIDS panic." In this situation, because of fear and misunderstanding, fellow employees act in concert to protest the continued employment of the AIDS victim by the organization. Other employees may take any number of actions from simply requesting reassignment for themselves or the AIDS victim, to refusing to work as long as the AIDS victim is employed. What is the organization supposed to do under these circumstances?

Employees generally have legal rights to protest what they consider to be unsafe working conditions under various federal or state labor laws as well as some occupational safety and health laws. Under the National Labor Relations Act, work stoppage by an employee or employees, who, in good faith, believe that they are protesting abnormally dangerous working conditions, will not be considered a strike.[22]

Normally, management can resolve these panics through an educational program covering the epidemiological facts about AIDS (preferably conducted by a medical doctor). Education about AIDS generally serves to reduce the level of fear among co-workers. Following this, if any protests occur, they should be treated on a case-by-case basis, and management should thoroughly investigate the related circumstances. If it is a normal working environment, then there is little chance of danger to fellow workers of working with an AIDS victim. If, however, there are co-workers who may be more highly susceptible to other viruses associated with AIDS victims— such as those who are pregnant, on steroids, or undergoing chemotherapy—then some kind of workplace accommodations such as transfers for those workers may be warranted.[23]

If a sound educational effort is unsuccessful, and if employee demands seem unreasonable, management should remember that employees generally have a responsibility to perform the assigned work, even if this means working with an AIDS victim. Situations may arise where, despite management's efforts at reasonably accommodating co-workers with concerns, some employees still refuse to perform the assigned work. At some point management may have no other choice than to discipline or dismiss. Attorneys disagree here regarding the rights of workers and employers, and there is no sufficient legal precedent regarding discipline of employees protesting the presence of AIDS victims. Management should keep abreast of the latest medical guidelines, act reasonably in trying to consider rights of both victims and co-workers, educate the workforce, and make a good faith effort at reasonable accommodations before taking adverse personnel actions against either the AIDS sufferer or other employees in the workforce.[24]

AIDS and employee medical benefits   Although AIDS is essentially a human tragedy with a high toll of emotional stress and suffering, the economic consequences of this disease cannot be ignored. New York City Mayor Ed Koch has warned of the potential for AIDS health care to "break the bank" for public health care facilities.[25] Some estimates run as high as $140,000 per AIDS patient.[26] In 1987 New York City spent around $1 million per week for the care of AIDS patients (around $100 million for 1986). Medical benefits for AIDS victims may come from at least two Social Security Administration programs: Supplemental Security Income, where benefits are related to medical condition and financial situations; and Social Security Disability, where benefits are based on medical condition and employment history.[27] AIDS costs will increase for taxpayers as the number of victims increases.

Some private health insurers are already trying to restrict coverage in what they consider to be high-risk populations. If this effort is successful, taxpayers will ultimately have to pick up these costs. Health insurance is likely to rise for government and private workers.[28]

Employers will have to make important decisions regarding coverage of AIDS-related conditions in medical benefits. Richard Simmons, a Los Angeles attorney, feels that employers have the legal right to decide whether or not to provide AIDS-related coverage in their employee medical benefits packages:

If we set aside federal, state and local regulation for a moment, it's clear that employers have the power to choose what benefits they will provide their employees, and what benefits they will not provide; and employers do this all the time. Many cover medical, but not dental; others cover dental, but not orthodontia. So there is nothing inherently unfair or unreasonable about the concept of covering some conditions and not others. Deciding what to cover is usually a matter of weighing the cost of coverage against the perceived benefit to the employer.[29]

Although all of the legal issues revolving around AIDS-related medical coverage are far from resolved, it is apparent that, in the near future, the courts will necessarily give employers some guidance in this area.

Summary

AIDS is a disease to be feared, especially by high-risk groups in the population, but it is a very difficult disease to contract. It is not a disease that is spread through casual contact that occurs in normal working conditions. Much of the fear of AIDS is based on misunderstanding and lack of medical information.

Legally, AIDS is likely to be considered a handicap, and employers will be prohibited from discriminating against AIDS victims based on their handicap. This means that in personnel processes—from pre-employment inquiries and screening to demotion or termination—one must constantly guard against discrimination based on an AIDS-related diagnosis.

Co-workers' concerns regarding working with AIDS victims are usually based on what they consider reasonable fears about a safe working environment, and must be treated with enlightened concern by management. Any resolution must give adequate consideration to the rights of the AIDS victim as well as the rights of fellow employees. Employer responses are called for which should be based on a sound educational program for co-workers, and on good faith efforts at reasonable accommodation for the AIDS victim and co-workers' concerns.

Notes

1. David A. Copus and H. M. Ginsburg, "AFRAIDS in the Workplace," *Commerce Clearing House Topical Law Reports* (June 1986): 6771-6778.

2. Centers for Disease Control, *Morbidity and Mortality Weekly Report (MMWR)* (Washington, D.C.: Department of Health and Human Services, 1981-1986).

3. David L. Wing, "AIDS: The Legal Debate," *Personnel Journal* 65 (August 1986): 114-119.

4. Commerce Clearing House, "AIDS: Employer Rights and Responsibilities," Human Resources Management/Equal Employment Opportunity (December 1985): 1-47.

5. Copus and Ginsburg, "AFRAIDS."

6. Commerce Clearing House, "Employer Rights and Responsibilties."

7. Center for Disease Control, *MMWR*.

8. Wing, "The Legal Debate."

9. Ibid.

10. International Personnel Management Association (IPMA), "Employers Face the AIDS Issue," *IPMA News* (February 1986): 3-11.

11. Ibid.

12. IPMA, "AIDS Case Settled," *IPMA News* (January 1987): 6-7.

13. Wing, "The Legal Debate."

14. U.S. Department of Justice, Office of Legal Counsel, Memorandum for Ronald E. Robertson, General Counsel, Department of Health and Human Services, Re: Application of Section 504 of the Rehabilitation Act to Persons with AIDS, AIDS-Related Complex, or Infection with the AIDS Virus (June 20, 1986): 1.

15. Ibid., 2.

16. Wing, "The Legal Debate."

17. Copus and Ginsburg, "AFRAIDS."

18. M. P. Rowe, M. Russell-Einhorn, and M. A. Baker, "The Fear of AIDS." *The Harvard Business Review* 64, 4 (July-August 1986): 28-36.

19. IPMA, "Employers Face the AIDS Issue."

20. Rowe et al., "Fear of AIDS."

21. Commerce Clearing House, "Employer Rights and Responsibilites."

22. Wing, "The Legal Debate."

23. Ibid.

24. Wing, "The Legal Debate"; Commerce Clearing House, "Employer Rights and Responsibilities"; Rowe et al., "Fear of AIDS."

25. Neal R. Peirce, "AIDS: High Costs for Government?" *Public Administration Times* 8, 24 (December 15, 1985): 2.

26. Allan Halcrow, "AIDS in the Workplace," *Personnel Journal* 64 (October 1985): 10-11.

27. Commerce Clearing House, "Employer Rights and Responsibilities."

28. Peirce, "High Costs for Government?"

29. Commerce Clearing House, "Employer Rights and Responsibilities."

Drugs and Drug Testing in the Workplace

Paul L. Cary

Problems posed by substance-using employees

Few would argue with the statement that America's work force is the heart of the nation's economy and that the health of its members is a matter of national priority. However, the productive capacity and the health of the work force are at risk due to the increase in drug misuse. Public and private employers are becoming more aware that employee use and abuse of alcohol and drugs affects efficiency in many different ways.

A 1983 study found that substance using employees, when compared to nonusers, were:

1. Four times more likely to be involved in accidents at work
2. Six times more likely to be involved in accidents away from work
3. Two and one-half times more likely to be absent from work more than a week
4. Five times more likely to file a workmen's compensation claim
5. Repeatedly involved in grievance procedures
6. Receiving three times more sickness benefits
7. Functioning at 67% of their potential.

These findings obviously translate into lower productivity and higher medical costs.

Reprinted with permission from *Missouri Municipal Review*, July 1987.

A substance abuse program for employers

A comprehensive occupationally based substance abuse program has several major elements. While the specific components of each program will vary depending on the size and nature of the organization, employee characteristics, number of work sites, and managerial style, the key building blocks of a sound program should include: a policy, a training and education program, an enforcement program, and a treatment component.

1. The written policy should address the city's needs and concerns and affirm management's commitment to the health and safety of its employees. At the same time it should clearly state why substance abuse is unacceptable and specifically how the city will address and handle it.

2. Once a policy is created it should be communicated to all employees. This communication should detail revisions in work rules that have resulted from the substance abuse policy. This communication process can be complemented with education and training programs about chemical dependency. Training is particularly critical at the middle management level, where supervisory personnel should be encouraged to identify and refer problem workers. Managers need to thoroughly understand their role so as to prevent discrimination, maintain confidentiality, and periodically report the program's progress to higher management.

3. Enforcing a substance abuse policy demonstrates the city's resolve regarding the substance abuse program. In most cases conducting chemical tests to detect alcohol and drug use by employees will be the enforcement method chosen. Employing appropriate procedures, including obtaining informed consent, identification of specimens, careful handling of specimens, testing by a competent laboratory, and discretion in interpretation of results build confidence and respect in the program. Testing not only identifies covert substance use but also documents abstinence in recovering employees.

4. Assistance for the chemically dependent employee is the final component of a complete substance abuse program. The decision on how to assist the drug using employee will, of course, be prefaced by the decision of whether the employee will be terminated or treated for their drug use. The considerations that must be taken into account are: costs of treatment versus costs of training new employees, nature of the job, past employment record, whether the drug use can be shown to have taken place on the job, and severity of employee drug problem. If treatment is proposed, it is important to under-

stand that there are a variety of programs that have different philosophies, treatment methods, and degrees of expertise in treatment of different types of clients.

Elements of a complete substance abuse policy

The purpose of a substance abuse policy generally is to answer the questions "who," "what," "where," "when," and "why" while the purpose of a procedure is to answer "how." The policy statement should clearly and concisely define the city's position on substance misuse as it relates to the administration of the city while at the same time informing the employees about the city's position. The policy statement should provide guidelines to management and supervisory personnel for handling suspected substance abuse cases. The policy statement should specify:

1. The need for a substance misuse policy
2. The city's position on use and possession of substances on city premises and by individuals on-the-job at noncity sites
3. Responsibility of both the city and employees to ensure public trust, public safety, and fitness for duty
4. The city's position on off-the-job use and possession of illegal substances
5. Sanctions that will be taken if the policy is violated (how the sanctions will be enforced should appear in city procedures)
6. The city's position on rehabilitation and treatment opportunities
7. Provisions for confidentiality.

Employee drug testing

Within the context of an overall plan to reduce or eliminate the impact of substance abuse on a city, drug testing has become a major weapon. Drug testing has been used for years by crime laboratories, as an adjunct to law enforcement, by hospitals and drug therapy programs, where toxicity was suspected, and more recently by the U.S. military. However, recent surveys indicate that hundreds if not thousands of occupational settings around the United States are now using drug tests. According to surveys, the percentage of Fortune 500 companies screening employees or applicants for drug use rose from 3% to 30% between 1982 and 1985. Many other companies are contemplating similar actions. With this increase has followed a proportional increase in protests, particularly from unions and civil liberties advocates. Drug testing is a highly controversial issue.

The most common type of drug testing is associated with pre-employment applications. The routine testing of all applicants (or those to whom a job offer has been made) is an effort to contain the drug problem by excluding from employment those individuals that test positive for drugs. At the same time, pre-employment screens pose far fewer employee relations or potential legal difficulties.

Another approach is the routine testing of employees as part of an annual physical. This nondiscriminatory screening reaffirms that an individual is qualified to continue his or her work responsibilities without unusual risk to self, fellow workers, or society. This strategy also seeks to reduce employee relations problems surrounding testing because the policy can be made to apply to every employee in a company, including the chief executive officer.

Sample drug policy statement

The city recognizes that the state of an employee's health affects his/her job performance, the kind of work he/she can perform, and may affect his/her opportunities for continued employment. The city also recognizes that alcohol and drug abuse ranks as one of the major health problems in the world. It is the intent of this policy to provide employees with the city's viewpoint on behavioral/medical disorders, to encourage an enlightened viewpoint toward these disorders, and to provide guidelines for consistent handling throughout the city regarding alcohol and substance usage situations.

The policy   The city intends to give the same consideration to persons with chemical (alcohol or other drugs) misuse patterns or dependencies as it does to employees having other diseases. The company is concerned with only those situations where the use of alcohol and other drugs seriously interferes with any employee's health and job performance, adversely affects the job performance of other employees, or is considered serious enough as to be detrimental to the city's business. There is no intent to intrude upon the private lives of employees.

Early recognition and treatment of chemical dependency problems is important for successful rehabilitation; service to the public; and reduced personal, family, and social disruption. The city supports sound treatment efforts: an employee's job will not be jeopardized for conscientiously seeking assistance. Constructive disciplinary measures may be used to provide motivation to seek assistance. Normal city benefits, such as sick leave and the group medical plan, are available to give help in the rehabilitation process.

Legal drugs (including alcohol)   The use of any legally obtained drug, including alcohol, to the point where such use adversely affects the employee's job performance, is prohibited. This prohibition covers arriving on city premises under the effects of any drug that adversely affects the employee's job performance, including the use of prescribed drugs under medical direction. Where physician-directed

Probable cause/reasonable suspicion testing is usually conducted only under certain circumstances. One circumstance would be when an employee's supervisor has a reasonable suspicion that the employee is intoxicated or under the influence of drugs or alcohol. "Reasonable suspicion" is a belief based upon articulable observations sufficient to lead a prudent supervisor to suspect that the employee is under the influence of drugs or alcohol (i.e. slurred speech, glassy eyes, poor coordination and/or reflexes, alcohol on breath, etc.) Another circumstance that would warrant probable cause testing would be when an employee is found in possession of an illicit or banned drug or alcohol or is arrested for the same out-

---

use of drugs adversely affects job performance, it is in the best interest of the employee, coworkers, and the city that sick leave be used. Any employee engaging in the misuse of alcoholic beverages on city premises is subject to disciplinary action, up to and including termination.

Illegal drugs

1. Illegal drugs, for the purpose of this policy, include (a) drugs that are not legally obtainable and (b) drugs that are legally obtainable but have been obtained illegally.
2. The sale, possession, purchase, transfer, or use of illegal drugs by employees on city premises or while on city business is prohibited. Arriving on city premises under the influence of any drug to the extent that job performance is adversely affected is prohibited. This prohibition applies to any or all forms of drugs whose sale, purchase, transfer, possession, or use is prohibited or restricted by law.

    a. Any employee engaging in the sale, purchase, transfer, possession, or use of illegal drugs on city premises or while on city business is subject to disciplinary action, up to and including termination.
    b. Any employee engaging in the sale, purchase, transfer, possession, or use of illegal drugs off-the-job, which could jeopardize the safety of other employees, the public or city equipment is subject to disciplinary action, up to and including termination.
    c. Any employee arrested for the sale, purchase, transfer, possession, or use of illegal drugs off-the-job, may be considered in violation of this policy. In deciding what action to take, the city will consider the nature of the charges, the employee's present job assignment, the employee's record with the city, and other factors relative to the impact of the employee's arrest upon the ability of the city to continue to conduct business.

side of work. Finally, a serious accident or incident in which safety precautions were violated or carelessness is attributed to the event could be grounds for drug testing.

Random drug testing is without doubt the most controversial. However, random drug testing is being conducted when the use of drugs poses obvious hazards to the public safety or the safety of fellow employees. Currently this type of testing has been limited to occupational areas such as police officers, fire personnel and transportation industry employees. Policies that involve random testing have met with strong protest and opposition on many occasions.

Lastly, predetermined testing can be used when monitoring employees during rehabilitation or treatment for drug use. In this instance, monitoring is often limited to a specific time period.

Drug testing: Choosing a laboratory

After a city decides to engage in a drug testing program, one of the first challenges is selecting a laboratory. Generally, two major types of laboratories are available. First are the large national or regional reference laboratories that offer drug testing services as well as a broad range of other clinical testing. Second are the smaller, specialized laboratories, often located in a local hospital, that perform drug testing and offer regionalized service through the mail or courier services.

The following list represents important considerations and activities in selecting a drug testing facility:

1. Require the laboratory to specify the type of accreditation or license under which it operates.
2. Perform an on-site inspection of the facilities.
3. Review the laboratory's procedures manual.
4. Consider analytical techniques used and policies for confirming test results.
5. Review staff qualifications.
6. Examine quality control programs.
7. Check additional service features such as rapid turnaround time, accessible technical assistance and expert testimony.

Drug testing

Urine tests are by far the most common tests used to detect employee drug use. Blood, saliva and breath have been used for occupational drug testing but are generally reserved for specific situations or limited testing procedures.

As in any forensic analysis or medico-legal examination where accuracy of results is crucial by virtue of its ramifications, confirmation of the original result is essential. Because of the potential impact of drug testing results on employees, it is essential that both rigorous screening methods and conclusive confirmation methods be incorporated into a drug testing program. A confirmation policy adds a greater level of fairness and certainty to the drug testing process while at the same time minimizing the legal issues concerning the validity of test results. The policy also enhances employee morale and confidence in the drug testing process.

The reporting of drug test results must be rapid, accurate, and confidential. Results can be reported by telephone, by mail, or both. Some laboratories have provisions for sending the data by electronic means. Generally, laboratories should be able to provide results within 48 to 72 hours after specimen pickup. One designated person within a city should receive all drug test reports and be responsible for notification of city officials who absolutely need to know the test results as defined by company policy. If results are sent by mail, the envelope should be clearly marked confidential and addressed to the person authorized to receive the results. If results are to be telephoned, the person receiving the results must be familiar enough with drug nomenclature to transcribe results accurately. As a rule, telephone reporting is less secure and more prone to mistakes. Laboratory reports should not appear in an employee's personnel file. These records should be segregated or filed only in medical files.

Legal issues in employee drug detection programs

The question of whether drug testing violates an individual's constitutional rights must be considered in light of three basic legal principles: the right to privacy and freedom from unreasonable search and seizure, protection against self-incrimination, and due process.

1. *Right to privacy/unreasonable search and seizure.* The U.S. Supreme Court has consistently held that the right to privacy protected by the Constitution extends only to protection against governmental intrusion. According to the court, employees do not have a reasonable expectation of privacy in the employer/employee relationship. Although the Supreme Court has not had occasion to rule directly on the question of urine testing, it has held that drug users could be excluded from certain types of employment. Some lower courts have held that employee urine tests do not violate the employee's right to freedom from unreasonable search and seizure and that such tests do not require the issuance of a warrant. However, the courts have put some limits on when such tests can be conducted.

2. Self-incrimination: The U.S. Supreme Court has ruled that blood and breath tests do not violate a person's legal protec-

tion against self-incrimination. Therefore, it is reasonable to assume that testing an employee's urine would also not violate this right.

3. Due process: Fundamental fairness requires that employers inform employees that urine drug testing may be required under certain circumstances as a condition of their employment. Additionally, employees should be clearly apprised if a urine test result is positive. In most cases, an employee will be entitled to a hearing before discipline can be imposed.

Routine or random testing of employees will probably be upheld only if it can be shown that such testing is necessary to ensure public safety. This would permit the testing of bus drivers, police officers, firefighters, and others in jobs requiring protection of public safety. In other situations, testing should be limited to those cases where there is reasonable suspicion based on specific objective facts that an employee is using illegal substances. "Reasonable suspicion" sufficient to support the ordering of a urine test would include on-the-job accidents, slurred speech, or the employee's arrest for drug use or sale. Additionally, the courts will probably uphold tests that are ordered as part of a routine, periodic physical examination required of all employees. Routine or even random testing of employees who have previously faced disciplinary action for drug-related offenses may also be upheld by the courts. However, this latter testing could not go on indefinitely, but would have to be limited to a reasonable period of time.

Job applicants may be required to submit to urine testing. However, to guard against charges of discrimination, it is best to test all applicants, or at least all applicants for particular jobs, rather than to test randomly.

Employees must be informed of any rule regarding drug testing and of the possible penalties resulting from positive test results. While the necessity of giving job applicants advance notice is not as clear, this would seem to be preferred as a matter of fundamental fairness and as a method of assuring the applicants that the testing is being conducted in a nondiscriminatory manner.

Employers' rights and liabilities

An employer has a duty to protect other employees and the general public if their safety is placed in jeopardy by a drug abusing employee. However, the need for immediate termination will vary from situation to situation and will depend on other alternatives available to the employer. One alternative is to establish a rehabilitation program for employees found to be using drugs. In addition to assisting the employee, such efforts will stand the employer in good stead if it later becomes necessary to terminate the employee.

Recommendations for public employers

1. Public employers must respect constitutional guarantees when developing drug-testing and control programs. Insure that employee rights to privacy, due process, and unreasonable search and seizure are protected unless there is a compelling state interest.
2. When testing must be done, do it in private, and respect the wishes of the individual to the extent possible.
3. Test only for cause. Confirm any positive result. Insure opportunity to appeal any decision that adversely impacts the employee.
4. Insure that a well-established laboratory is selected to conduct testing. Investigate its references.
5. Testing is more likely to be supported by the courts if the purpose of the test is to corroborate other evidence, if it is a part of an employment inquiry, and if it is based on reasonable suspicion. The courts are less likely to support random testing, and testing as a part of a criminal investigation, unless there is reasonable suspicion.
6. Applicants do not have a property interest in the positions applied for. Drug testing can be included in the preemployment physical.
7. Employees in positions that have a safety interest may have fewer rights afforded them than employees in positions not involving a safety interest.
8. Due process requires that public employees know of policies that may adversely affect them. Labor organizations should participate in developing the framework for testing, regardless of whether labor supports it. All policies should be written.
9. Adverse actions that a public employer can take should be clear. Labor organizations should be familiar with them so they can properly represent members, and so that modifications or improvements can be sought during bargaining.
10. Employers should insure that their health benefit plans have drug-treatment provisions.
11. Confidentiality is most important. Distribute information on a need-to-know basis. On the other hand, confirmed findings must not be concealed. Avoid being a contributor to a negligence action that may result if an employee who is a drug user causes harm to others.
12. Weigh discipline versus treatment. Must discipline and discharge result from confirmed tests? Is it not cheaper to rehabilitate than to recruit, select, and train, a replacement? Keep in mind, too, that referral to treatment is less likely to lead to litigation.

Source: William A. Nowlin, "Employee Drug Testing: Issues for Public Employers and Labor Organizations," *Journal of Collective Negotiations in the Public Sector,* vol. 16, no. 4 (1987): 305–306. ©1987, Baywood Publishing Company. Reprinted with permission.

In public-sector employment where the employee is involved in law enforcement, off-the-job drug use is generally accepted as grounds for discharge regardless of any effect on the employee's ability to perform the job. In other areas, a relationship between the offense and the job must usually be established. This relationship might include the following: potential harm to members of the public or to the city's reputation; inability to perform the duties of the job or appear at work; or refusal, reluctance, or inability of other employees to work with the drug abuser.

The greatest liability would result from inaction by a city that is aware of a drug abuse problem if this inaction resulted in the drug abuser harming another employee or a member of the public. Another source of liability is if the city does not respect employee's rights to confidentiality regarding the test results. Therefore, test results should be communicated only to those who need to know them.

Test results upheld in court

Testing does not necessarily have to be performed by medical personnel for the results to be upheld in court. However, the person conducting the test must be trained in its use.

While employee urine testing is relatively new, both courts and labor arbitrators have consistently permitted the use of drug test results as evidence in cases where the following had occurred: the employer had a reasonable rule regarding drug screening, the rule had been communicated to the employee, and the rule spelled out explicitly the circumstances in which urine would be tested and the penalty if drug use was found. Whether the test results alone are sufficient for legal purposes depends on a variety of factors. In general, it is best to have all test results confirmed and to introduce other testimony to support the city's position. A combination of medical evidence and lay testimony provides the best assurance that an employee's discipline or discharge will be upheld in court.

The following evidence will strengthen a court case in which urine test results are used:

1. Evidence that employees were informed of the rule regarding drug use and of the possible penalties that could be imposed if drug use was found.
2. A demonstrated relationship between drug use and the employee's duties, the employer's mission or reputation, danger to public safety, or danger to the safety of fellow employees.
3. A showing that similar punishments were routinely handed out for similar offenses.
4. Clear procedures and records showing the "chain of custody" of the urine specimen tested.

5. Confirmation of all test results, preferably by use of an alternative scientific method, or at a minimum, evidence that positive results have been found on more than one occasion involving the same employee.

Employee drug education and treatment

No effort to combat drug abuse in the workplace is complete without employee and employer drug education. Drug education is both a form of prevention and means for involving employees in early intervention. Employee education can be accomplished in a variety of ways including: guest speakers, face-to-face employer-employee presentations, educational material (wall posters, newsletters, direct mailing, payroll pamphlets, etc.) and extended retreats for key employee training, such as supervisors. Prevention, which is a major goal of drug education, is the most cost effective way of alleviating drug problems, and it is in everyone's best interest to develop a comprehensive drug education plan.

Substance abuse is said to affect between 3% and 25% of all American workers. There is little doubt that if a drug testing program is initiated, positive test results will be forthcoming. The time to decide what to do about employees testing positive for drugs is before the testing program begins. The two choices an employer has are termination or treatment. Most employers have chosen to permit each employee at least one positive drug test without punitive action, provided that the employee receives appropriate help.

If treatment is chosen there are many different approaches. Large cities may have internal employee assistance programs. A city can use existing private or public agencies. Rehabilitation or counseling may be directly tied to the city or employees may be required to procure their own services. Regardless of the format, a good treatment program should be designed to restore physical health, produce permanent changes in behavior and guide the restructuring in the individual's perception of himself and his area of control.

With the availability of new drug detection technology, employee drug testing programs have become almost commonplace and have demonstrated a positive effect in reducing drug use by early identification of affected employees. Employers considering the use of drug testing to combat substance abuse should realize the complex issues associated with such a decision. However, no city needs to accept substance abuse as a cost of doing business. The ability to provide a drug-free work environment for other employees and the safety of the public is a goal that is in the best interest of all involved.

Smoking in the Workplace: A Growing Dilemma

Richard H. Deane

Involuntary smoking is a cause of disease, including lung cancer, in healthy nonsmokers.[1] With that conclusion from his 1986 Annual Report, the Surgeon General of the United States initiated what may be the final chapter in the workplace smoking debate. This debate focuses on balancing the rights of smokers and nonsmokers in the work environment. Thus managers—caught in the middle—are forced to address the salient issues and develop a plan of action.

Health and productivity issues

The health hazards of smoking have been recognized for many years. Only in recent years, however, have the hazards of "passive" or "secondhand" smoke become clear. Statistically speaking, for most adults the greatest exposure to passive smoking occurs in the workplace. Such exposure may result in only minor physical discomfort, but it can also result in reduced lung functioning and cancer.[2]

In addition to direct health hazards, passive exposure to tobacco smoke can result in considerable indirect costs to employers. These costs include absenteeism, increased insurance premiums, lost wages and productivity, property damage, cleaning and other maintenance costs, and employee morale problems. One study purports to document and quantify these indirect costs at $4,611 per employee per year.[3] Although other research challenges the viability of accurately measuring these indirect costs, it is clear that workplace smoking has serious negative consequences in the work environment.[4]

Legal issues

Negotiations between employers and employees have historically been the primary basis for resolving workplace smoking issues. In recent years, however, non-smokers have increasingly turned to courts and legislatures in the hope of supplanting this informal negotiation process.

Constitutional and common law issues   In the absence of specific legislation, the courts have been reluctant to invoke the constitution or common law to resolve grievances involving smoking in the workplace. Perhaps the most notable counterexample is the New Jersey case *Shimp v. New Jersey Bell Telephone*, which required an employer to restrict smoking in the workplace.[5] Most often, however, lawsuits to require a "smoke-free" work environment based on the constitution or common law have met with little success.[6] To date, no federal legislation has been interpreted to limit workplace smoking. The Occupational Safety and Health Act has been asserted, without success, as a basis for restricting workplace smoking.[7] It is argued that various federal and state statutes prohibiting discrimination against the handicapped provide a basis for restricting smoking in the workplace. While such statutes might provide support to an employee who is hypersensitive to tobacco smoke, they would not provide grounds for the vast majority of non-smoking employees who are merely irritated by secondhand smoke.[8]

It is important to note that most common law claims in the courts have not been supported with *clear* evidence that passive smoke in the workplace is unreasonably hazardous. This has been a fatal weakness in most cases filed by nonsmokers. The recently released report of the U.S. Surgeon General may, in fact, provide the necessary support for a common law cause of action in future cases.

Even less judicial support exists for the rights of smokers in the workplace. Employers apparently have the right to discriminate against smokers by restricting smoking to selected areas of the workplace, banning smoking entirely in the workplace, or restricting hiring to nonsmokers. Furthermore, disciplinary actions against employees for violating nonsmoking rules would appear to be enforceable.[9] An employer's inconsistent application of sanctions against nonsmokers would, of course, be suspect and therefore subject to closer judicial review. In short, there is no inherent, fundamental "right" to smoke in the private workplace. Thus, such a fallacious premise cannot be used as justification for employer inaction in adopting workplace smoking rules.

To summarize, the courts have thus far been reluctant to intervene in the private workplace by ordering restrictions on smoking, especially where the employer has made "reasonable" efforts to accommodate nonsmokers and smokers alike. The employer's common law duty apparently is to provide a reasonably safe workplace, not one that is necessarily "pleasant." However, as the dangers of secondhand smoke are increasingly documented, the courts are likely to become more active in this issue.

Legislative actions   Proponents of workplace smoking restrictions have been active in lobbying for state and local laws. A number of state laws and local ordinances that address the issue of workplace smoking have, in fact, been enacted. Depending on interpretation, there are about 10 state laws and at least 60 local laws (many of which are in California) directed at public and workplace smoking. While these laws vary considerably in terms of coverage, they tend to replace employer decision making with directed actions. The weakest of these laws requires that employers merely develop and post written rules addressing smoking in the workplace. Stronger laws presume that nonsmoking should be the norm in the workplace. The most stringent of these laws dictate the specific types of work areas—such as restrooms—that must be designated as nonsmoking.

Few lawsuits to date have challenged state and local laws restricting workplace smoking. Substantial enforcement problems as well as constitutional challenges may arise as the laws are implemented. For example, certain laws require employers to make "good faith" efforts to establish policies and accommodate nonsmokers. Such wording may be challenged on the basis of vagueness, that is, the employer has no specific direction in terms of legislative intention. However, as a general rule, the courts have been quite willing to enforce workplace smoking rules enacted by an employer.

In addition to increased judicial intervention, the report of the U.S Surgeon General could also have a strong impact on lobbying efforts for tougher workplace smoking laws. Now that state and local governments have clear evidence that secondhand smoke is dangerous, additional laws that restrict public smoking are likely to be forthcoming.

Labor union position   Interestingly, workplace smoking has long been the subject of the collective bargaining process. Historically, it was not uncommon for an employer to allow smoking privileges for white-collar workers while restricting those for blue-collar workers. In most cases the justification for such blue-collar smoking restrictions was workplace safety or productivity. Workplace smoking as a collective bargaining issue arose as a negative reaction to such policies. The arbitration process and the courts have generally upheld any such workplace smoking restrictions that appear in collective bargaining agreements.

In today's work environment, union members themselves have widely differing views on workplace smoking. For this reason, workplace smoking restrictions do not appear to be an important union issue.

Developing a plan of action

Today, company policies addressing workplace smoking vary widely, due partly to the fact that smoking is a relatively new employee relations issue facing management:

At one end of the spectrum, most companies have simply not formally addressed the smoking issue, thereby encouraging employees to "work out problems themselves." This failure to address the issue of workplace smoking is, in fact, a policy, albeit a bad one, in light of the growing evidence of the dangers of secondhand smoke.

About 30% of U.S. companies have instituted some type of ban—partial or full—on workplace smoking. Overall, the results of these policies are encouraging.

At the other end of the spectrum, a very small number of companies hire only nonsmokers. This practice is questionable because of the large number of potentially good employees (30% of the work force) that are thus eliminated from employment consideration.

A situational approach would seem to be most appropriate in developing a smoking policy. That is, no one single policy would appear to be "best" for all companies (or perhaps not even all divisions of the same company).

In addition to general employee health considerations, the following factors should be considered in developing a smoking policy:

Management attitude   Any policy must have top management support.

Company products   Certain products or services, such as food production, may suggest the need for a stronger smoking restriction policy.

Company processes   Some production processes—painting operations, for example—obviously dictate strong smoking restrictions.

Employee attitudes   How do employees feel about strong smoking restrictions?

Customer relations   Do employees have a high degree of customer contact? How will a smoking policy impact customers, vendors, and visitors?

Legal requirements   Any policy (or nonpolicy) must be in conformance with all legal requirements. A legal requirement can often offer a springboard for action for the company.

Flexibility in work assignments   Is there flexibility to reassign workers to work groups based on smoking preferences? Can workers choose work groups based on smoking and other factors?

Physical layout of work space   Certain "open area" work environments make smoking an acute problem. Is there flexibility to redesign the work space to accommodate smoking?

Ventilation of work facility   What is the current ventilation capacity at the facility? Are improvements in the general ventilation system feasible? Would local ventilation, such as desktop air cleaners, be helpful?

Sample smoking policy at XYZ corporation

Purpose and background   The purpose of this document is to outline the XYZ Corporation's policy on smoking in the workplace. This policy was developed by the XYZ Smoking Committee, after soliciting written input from all employees and conducting open hearings that all employees were invited to attend.

The Surgeon General of the United States has declared that smoking represents the greatest health threat to the American worker. The evidence is clear. Smoking represents a significant risk not only to the smoker, but to the nonsmoker in the work environment too. The intent of this policy is not only to foster the safety and health of our employees but to accommodate the rights of smokers and nonsmokers alike. While the policy does not totally prohibit smoking on the XYZ premises, it does restrict smoking to certain areas. We must constantly strive to find a reasonable accommodation between those who do not smoke and those who do.

General policy statement   It is the policy of XYZ to protect the rights of smokers and nonsmokers in company buildings and facilities. When these rights conflict, management and employees should try to find a reasonable compromise. When this is not possible, the rights of the nonsmoker shall prevail.

Smoking is *always* totally banned at XYZ in all areas where:

1. Flammable or otherwise hazardous materials are stored or in use
2. Computers (not including desktop personal computers) are operated
3. Sensitive equipment is operated
4. Critical records and supplies would be exposed to a hazard from fire, ashes, or smoke
5. Combustible fumes can collect.

Smoking will ordinarily be banned at XYZ in common work areas, such as photocopy rooms, restrooms, libraries, first aid stations, lobbies, elevators, and stairwells.

Smoking is prohibited in customer reception areas and any other areas used by customers. Customers are requested not to smoke in these areas.

Insurance   Does a smoking policy have a direct or indirect effect on a company's insurance rates? (Certain insurance companies offer discount health insurance rates to firms with restrictive smoking policies.)

Union agreements   Would a smoking policy be affected by a union agreement?

Employees may designate their own private office as smoking or nonsmoking. Signs to identify "No Smoking" areas are available from the personnel office.

In work areas shared by two or more persons, an effort will be made to accommodate individual preferences. On request, managers shall attempt to separate persons who smoke from those who do not.

Smoking is permitted in company vehicles only on the consent of all occupants of the vehicle.

Smoking is not permitted in enclosed meeting rooms and training rooms.

In XYZ cafeterias, employee lounges, and auditoriums, smoking is permitted only in designated areas. These areas will be established when proper ventilation is available.

Employees and visitors are expected to honor the smoking and nonsmoking designations and to be considerate of other persons in the vicinity.

An employee smoking within a designated smoking area must use a "smokeless" ashtray. It is the responsibility of the employee to purchase the ashtray and to keep it in good working order. A listing of acceptable smokeless ashtrays has been compiled by the XYZ Smoking Policy Committee and is available through the personnel office.

Enforcement   XYZ intends to fully and consistently enforce the smoking policy described in this document. Enforcement is the responsibility of all employees at XYZ. It is suggested that resolution of policy violations be informally handled among employees and immediate supervisors. If the policy is repeatedly violated, employees may contact their company grievance officer. The same disciplinary procedures and penalties apply to violations of the smoking policy as apply to any other company policies. See the XYZ Personnel Manual for details.

This document shall be incorporated into the XYZ employee handbook.

Education and training   Information and counseling on the dangers of smoking or smoking cessation programs is available from the personnel office. The company will pay 50% of the cost for any employee wishing to attend an approved smoking cessation program.

Although the foregoing checklist is not exhaustive, it does provide a good starting point for policy planning. The list is not exhaustive simply because each company has too many unique, local characteristics that could impact the development of a smoking restriction policy.

Elements of a smoking policy

The follow should be included in a firm's workplace smoking policy:

Statement of purpose and background   Identifies the reasons why a smoking policy is being implemented (health hazards, dangers, legal requirements, and so forth).

General policy statement   Includes a general statement that summarizes the approach the company is taking, for example, nonsmoking is the "norm." It should also identify:

1. Special areas where smoking is absolutely banned (for example, around certain hazardous or sensitive equipment, food preparation areas)
2. General rules for common work areas, meeting rooms, auditoriums, lounges, restrooms, customer reception areas, hallways, and private offices.

Enforcement   Outlines enforcement responsibilities and procedures, including an opening statement regarding the intention of management to consistently enforce the policy.

Education and training   Highlights the availability of company-furnished information on the dangers of smoking and smoking cessation programs.

Carrying out the policy

Like any change in managerial policy, carrying out smoking restrictions in the workplace will not always be easy. Bearing this in mind, smoking policies must be implemented with deliberation and care. Here are a few suggestions:

1. Get employees, including management, involved in the planning stages of the policy. An employee committee of smokers and nonsmokers may be helpful at the policy formulation stage.
2. Pledge the support of top management to the program. Make sure employees know that top management is involved.
3. If appropriate, inform employees that the policy has union support.
4. Stress the important health reasons for the policy.
5. Promote nonsmoking as the norm where conflict arises.

6. Do not attempt to put a smoking policy into action overnight. There should be a reasonable lead time between the announcement of the program and the program's implementation.
7. Make sure the details of the policy are clearly stated in writing. Send a copy of the written policy to every employee.
8. Conduct meetings with middle managers and supervisors to review and discuss the policy before implementation.
9. Discuss the smoking policy with each newly hired employee during orientation. For new employees who smoke, point out the general areas where smoking is permitted.

Remember that accommodation and communication represent half the solution; consistency in enforcement represents the other half.[10]

Notes

1. U.S. Department of Health and Human Services, *The Health Consequences of Involuntary Smoking: A Report of the Surgeon General* (Washington, D.C.: 16 December 1986, prepublication edition).
2. Office of Technology Assessment, U.S. Congress, *Passive Smoking in the Workplace: Selected Issues* (Washington, D.C.: Government Printing Office, May 1986), 15.
3. William L. Weis, "Can You Afford to Hire Smokers?" *Personnel Administrator*, May 1981, 27.
4. Lewis C. Solomon, "The Other Side of the Smoking Worker Controversy," *Personnel Administrator*, March 1983, 72–73.
5. *Shimp v. New Jersey Bell Telephone Company*, 368 A.2d 408, 411 (New Jersey Supreme Court Ch. Div. 1976).
6. *Gasper v. Louisiana Stadium and Exposition District*, 418 F. Supp. 716 (E.D. La. 1976), aff'd, 577 F.2d 897 (5th Cir. 1978). This case did not involve a workplace issue specifically, but is perhaps the leading case addressing the constitutional issues of a smoke-free environment.
7. 29 U.S.C. Section 651 et seq. See *Federal Employees for Non-Smokers' Rights v. United States*, 446 F. Supp. 181 (D.D.C.), aff'd, 598 F.2d 310 (D.C. Cir. 1978), cert. denied, 444 U.S. 926 (1979).
8. 29 U.S.C. Section 701 et seq. See *Vickers v. Veterans Administration*, 549 F. Supp. 85 (W.D. Wash. 1982).
9. Ibid.
10. American Lung Association, "Taking Executive Action" (1985). See also the "Freedom From Smoking" program (1986) offered by the American Lung Association, New York, New York.

Sexual Harassment: New Approaches for a Changed Environment

Robert K. Robinson, Delaney J. Kirk, and James D. Powell

Anyone feel the tremors? The ground is definitely shifting in the area of sexual harassment. Two convergent trends are dictating that employers pay much more attention to this volatile issue. Both an expanding definition of what constitutes harassment and an increasing unwillingness of individuals (especially women) to tolerate harassment are harbingers of change.

This article will define "hostile environment" sexual harassment in terms of the 1986 Supreme Court decision and explore its implications for future employer liability suits. Additionally, the results of a survey conducted by the authors will be presented, which indicate that sexual harassment is a widespread problem and that attitudes may be shifting from passive acceptance toward active resistance. Finally, the impact of the *Vinson* ruling on traditional employer defenses against sexual harassment complaints will be examined and recommendations will be provided for reducing liability in such instances.

A changed definition of harassment

On June 19, 1986, the Supreme Court reached a landmark decision that greatly expands protection for working women against sexual harassment in the workplace. The case, *Meritor Savings Bank vs. Vinson,* marked the first time that the high court had ruled on the issue of "hostile environment" claims of sexual harassment. With this ruling, the Court opened the door to a potentially greater number of sexual harassment claims.

Reprinted by permission, *SAM Advanced Management Journal,* Autumn, 1987, Society for Advancement of Management, Cincinnati, OH 45206.

Background of the case   Mechelle Vinson began working for
Capital City Federal Savings and Loan Association (later Meritor
Savings Bank, FSB) on September 9, 1974. On November 1, 1978, she
was terminated by her employer for excessive use of sick leave—she
had failed to come to work since September 21, 1978. During her four
years with Capital Savings, Ms. Vinson had received four promotions—from teller-trainee through assistant branch manager. Just
prior to her termination she had been told that she was scheduled to
be promoted to branch manager in December of that year. In her
testimony, Ms. Vinson stated that she received all of these promotions strictly on merit—a point on which the court agreed. There
was, therefore, no evidence of tangible benefits being withheld from
Ms. Vinson.

On November 22, 1978, Ms. Vinson filed a complaint with the
Equal Employment Opportunity Commission (EEOC) alleging that
she had left her former employer because of the hostile work environment created by the sexual advances of her supervisor. According to Ms. Vinson, her supervisor began making sexual demands of
her shortly after she completed her probationary period as a teller-
trainee. In response to these advances, she agreed to have sexual
intercourse with her supervisor some 40 or 50 times during the next
two years. The supervisor also allegedly persisted in fondling and
touching her during working hours in the presence of her co-workers. Ms. Vinson stated that her supervisor's sexual demands did not
stop until she began going with a steady boyfriend in 1977.

Even though Ms. Vinson's employer, Capital City Federal Savings and Loan, had a company policy prohibiting sexual harassment
and a procedure for reporting violations, Ms. Vinson made no formal complaint. According to her testimony, she was afraid to use
the complaint procedure because she feared reprisal from her supervisor. Her employer contended that unless it knew about the
misconduct, it could not take corrective action.

The U.S. District Court, District of Columbia, the court which
had original jurisdiction in the case, decided in favor of the defen-
dant (Capital City Savings) on February 1980. Following conven-
tion, the District Court held that the employer should not be liable
for the sexual harassment of its supervisors unless it knew about
the incident. The court agreed that the employer could hardly be
expected to correct the situation without first being aware of its
existence. This rationale had been used in previous court decisions
involving unreported incidents of sexual harassment.

It should be noted that even prior to the *Vinson* case, notice by
the employee was not the sole criterion for alleviating employers
from liability. If the sexual harassment was so blatant or pervasive
that the employer *should* have known of its existence, then the employer would be liable. This condition is commonly referred to as

constructive knowledge. In this particular instance, the District Court found no evidence of constructive knowledge.

The District Court further held that Ms. Vinson was not a victim of sexual harassment, even if she was pressured to have sex with her supervisor, because that relationship was voluntarily entered into and had no connection with her employment opportunities. In short, the District Court felt that Ms. Vinson had no grounds for suit under Title VII of the Civil Rights Act (1964).

The U.S. Court of Appeals, District of Columbia Circuit, saw the case in an entirely different light. On January 25, 1985, the Court of Appeals held that Ms. Vinson was indeed a victim of sexual harassment and, therefore, sex discrimination. That court contended that sexual harassment is not limited only to those *quid pro quo* incidents that involve the loss of tangible employment benefits (raises, advancement, promotion, etc.). Sexual harassment may also involve sex-oriented conditions in the workplace that result in an intimidating or abusive psychological and emotional work environment. Because Title VII prohibits arbitrary barriers to sexual equality in the workplace with respect to "compensation, terms, conditions, or privileges of employment," some federal courts have interpreted "conditions" to include the state of psychological well-being in the workplace. For example, if a supervisor is causing a female worker to feel embarrassed or ashamed because of unwelcomed sexual advances, and does not create a similar offensive environment for male employees, that supervisor has discriminated against the female worker because of her sex. The supervisor, through his action, has created a hostile environment for the female employee.

Using the EEOC's *Guidelines on Discrimination Because of Sex,* which broadly defines employer liability, the Court of Appeals further held that an employer was absolutely responsible for its supervisors' sexual harassment of its employees, in *all* instances, even if the employer had no knowledge of the harassment. Thus, even though the employer had policies prohibiting such behavior and a procedure by which employees could report violations of those policies, the employer was still ultimately liable. In other words, the existence of a company policy against sexual harassment was not a defense in court.

The Supreme Court's decision   Based upon the two lower court decisions, the U.S. Supreme Court heard the *Vinson* case on final appeal in March 1985. A decision followed on June 9, 1986, with the following key findings presented by the court:

1. Hostile environment claims of sexual harassment are a form of sex discrimination actionable under Title VII.

2. The "voluntariness" of an employee's participation in a sexual relationship with an employer's agents or supervisory personnel does not preclude that employee from filing a claim of sexual harassment. What is at issue is not that the employee gave in to the sexual demands of her or his supervisor, but whether or not those demands were "unwelcomed."
3. Employers are *not* automatically liable for sexual harassment committed by their supervisors [contrary to what the Court of Appeals contended]. However, the mere existence of a grievance procedure, policies against sexual harassment, or an employee's failure to use that procedure does not insulate that employer from liability.

Impact on employers   The most likely result of the *Vinson* decision will be an increase in the number of sexual harassment suits using hostile environment claims. The significant problem confronting employers in such cases is defining the conditions that constitute psychological or emotional abuses in the workplace. Under *quid pro quo* sexual harassment claims—the other form of sexual harassment—an employer could readily defend itself by showing that the complainant had received equal economic treatment. The plaintiff, of course, would attempt to show the loss or threatened loss of an employment benefit.

Because hostile environment claims are *not* rooted in such tangibles as promotions, raises, or other employment benefits, it will be difficult for an employer to show that the aggrieved employee has suffered no mental harm or anguish. This makes employer defenses more tenuous.

On the other hand, the employee has to establish only three conditions in order to bring a hostile environment suit against an employer.

1. The employee belongs to a protected group—the employee is either a man or a woman.
2. The employee was subject to unwelcome sexual harassment. Under EEOC regulations, harassment is broadly defined as "sexual advances, requests for sexual favors, and other verbal or physical conduct of a sexual nature ... " To be unwelcomed, the employee must show that he or she did not encourage the harassment and regarded the conduct as undesirable or offensive.
3. The harassment complained of was based upon sex. The plaintiff must show that but for her [or his] sex, she [he] would not have been subjected to the sexual harassment.

As an interesting point of information, the courts hold that sexual harassment does not occur under circumstances where a supervisor makes sexual advances to employees of both sexes. In a legal sense, if men and women were accorded like treatment, the employee's sex was not the determinant of the harassment.

Though the Supreme Court held that employers were not absolutely liable for the conduct of their agents, it did not provide sufficient guidance as to when they are and are not liable. The question of employer liability remains shrouded in ambiguity. All that is evident is that policies, grievance procedures, and ignorance of the misconduct are not sufficient, *by themselves*, to qualify as an employer defense. Nevertheless, the employer should not automatically assume they are useless.

Finally, an employee's apparent tolerance or acceptance of a supervisor's sexually oriented behavior does not protect the employer. The mere fact that an employee has consented to sexual demands by her or his supervisor is no proof (according to the Court) that the sexual demands were "welcomed" by the employee. The length of time during which these sexual liaisons take place seems to be equally irrelevant in the eyes of the court. Vinson's alleged sexual relations with her boss continued from May 1975 to 1977 and had ended nearly a year before she filed a formal complaint. As long as a supervisor or any other agent of an employer is engaging in any sexual activity with an employee, the employer faces the threat of a sexual harassment suit at some future date. The next issue is the prevalence of sexual harassment.

How widespread is sexual harassment?
In the last few years sexual harassment has become a very real problem that shows no sign of disappearing. Cornell University discovered in a survey of 155 respondents that 92 percent believed sexual harassment was a serious problem and 70 percent had actually experienced sexual harassment.

In an October 1986 survey by the authors, of business and professional women ages 23 to 77, 71 percent of the women reported being sexually harassed on the job. Of these women, only 33 percent

Table 1. Responses of women surveyed who had experienced sexual harassment. (Respondents were instructed to check all that applied.)

Response	%
Embarrassed	58
Angry	50
Confused	33
Ashamed	25
Guilty	17
Intimidated	8
Indifferent	8

reported the harassment, although the majority felt angry and embarrassed. Table 1 lists the responses of the women to the sexual harassment.

When the respondents were asked if the sexual harassment had altered their work habits, 67 percent replied yes. Comments included, "I became less friendly to male co-workers" and "I've spent days too furious to work." The women surveyed said they would not tolerate sexual harassment again and would take legal action against the harasser. This may be the trend in the future.

The women were also asked if the company they worked for had a written policy against sexual harassment. Sixty-five percent said their employer did not have a formal policy; 18 percent replied that their company did have a written policy; and 17 percent did not know. Although a written policy explicitly stating that sexual harassment will not be tolerated is not an adequate defense against legal action, it does indicate that the employer is concerned about its employees and is attempting to provide an environment free from harassment.

What's an employer to do?

Although policies and procedures proscribing sexual harassment offer no guarantee against a company being held liable in court, employers are advised to establish them. Policies prohibiting sexual harassment can benefit employers in two ways. First, they may have a preventive effect. If employees, including management, are aware that certain behaviors or actions will not be tolerated by their employer, they are less likely to engage in them.

Secondly, if the company's policies provide a grievance procedure to report suspected violations, the employee who feels harassed is more likely to seek redress within the organization. This keeps the problem "in house" rather than in the court systems.

It is further recommended that the policy specifically identify a member of top management who is ultimately responsible for monitoring the program. As an incentive for managers throughout the organization to fully support sexual harassment prohibitions, the direct superior of any member of the management team should be held accountable for the misconduct of that individual. This should not be perceived as adding to the superior's managerial burden, as any manager is ultimately responsible for everything his or her subordinates do or do not do.

The policy should also outline a reporting procedure that does not require an employee to initiate action through the very person who is harassing her or him. The key to an effective reporting procedure lies in winning the trust of the employees who are expected to use it. To gain their trust, it can not be stressed enough that all members of the management team must support the employer's sexual harassment policies. It takes only one unsupportive manager or supervisor to render the whole process useless. All managers must understand that maintaining an abuse-free work environment is an integral part of their job description. Strict adherence to the employer's policies proscribing sexual harassment must be a condition of employment for every employee (including management).

Even though sound policies against sexual harassment are a necessary (but not sufficient) condition for a successful legal defense, it is the organizational support and implementation of these policies that will ultimately determine their sufficiency. If an employer's true intention is to provide a harassment-free work environment, its policies must be disseminated throughout the organization. Rules that are not known or understood are not going to be followed.

Training seminars for all management and supervisory personnel should be conducted to ensure that they are aware of the policies and of their individual responsibilities for compliance. Policy statements should include a procedure for reporting violations in confidence. They should also clearly state the consequences to be incurred by *any* employee who engages in prohibited acts.

Conclusion

Sexual harassment is a very real problem which shows no signs of going away. Sexual harassment affects not only the moral and organizational climate in a firm, but may also be expensive in terms of legal costs and damage to an employer's image.

It appears that employers will be increasingly subjected to hostile environment claims against their supervisors and agents. To counteract this threat, employers must be able to prove to both their employees and the courts that they sincerely desire to have a harassment-free work environment. Such proof will not be established by the mere existence of anti-harassment policies, but rather by the broadest possible dissemination and strictest enforcement of those policies.

The benefits of any policy which enjoys strong management support and is widely known by all employees are three-fold. First, employees are more aware of the type of prohibited behavior that is likely to create hostile work environments and are less likely to engage in it. This satisfies the preventive objective of the policy.

Second, affected employees (those who believe, either correctly or incorrectly, that they are the victims of sexual harassment by their supervisors) will have confidence that employers will resolve their problem. Thus, there is no reason for them to redress their grievances in the court system.

Three, strongly supported and implemented policies will constitute the employer's best defense in situations where legal action has been taken.

How to Comply with the Immigration Reform Act

Larry Besnoff

Employers who read about the Immigration Reform and Control Act of 1986 (IRCA) may conclude that the Immigration and Naturalization Service (INS) has thrown its hands in the air and dumped all of its enforcement responsibilities in the laps of the private enterprise. Congress appears to have decided that the only way to stop the increasing flow of illegal aliens into the United States is to cut off the jobs they immigrate to the United States to acquire. Employers now become the eyes, ears, and enforcers for the INS. For the first time, employers are subject to civil and criminal sanctions for knowingly hiring undocumented aliens.

Many employers have complained that the burdens on them are unfair and unworkable. So plans are already being made to change IRCA's most onerous provisions. Until then, there is a need for all managers to be full acquainted with the act's provisions.

Highlights of the new act

As of November 6, 1986, all employers must:

1. Actually *see* written proof of identity and right-to-work in the United States before hiring any new applicant. This requirement applies to *all applicants* whether U.S. citizens or not.
2. Complete a written form for every new hire certifying that the necessary documents were examined.
3. Not discriminate on the basis of citizenship.

Reprinted, by permission of the publisher, from *Management Solutions*, August 1987, © 1987 American Management Association, New York. All rights reserved.

Penalties for hiring an alien not authorized to work in the United States or lawfully admitted for permanent residence are progressive.

1. *Recordkeeping*—$100 to $1000 (even if you never hire an illegal alien)
2. *First offense*—$250 to $2000 per alien
3. *Second offense*—$2000 to $5000 per alien
4. *Third offense*—$3000 to $10,000 per alien
5. *Pattern of violations*—$3000 per alien and/or up to 6 months' imprisonment

The recordkeeping fine can be assessed if an employer fails to verify the status of an applicant, even if that applicant later proves to be a U.S. citizen.

INS began issuing citations in May 1987. During the year, however, no fines will be collected. Congress has three years to repeal the sanctions provided for in the act, but an employer cannot "get around" the fines by having an employee obtain a bond or post security to reimburse the employer for any fines incurred.

Before any applicant is hired

Based on the act and March 1987 regulations, there are three things an employer must do before hiring any new employee.

1. Request, inspect, and copy written proof of both identity and authorization for employment. A single document can establish both, or an applicant can produce two documents.

   A document that can establish *identity* is an original driver's license issued by any state bearing a photograph of the individual, or containing personal identifying information which, at a minimum, includes full name, date of birth, sex, height, color of eyes, and residence address.

   Documents that establish *employment authorization* include a Social Security account number card, issued by the Department of Health and Human Services or previously issued by Health, Education, and Welfare (other than such a card specifying on the face that the issuance of the card does not authorize employment in the United States), an unexpired re-entry permit (INS Form I-327), an unexpired Refugee Travel document (INS Form I-571), a certificate of birth issued by the Department of State (Form FS-545), a certificate of birth abroad issued by the Department of State (Form DS-1350), and an original or certified copy of a birth certificate issued by a state or recognized subdivision establishing birth in a state.

Documents that can establish *both identity and employment authorization* are a United States passport, a certificate of U.S. citizenship, issued by the U.S. Immigration and Naturalization Service (Form N-560); a certificate of naturalization (Form N-550); an alien registration card or resident alien card (the "green card"), provided that it contains a photograph of the bearer (Form I-151 or I-551); and a temporary resident card or employment authorization card, issued by the U.S. Immigration and Naturalization Service, provided that it contains a photograph of the bearer (Form I-688 or I-688A). An unexpired foreign passport will also satisfy the requirement provided it contains an unexpired stamp therein which reads, "process for I-551 . . ." or has attached thereto a Form I-94 in the same name (with identical biographic information) on which is an employment authorization stamp so long as the period of endorsement has not yet expired and the proposed employment is not in conflict with any restrictions or limitations identified on Form I-94.

2. Have each applicant complete Part One of Form I-9. The form should be completed *prior* to employment and no later than three business days after date of hire.

3. Complete Part Two of Form I-9. After examining Part One on Form I-9, which has been completed by the applicant, an employer must examine the documents provided by the applicant to ensure that they appear to be genuine and meet the requirements of the act. The employer must attest in writing that the applicant is eligible for employment. An employer may give an applicant up to three business days to produce the required documentation after hire. The use of day labor to evade these requirements is forbidden.

Copies of Form I-9 must be maintained by the employer and made available for inspection by the INS or the U.S. Department of Labor for three years after the date of hire or one year after termination of employment. The documents should be kept in a special file separate from the personnel file. In the event of a request for these documents, the employer has three business days to provide the documents.

Anti-discrimination provisions

The new law contains four expansions of previous equal employment opportunity law.

1. *Legal aliens*, for the first time, are protected against employment discrimination based upon national origin or citizenship.

2. All employers with *four or more employees* are covered under IRCA, while Title VII of the Civil Rights Act of 1964 covers only employers with more than 14 employees (Title VII protects employees against discrimination in employment based upon race, sex, religion, or national origin).
3. A new protected class, *citizenship*, is created.
4. A new department, the U.S. Department of Justice Office of Special Counsel for Immigration Related Unfair Employment Practices, is created to receive charges of employment discrimination.

Citizens of the United States, temporary and permanent resident aliens, refugees, and persons granted asylum who evidence an intention to become a citizen, may file employment discrimination charges under IRCA.

IRCA does not amend Title VII to include citizenship. An employee who works for a company with more than 15 employees who has a citizenship discrimination complaint must go to the new Special Counsel's office within the U.S. Department of Justice. A person cannot file duplicate charges with both the Equal Employment Opportunity Commission and the Special Counsel. Complaints raising national origin discrimination must be filed with the Equal Employment Opportunity Commission.

Charges must be filed with the Special Counsel within 180 days of the discriminatory event. Administrative procedures provide for an investigation and a hearing before an administrative law judge. Remedies range from civil fines of $1,000 to $3,000 per person and may include back pay and attorneys' fees. The complainant can file a lawsuit in federal court if the Special Counsel fails to act.

Based upon the federal government's history of lackadaisical enforcement of Title VII claims against state and local governments, employers should expect the Special Counsel to be more of a kitten than a snarling lion. This is especially true if discriminatory intent by the employer will be required to prove a case, as some comments from the White House have suggested.

The entire program can be repealed by Congress in three years.

One of the confusing aspects of IRCA is that it permits an employer to hire a U.S. citizen over an alien if the two are equally qualified. While this action will not violate IRCA, the Equal Employment Opportunity Commission specifically issued a news release stating that rejecting an applicant because of citizenship could violate Title VII because of the use of national origin as a basis. This is a conflict that will have to be resolved in the courts.

Grandfather clause

Much publicity to date has been focused on the provision for "grandfathering" all illegal immigrants who can prove they have resided continuously in the United States since January 1, 1982. A twelve-month period was provided to allow application for temporary resident status that could later become permanent resident status. Applications were accepted starting May 5, 1987. More than 100 new offices are expected to be opened solely to process these claims.

Employers should advise all employees of this special procedure so that good employees are given the opportunity to obtain residency status. Documents showing residence for the five years might not be retained by an employee. But an employer may have sufficient records in the personnel file that could independently substantiate continuous residence.

Unanswered questions on the Grandfather clause abound:

1. When more than one family lives in a home, how can the family whose name is not on the lease or utility bills establish residency?
2. How can employees who used false names or false Social Security numbers establish an accurate work history?

Effect on business

No one knows the true number of undocumented aliens in the United States. The "flood" has been estimated at 3 to 5 million by the Census Bureau and as high as more than 10 million by others.

However, it is fair to assume that the illegal aliens are working, since they usually have little assets and no access to the social welfare system. According to a recent report, most aliens work in manufacturing, while others are in agricultural, mining, construction, food, retailing, and personal services.

If the number of illegal immigrants is reduced, what effect will that have on industry? Employers using low-paid illegal aliens to remain competitive may be forced to pay higher wages and this may price their products out of the market.

Is the documentation requirement realistic? In industries where employees are constantly hired, laid off and then rehired, must an employer demand to see documents every time an employee is rehired? INS will allow the initial Form I-9 to cover later rehire if the individual is rehired within one year and if the employer inspects the previous Form I-9 and finds the individual is still permitted to work.

Should an employer keep copies of the documents produced? Probably not. A better solution is to maintain a record of the documents on the Form I-9 that contain sufficient identifying information.

Effect on unions

Some unions are in favor of the new law. Those unions that have lost membership because employers could hire aliens for lower wages than would be paid to unionized American workers like the strong enforcement provisions. They look to increased membership. On the other hand, if a large number of employed aliens qualify for amnesty, it could generate a pool of prospective union members who are not afraid of deportation. We can expect to see unions jointly organizing and offering to help aliens qualify for amnesty. Unions are already establishing referral centers to help aliens with paperwork, handing out leaflets on employees' rights under IRCA at entrances to non-union plants, and giving guidance to non-union members.

Many unions have also already expressed an interest in Qualified Designated Entity (QDE) status, which would permit them to file claims for amnesty on behalf of aliens.

Recommendations

One thing is certain, IRCA has a long way to go before it becomes workable and livable for the business community. Changes in the requirements and paperwork should be expected in the meantime:

1. Take no action with respect to employees hired before November 6, 1986.
2. Stay alert for final regulations, judicial decisions, and congressional action that might change employer obligations.
3. See that all employees involved in the hiring process are educated about IRCA. Set up a system for handling the paperwork responsibilities.
4. Make sure all new employees are required to produce documentation and sign Form I-9. Don't invite discrimination lawsuits because of unequal policies. Don't ask only applicants who look or sound foreign to comply.
5. Do not hire anyone until all necessary documents have been produced.
6. Keep copies of the Form I-9 for at least three years from date of initial hire.
7. Don't copy or keep the underlying documentation produced by the new employee.
8. State an intention to hire only authorized workers in your personnel handbook and all other company documents.
9. Do not overreact and reject all applicants solely because they speak with an accent or appear to be "foreign."
10. Don't ask any applicant for place of birth or citizenship status. Do ask if the applicant is a U.S. citizen or an alien authorized to work in the United States.
11. Assist your employees to acquire amnesty status.
12. Don't fire anyone who has applied for amnesty. Wait for the decision of the INS; you need not evaluate the claim.

13. Assign one person the task of verifying the authenticity of documents produced to show authorization to work and identity.
14. Assign responsibility for handling employment discrimination claims filed with the Department of Justice to one person to ensure uniform processing.
15. Don't hire anyone you know is not permitted to work or live in the United States.

For Further Reference

Part 1: Changes in the Work-force and Workplace

Bardwick, Judith M. "How Executives Can Help 'Plateaued' Employees." *Management Review* (January 1987): 40–46.

Biles, George E., and Randall S. Schuber. *Audit Handbook of Human Resource Management Practices.* Alexandria, VA: American Society for Personnel Administration, 1986.

Blair, Edward. "Bootstrapping Your HRIS Capabilities." *Personnel Administrator* (February 1988): 68–72.

Capozzola, John M. "Affirmative Action Alive and Well under Court's Strict Scrutiny." *National Civic Review* (November–December 1986): 354–362.

Feuer, Dale. "The Skill Gap: America's Crisis of Competence." *Training* (December 1987): 27–35.

———. "Workplace Issues: Testing, Training, and Policy." *Training* (October 1987): 66–67.

Flamholtz, Eric G., Yvonne Randle, and Sonja Sackmann. "Personnel Management: The Tone of Tomorrow." *Personnel Journal* (July 1987): 42–48.

Grensing, Lin. "An AA Primer." *Management World* (January 1987): 34–35.

Gridley, John D. "Six Steps to a More Efficient HRIS: A Pre-Vendor Evaluation." *Personnel*, vol. 64, no. 4 (April 1987): 8–12.

Harris, Donald. "Beyond the Basics: New HRIS Developments." *Personnel* (January 1986): 49–56.

Harvey, L. James. "Nine Major Trends in HRM." *Personnel Administrator* (November 1986): 102–109.

Holzer, Marc. "Workforce Reduction and Productivity." *Public Administration Quarterly* (Spring 1986): 86–98.

Hooper, John A. "A Strategy for Increasing the Human Resources Department's Effectiveness." *Personnel Administrator* (June 1984): 141–48.

Jacobs, Dorri. "Maintaining Morale during and after Downsizing." *Management Solutions* (April 1988): 4–13.

Kauffman, Nancy. "Motivating the Older Worker." *SAM Advanced Management Journal* (Spring 1987): 43–47.

Kohl, John P., and David B. Stephens. "Expanding the Legal

Rights of Working Women." *Personnel* (May 1987): 46–51.

Leote, Dennis M. "Piecemeal Planning Hinders HRIS Performance." *Personnel Journal* (March 1988): 65–69.

Lester, Rick A., and Donald W. Caudill. "The Handicapped Worker: Seven Myths." *Training and Development Journal* (August 1987): 50–51.

Olivetti, L. James. "Information Resources in HRD." *Training and Development Journal* (January 1988): 38–44.

Perry, Stephen G. "The PC-Based HRIS." *Personnel Administrator* (February 1988): 60–63.

Robert, James M. "Downsizing to Meet Strategic Objectives." *National Productivity Review* (Autumn 1987): 324–330.

Schachter, Jim. "Firms Begin to Embrace Diversity." *Los Angeles Times* (April 7, 1988): 1, 14, 16.

Shipper, Francis C., and Frank M. Shipper. "Beyond EEO: Toward Pluralism." *Business Horizons* (May–June 1987): 53–61.

Tatel, David, and Elliot Mincberg. "The Supreme Court's 1987 Decision on Voluntary Affirmative Action." *Public Management* (December 1987): 3–5.

Part 2: Employee Performance, Motivation, and Training

"Attitude Surveys: Organization and Managerial Assessment?" *Management Solutions* (September 1987): 5–11.

Becker, Christine S., ed. *Performance Evaluation: An Essential Management Tool.* Washington, D.C.: International City Management Association, 1988.

Brown, Abby. "Today's Employees Choose Their Own Recognition Award." *Personnel Administrator* (August 1986): 51–58.

Brown, Dan G. "Development of

Performance Standards: A Practical Guide." *Public Personnel Management* 16, no. 2 (Summer 1987): 93–114.

Clark, Susan G. "Guidelines for Employee Development and Training Programs." *MIS Report* 18, no. 1 (January 1986).

Doyel, Hoyt, and Thomas Riley. "Considerations in Developing Incentive Plans." *Management Review* (March 1987): 34–37.

England, Robert E., and William M. Parle. "Nonmanagerial Performance Appraisal Practices in Large American Cities." *Public Administration Review* (November–December 1987): 498–504.

Goddard, Robert W. "The Potential in Problem People." *Management World* (June–August 1987): 19–21.

Grant, Philip. "A Better Approach to Performance Reviews." *Management Solutions* (March 1987): 11–16.

Grant, Philip C. "Rewards: The Pizzazz Is the Package, Not the Prize." *Personnel Journal* (March 1988): 76–81.

Greiner, John M. "Motivational Programs and Productivity Improvement in Times of Limited Resources." *Public Productivity Review* (Fall 1986): 81–101.

Guinn, Kathleen. "Performance Management: Not Just an Annual Appraisal." *Training* (August 1987): 39–42.

Haislip Jr., Otis L. "How to Treat Training as an Investment." *Training* (February 1987): 63–66.

Jackson, Tom, and Alan Vitberg. "Career Development, Part 1: Careers and Entrepreneurship." *Personnel* (February 1987): 12–17.

———. "Career Development, Part 2: Challenges for the Organization." *Personnel* (March 1987): 68–72.

———. "Career Development, Part 3: Challenges for the Individual." *Personnel* (April 1987): 54–57.

Jennings, Lois. "How Do You Determine the Use of New Training Technologies?" *Training and Development Journal* (August 1987): 22–26.

Klubnik, Joan P. "Putting Together a Career Development Program." *Management Solutions* (January 1988): 31–36.

Kovach, Kenneth A. "What Motivates Employees? Workers and Supervisors Give Different Answers." *Business Horizons* (September–October 1987): 58–65.

Krupar, Karen R., and Joseph J. Krupar. "Jerks at Work." *Personnel Journal* (June 1988): 68–75.

Lawrie, John. "Are Employees Using What They Learn?" *Personnel Journal* (April 1988): 95–97.

Lee, Chris. "Where the Training Dollars Go." *Training* (October 1987): 51–65.

Lehrer, Sande. "Motivating Subordinates: Making It Work." *The Bureaucrat* (Summer 1986): 49–52.

Madlin, Nancy. "Computer-Based Training Comes of Age." *Personnel* (November 1987): 64–65.

Michaels, Mark. "The New Game of Motivation." *American City and County* (February 1986): 36–44.

Mirabile, Richard. "New Directions for Career Development." *Training and Development Journal* (December 1987): 30–33.

Mischkind, Louis A. "Is Employee Morale Hidden behind Statistics?" *Personnel Journal,* vol. 65, no. 2 (February 1986): 74–79.

O'Dell, Carla, and Jerry McAdams. "The Revolution in Employee Rewards." *Management Review* (March 1987): 30–33.

Paul, Celia, and Ann W. Sanger. "Charting Your Career Goals." *Management Solutions* (December 1987): 22–26.

Perry, Manuel, Joan More, and

Nancy Parkison. "Does Your Appraisal System Stack Up?" *Personnel Journal* (May 1987): 82–87.

Pulich, Marcia Ann. "What to Do with Incompetent Employees." *Supervisory Management* (March 1986): 10–16.

Sherwood, Andrew. "A Baker's Dozen of Ways to Motivate People." *Management Solutions* (May 1987): 14–16.

Smallwood, Norman, and Joe Folkman. "Why Employee Surveys Don't Always Work." *Personnel* (August 1987): 20–28.

Tartell, Ross. "What to Look for When You Buy Training." *Training and Development Journal* (January 1987): 28–30.

Taylor, Robert R., and Lois Smith. "Performance Standards: Developing an Employee Appraisal System to Enhance Productivity in a County Government." *Public Administration Quarterly* (Summer 1987): 217–238.

Vogt, Judith F., and Bradley D. Hunt. "What Really Goes Wrong with Participative Work Groups." *Training and Development Journal* (May 1988): 96–100.

Warfle, Dawn Marie. "Adult Learning: Implications for Executive Development Programs." *Public Management* (July 1987): 2–4.

Weiss, Donald H. "How to Handle Difficult People." *Management Solutions* (February 1988): 33–38.

Wilkinson, Harry E., Charles D. Orth, and Robert C. Benfari. "Motivation Theories: An Integrated Operational Model." *SAM Advanced Management Journal* (Autumn 1986): 24–31.

Part 3: Employee Issues

Brown, Michael. "AIDS Discrimination in the Workplace: The Legal Dilemma." *Case & Comment* (May–June 1987): 3–10.

Cathcart, David A., and J. Kevin Lilly. "The Immigration Reform and Control Act of 1986—Key Compliance Issues." *Employee Relations Law Journal* (Autumn 1987): 224-248.

Colosi, Marco L. "Do Employees Have the Right to Smoke?" *Personnel Journal* (April 1988): 72-79.

Darnell, Tim. "Drugs and Booze—A Personnel Nightmare." *American City and County* (March 1988): 28-31.

———. "Drugs and Booze: Combatting the Problem." *American City and County* (April 1988): 46-50.

Feuer, Dale. "AIDS at Work: Fighting the Fear." *Training* (June 1987): 61-71.

Franklin, Geralyn McClure, and Robert K. Robinson. "AIDS and the Law." *Personnel Administrator* (April 1988): 118-121.

Garvey, Margaret S. "The High Cost of Sexual Harassment Suits." *Personnel Journal* (January 1986): 75-79.

Goddard, Robert W. "Shedding Light on Employee Privacy." *Management World* (January 1987): 18-20.

Harris, Donald. "A Matter of Privacy: Managing Personnel Data in Company Computers." *Personnel* (February 1987): 34-43.

Hoerr, John, et al. "Privacy." *Business Week* (March 28, 1988): 61-68.

Hubbartt, William S. "Smoking at Work—An Emerging Office Issue." *Administrative Management* (February 1986): 21-23.

Kruchko, John G., and Paul M. Lucky. "Drug Testing in the Public Sector." *American City and County* (April 1988): 52-54.

Kuzmits, Frank K., and Lyle Sussman. "Twenty Questions about AIDS in the Workplace." *Business Horizons* (July-August 1986): 36-42.

Linenberger, P., and Keavenly, T. "Sexual Harassment." *Human Resource Management* (Spring 1981): 11-17.

Lutgen, Lorraine. "AIDS in the Workplace: Fighting Fear with Facts and Policy." *Personnel* (November 1987): 53-57.

Machlowitz, David S., and Marilyn M. Machlowitz. "Preventing Sexual Harassment." *ABA Journal* (October 1, 1987): 78-90.

Manley, Marisa. "Coping with the New Immigration Law." *INC* (August 1987): 91-94.

Masi, Dale. "Company Responses to Drug Abuse from AMA's Nationwide Survey." *Personnel* 64, no. 3 (March 1987): 40-46.

McKendrick, Joseph. "Smoking Policies Take Off." *Management World* (January-February 1988): 12-13.

Munchus III, George. "An Update on Smoking: Employees' Rights and Employers' Responsibilities." *Personnel* (August 1987): 46-50.

Nowlin, William A. "Employee Drug Testing: Issues for Public Employers and Labor Organizations." *Journal of Collective Negotiations* 16, no. 4 (1987): 295-309.

Post, Linda Currey. "Drugs, Drink, Disease: Personnel Issues of the '80s." *Outlook* (Winter 1988): 16-20.

Rosen, Theodore H. "Identification of Substance Abusers in the Workplace." *Public Personnel Management* 16, no. 3 (Fall 1987): 197-207.

Ross, Cynthia S., and Robert E. England. "State Governments' Sexual Harassment Policy Initiatives." *Public Administration Review* May-June 1987: 259-262.

Schachter, Jim. "Firms Walk Tightrope on Privacy Issues." *Los Angeles Times,* Part IV (December 20, 1987): 1, 6, 9.

Scott, Craig R. "The Smoking Controversy Goes to Court." *Manage-

ment World (January–February 1988): 13–14.

Sepanik, Jani. "Drug Testing, Sexual Harassment, Smoking: Employee Rights Issues." *MIS Report* 20, no. 3 (March 1988).

"The Workplace and AIDS: A Guide to Services and Information, Part II." *Personnel Journal* (February 1988): 101–111.

Thornton, Terry. "Sexual Harassment: Discouraging It in the Work Place." *Personnel* (April 1986): 18–33.

U.S. Chamber of Commerce. *The New Immigration Law.* Washington, D.C., n.d.

Watson, Tom. "Drug Testing Laws Are Catching On." *Governing* (June 1988): 60–63.

Weiss, Lisa K. "Cutting the Cost of Substance Abuse Treatment." *Compensation and Benefits Review* (May–June 1987): 37–44.

"Workplace Smoking Policies: 16 Questions and Answers." *Personnel Journal* (April 1988): 80–82.

Wrich, James T. "Beyond Testing: Coping with Drugs at Work." *Harvard Business Review* (January–February 1988): 120–128.

Practical Management Series

**Personnel Practices for the '90s:
A Local Government Guide**

Text type
Century Expanded

Composition
Unicorn Graphics
Washington, D.C.

Printing and binding
R. R. Donnelley & Sons Company
Harrisonburg, Virginia

Cover design
Rebecca Geanaros